CONFESSIONS OF A Tropical Fish Addict

Ross Socolof

A history of the tropical fish industry in Florida with observations and comments by the author.

Published by:
Socolof Industries
P.O. Box 1987
Bradenton, Florida 34206

This book is dedicated to my wife,
Loise Socolof
who gives meaning and cohesion to my life

ISBN 978-1-932892-15-4

Second edition
First edition published in 1996

Cichlid Press
P.O. Box 13608
El Paso, TX 79913

Cover photo front *Pseudotropheus socolofi* and on back *Thorichtys socolofi* — both fish named after the author, and photographed by Ad Konings in Lake Malawi (Tumbi Point, Mozambique) and in the Río Tulijá (Mexico) respectively.

Introduction

You are about to have a "conversation" with a man who is a lucky, inquisitive, and rare individual. He has spent his lifetime doing exactly what he loves doing. He has been fortunate in his business endeavors, his adventures, his studies, his credits, and his life because he has loved it all. It was never work.

Sometime ago a young fish fancier said to me, "you're so lucky – you get to talk to Ross all of the time". I've been proud and happy to be included, and am pleased that Ross has finally put some of his life on record. This book is truly a reminiscence, not always in chronological order, but a lot about the man, the industry pioneers, the business, and his joy, working with and caring for tropical fish.

Read on, learn, and enjoy!

Loise Socolof

Confessions of a Tropical Fish Addict

Tropical fish keeping, breeding, raising, buying and selling has been my passion for sixty five years. My children, grandchildren, great-grandchildren, childhood chums, and relatives have almost no idea of what my life has been about. I want them to know. My fondest hope is that you all can get as much pleasure from your lives as I have from mine.

I am not a professional writer. I have been writing articles, sections of books, and making speeches about fish for years. This has been easy and has been fun. A record of the people and personalities connecting my life and fish is not so easy. I have enjoyed recalling all of it. I hope you will enjoy reading about it. This record is not about my entire life. It is only about a lifelong involvement with tropical fish and the people who have touched my life with fishes. If I am able to interest, inspire, or amuse by what I write I will have accomplished my wish.

The important message I am trying to give is to live your life fulfilled. It is the only life you are likely to have. Anyone spending a lifetime unhappy and uninspired during their working hours is a fool. The time it took you to read that sentence; is gone forever. Time is not renegotiable, recyclable, or for sale. Don't waste it. A road sign posted on a dirt road read as follows: "Choose your rut carefully, you'll be in it for the next seventeen miles". That's the message. Life is what happens to you while you're making other plans. People are divided into three groups. Those that make things happen. Those who watch things happen, and those who wonder what happened.

I wasn't born smart. A good(?) friend told me years ago that I had a great business asset. I looked stupid. It took me years to realize that I only look stupid. I cast off work that I did not enjoy for work that I knew I would enjoy. This was the most courageous thing I have ever done. Every day since then I have looked forward to my workday. In business for your self you make plenty of mistakes, but they are your mistakes. The bonus is the sense of fulfillment that comes when you correct them. There is another big bonus in being self-employed. You eliminate the fear of getting fired or threatened for your mistakes. Of course, you will not get fired if you are the boss, but you may go bankrupt. You can not over do this wonderful luxury.

Keeping and breeding tropical fish has been a life long obsession. It has been great fun and emotionally rewarding. I will give hundreds of thousands of dollars worth of free information in this book for the reader who wants to turn an expensive hobby into a paying proposition. This statement is conservative. The money represents what it cost me to learn not to repeat expensive and dumb mistakes. I gift it to you. It really is no fun to enmesh yourself in an unprofitable business. The most fun is to win at what you are doing. The pleasure is making money. It is easy to do this breeding tropical fish. At the very least you can pay for an expensive hobby, and at the same time provide a service. I have learned "what not to do". This is the result of surviving a lot of bad decisions. The net result, many years later, is positive. The degree of the benefits I pass on to you depends on how much you want. If you want to get your hobby to pay for itself, read on. If you want to make extra money for an earlier retirement, read on. If you need to augment a belt-tightening retirement income, read on. If you want your own small business (full time), read on. If you are really addicted and want to build a large tropical fish business, and employ many people while building a significant estate, then read on. If you do not like tropical fish (and are not a relative) drop this book and run like hell.

My short term memory is giving me problems. Yesterday, I went to Loise (my wife and partner), and announced that she had better pay attention as I wanted to tell her something really important. When I knew that I had her attention I looked back at her with a blank face and said "I forgot what". I still haven't remembered WHAT, but I did decide that NOW is the time to start this project. Someone once told me that an autobiography reveals nothing bad about the author except his memory. In my case the only memory problems I have are the things that happened this week. The rest remains crisp and sharp.

I have felt a great need to write this book. Long ago I discovered that your brain does not remember mental and physical hurts for lengthy periods of time. This does not imply that I have not had my share of misery. What does amaze me now is the realization of how insensitive one becomes to negatives as time passes. Terrible happenings, in time, can become really funny. Sitting here now laughing at the crazy things

I have been involved in is fun. It keeps me smiling so much my fingers have trouble finding the keys.

I incurred a life long addiction to tropical fish in 1931. I was six years old at the time. Things were desperately bad economically. Welcome to the Depression. What happened in 1931 affected my life more than anything else ever did. Cousin Carl Kaplan came to live with us. His mother was my mother's sister (Aunt Beatrice). She needed help. My parents took Carl home. He stayed for years. Cousin Carl became the older brother I never had. He lived with us until sometime before World War Two. I not only got an older brother, but got a brother obsessed with tropical fish. I loved my cousin Carl (still do). I now vividly remember hours and hours spent in our magic basement (in Manhattan Beach, Brooklyn, New York City) "doing" tropical fish. I immediately bonded to Carl and to tropical fish. In the next years the two of us spent uncounted hours in the fish room. Carl was a patient teacher. I can still taste foul water choking me while trying to learn how to siphon. I learned how to siphon. In those years you siphoned with a thick rubber hose. It was all I could do to get my mouth open wide enough to siphon. Carl's most prized possession was a double piston Marco air pump. I can still hear the never ending chuga, chuga, chuga. It pumped air into thirty or forty refrigerator liners, bathtubs, and aquariums via spaghetti-like rubber tubing that connected all with many brass valves. It took a delicate touch to adjust them to provide air to all the containers. I never was allowed to touch them. Today, whenever I see a valve needing adjustment, I look over my shoulder to be sure Carl is not there before gathering enough courage to touch it.

Carl made remarkable, gigantic aquariums. Not good or pretty, but remarkable. Easy. Stick five sheets of glass together with Silastic. Actually, it wasn't quite like that then. I often have wondered where Carl got his design. I suspect from a lunatic. I realize now his were the legendary "aquariums from hell". Would you believe all one piece of poured concrete with the front open. A broad lip there received a massive piece of plate glass that Carl could salvage from construction sites where remodeling was being done. Glass cutting became an art form. Usually his concrete aquariums were made to fit the piece of glass available. He made a large aquarium when he found the glass. No two matched. The aquariums always leaked, but never at the same time or in the same place. Drips, not torrents. The glass was affixed (when he could afford it) with "Pecora" a black, gooey cement which worked better than homemade or toxic putty type adhesives. What good the glass did I am not sure. It certainly was not to observe fish. The tanks were deep. I never remember seeing much unless fish banged their heads against the glass by mistake or while getting fed. We fed a lot of glass worms, Daphnia, and *Tubifex*, all easily collected at that time. The dry food we fed was an ever varying mix of shrimp meal, dried bugs, dried blood, dried clams, oatmeal, and as much "Longlife" dried food as Carl could afford. The concrete in his homemade aquariums was about three inches thick in every direction. The concrete was strengthened with chicken wire which was put in the mold before pouring the cement. It worked.

The house soon overflowed with fish and trophies. In those days the Greater New York City Aquarium Society awarded three places in competitions. They were beautiful medallions of (real) gold, silver, or bronze showing a beautiful Japanese Oranda or an angelfish. Carl won more than his share of them. I had one for years and lost it. I would trade a dog or even a grandchild for another one.

We raised angelfish. We raised Siamese fighting fish, barbs, tetras, livebearers, Egyptian mouthbrooders, and danios.

I remember a visit to Albert Greenberg's Everglades Water Gardens in Tampa, Florida in 1935. My wonderful father bought me a pair of the new cornflower blue Bettas from Mr. Greenberg. We raised regular and giant danios in tanks with the bottoms covered with marbles (to keep them from eating the eggs). We never raised *Rasbora heteromorpha*, but we sure tried. We raised a lot of livebearers. The colorful hybrid Xiphophorines were improving fast. The Germans were shipping in wonderful fish. I remember our greatest single investment. It was a pair of albino swordtails. A man on Ocean Parkway in Brooklyn hit it lucky. He got the "first ever" albino swordtails and he made big money from his great good luck. He sold us a pair for $7.50. In today's world that would be something like three to five hundred dollars.

Saturday was Carl's fish "business" day. I looked forward to it all week. We went everywhere in our world (Staten Island, Newark, Long Island, Manhattan, and other distant and strange places) that could be reached by public transportation for a nickel. We carried with us metal pails with tight lids and traded our fish for different fish, fish food, and

Cousin Carl Kaplan who started it all, at 79.

Dr. Jacques Géry's wonderful "Anti-Portrait" made out of fish parts.

other equipment that we needed. I never remember Carl spending "real money". We had regular customers for all of our fish close to home, but the quest was for new varieties. We went far afield hunting for new fish. We kept our best produced fish as bait to get something new.

The great event came when Carl was sixteen and able to buy a secondhand car. I often think of the $15.00 he paid for the car. Today I spend that and more on a tankful of gasoline. I would believe it if I found out that Carl got a free tank of gas with his $15.00 car. I must ask him. The car was not a thing of beauty, but it ran. It took us on wonderful outings to magic fish hatcheries, places we could never have reached by subway or bus. Today, more than sixty years later, I can pick up a sixty year old copy of Aquatic Life or The Aquarium Magazine and have a voyage backward in time, reading the advertisements, for (long gone) hatcheries and stores where we bought, traded, and sold our tropical fish. I still see in my mind's eye many of these hatcheries. There were few real pet shops around. Most of our visits were to small, commercial hatcheries. There was Henry in Flushing and Henry the Hunchback in Queens, Mr. Huffmire at Flatlands Hatchery in Canarsie, Mr. Richard Buettner and later Fred Cochu at Empire Tropical Fish, Huber in Staten Island, Rabinow on Myrtle Ave., and both Visel & Kissel in Brooklyn. I remember an all day (two flats) excursion to see Mr. Lingg in Yonkers.

Today the vast majority of the fish sold are produced in Florida or the Far East. There was no commercial air transportation available in the 1930s. Fish came from the few producing centers by rail in metal fish cans. New Orleans was a bigger producer than Florida. Bill Sternke in Opa Locka, Florida was the only real tropical fish producer in Florida in the late 1920s. It reversed in the mid 1930s. Otto Beltz in St. Louis produced and shipped lots of fish. The only source for new fish was from overseas by steam ship. The tank-raised fish came from Germany, and from local breeders most of whom were German immigrants. Wild-caught tropical fish came from people like Fred Cochu, Mertins, Henrik Hansen (much more about him later), and Auguste Rabaut. These suppliers would travel to the United States with the fish that they obtained in South America, Africa, Europe, and the Far East. There were lots of people like Henrik Hansen who were employed by various steamship lines. Rabaut and Cochu were paying passengers who rented cabins to maintain their fish. Hansen was the best known of the steamship employees who dealt in tropical fish. The others now remain nameless. As an adjunct to their income these people bought, transported, and then sold their fish at all of the world's major ports. The customers invariably were the larger wholesalers (Schomburg in New Orleans, Greenberg and Woolf in Tampa, Paramount in New York, etc.).

Breeding fish at home for local resale is one of the things that has not changed in the past one hundred years. It still makes good sense. The trick is to breed what your local market can use. Angelfish, for example, are always good, but not if your market is already supplied (locally) with good and fairly priced angelfish. What you must do is pick a list of items you would enjoy breeding and then have your local retail outlets look at your list to see what they can use. If Angels do not work, something else will. It also will work in reverse. Ask your local buyers what items they have trouble getting and tell them what you plan to do. Stay involved in the hobby and join one of the national organizations. The American Cichlid Association is a good example. The A.C.A. puts out a Journal and a Trading Post. This is where you can get new items before any of the major commercial breeders have them. You can also sell and ship profitably to members using this method.

I enlisted in World War Two when I was seventeen years old. Three years later I was discharged. I went to work for the family grocery business in New York City. My Grandfather, Joseph Socolof, had started his Sweet Life Food Company in 1883. Grandpa Joe called the company Sweet Life, because that is how he felt about his new homeland. The "Sweet Life" label is still very popular through most of New England and New York State. In 1931 my father (Harry R. Socolof) joined Mike Kullen, a former Kroger Company vice-president who had conceived the idea for what became the world's first supermarket. Both men were imaginative merchants and together this new innovation (the supermarket) blossomed and thrived. They were 50/50 partners. Their first store opened in 1931. The cornerstones of their advertising was, "How Does He Do It?" and "Why Pay More?" repeated over and over in every advertisement. A huge volume of business resulted from this combination of low prices and no credit. The disbelievers became instant converts to the new system. The chain was called "King Kullen". The stores are still in business in and about New York City. The only vivid memory I have of that time were the days after President Roosevelt closed the banks. All the cash from all the stores was kept, in our home, under my parents' bed until the banks opened again. There was a constant crew present that guarded the money at the house. That was great fun for a child.

Grandpa Joe left Russia in 1879. I have been told two stories explaining his exodus from Russia. First he had gotten the Rabbi's daughter pregnant and had to marry her. He left soon afterwards. The second, and perhaps more believable, was that he was being forced into the Tsar's army to fight the Turks. Either reason would have been enough to motivate him to leave Russia. He left taking his younger brother, Isaac, with him. Together they walked out of Russia from their little Shtetle (village) in the Ukraine (near Kiev). They actually walked across Europe to the English Channel. It took them a year. Eventually they got to London. Grandpa's stay in England was just long enough for him to learn perfect English. Joseph Socolof spoke English with a British accent, with no trace of a Russian accent. In London the brothers worked and saved. The goal was enough money to buy (steerage) passage to New York. Grandpa told me that he ate dog biscuits for three months before finding out what they were. They had been the cheapest food available. That was why they started eating them. He kept right on eating them and saving money. By early 1881 they were in New York City. They found a place to stay with Russian townspeople who had emigrated earlier.

Grandpa Joe quickly enlisted in the United States Army for a two years' hitch. Army service gave him citizenship upon his discharge. He saved almost all his pay. Isaac was to stay in New York and go to school. The Army sent Grandpa Joe to the Black Hills of North Dakota to fight Indians. He told me that he never really knew, at that time, what it was all about. He loved the time he spent as a soldier. He loved the food. I inherited this aberrant gene from him as I also loved Army food. He enlisted again when we declared war on Spain in 1898. This time he got as far as Tampa and then that war ended. He made Sergeant that time. He was a great fan and supporter of Theodore Roosevelt. In 1883, when discharged from the Army, he used his savings to buy a small grocery store in Brooklyn. He barely survived. The seller unmercifully cheated the "Greenhorn" Socolof. He found bags with sand instead of flour, sawdust instead of pepper, and jars with water instead of oil. His brother, Isaac, had left New York signing on as cabin boy on a ship bound for South America. He left that boat in Buenos Aires. The brothers never saw each other again. They exchanged a few letters, and then that stopped. The family is still in Argentina. In 1936 Grandpa Joe took a boat to Argentina to try to find Isaac or his family. Isaac had married and had five daughters. He had died some years earlier. The only family name that I can remember now was Glazer. Just before World War Two some of these Argentinean relatives visited my parents. I was too young to pay attention. Now, as all the other players are dead, contact again has been lost. I have made several attempts to track them. No luck yet.

Grandpa Joe retired to Coral Gables in Miami in 1939. His Sweet Life Food Corporation had become a huge business. He had outlived three of his wives and married his fourth wife when in his mid eighties. Joe took the future "Grandma Ray" on a trip around the world before tying the nuptial knots (to see if they were compatible). He loved to drink and he loved pretty women. He was still chasing, my wife, Loise, who is a very pretty woman, around the table in his mid nineties. I think he had forgotten why. Loise and I visited him often. He always had a new alcoholic concoction for us to sample. He was a Russian, and a lifelong Vodka drinker. As he got older his taste buds dulled and he switched to other alcoholic potions. A combination of Peach Brandy, Crème de Menthe, and Cherry Heering was his favorite. He remained vital to the end. He still quoted page after page of Shakespeare from memory. His driving got very erratic. He turned in his license when he was ninety-eight. On his ninety-third birthday he decided he had paid enough income taxes. This decision was stimulated by the insurance companies paying off his life insurance policies. He decided that the I.R.S. should also stop asking him to pay taxes. He returned all tax notices, letters, and threats to the IRS marked "deceased." This went on for almost seven years and caused great anxiety for the family. No one would ever cross the patriarch, but then again the I.R.S. was not an outfit to irritate. He loved it and, I am sure, thought he'd beaten the system when he died. I had more than one call from the I.R.S. asking if I had a grandfather named Joseph, and if he still lived, and if so where he was. My memory, and that of every other family member, always failed. The I.R.S. never caught up with him (while he lived). He really enjoyed this last adventure. Of course, they got his estate good when he died, but he made it out of this life just before his one hundredth birthday without knowing.

By 1946 when I got back from my wartime travels in the Pacific, as a guest of the U.S. Army, the family grocery business was huge. My father was the president. Grandpa Joe was chairman of the board and retired. A number of older relatives helped fill most of the other executive positions. As the only son I had no chance to consider anything other than to enter the business. I had no interest in the wholesale grocery and supermarket business, but I also loved my father and did as I was told. The family needed a replacement for the head food buyer who was a brother of Grandpa Joe.

Quickly I became the company's vice president and this obviously because of my great genius, acumen, experience, and also, my father owned the business. I never enjoyed a minute of it. For years I fantasized and schemed about getting away. I became the head buyer, learned the skills, put in long hours, and bought mega-millions of dollars worth of groceries for the Sweet Life Food Corporation. This lasted for nine years.

I could, and did again, keep tropical fish. I bought a new three bedroom, two bath row house ($6,500 with a 4% "G.I." mortgage) in Kew Gardens in Queens. An unfinished basement made an ideal hatchery. I soon had forty tanks going. I managed to get three pairs of Oscars breeding and turned out enough baby Oscars and other fish to support my addiction. The selling price for Oscars was ten cents each. I bartered them with local shops for other fish and equipment.

I made a great friend at that time. This was Jack Pearlman who was some years older than I, and also a vice president of the Sweet Life Food Company. He lived four blocks away. We went back and forth to work together. He was a fisherman and so am I. We spent most of each weekend fishing. We fished everywhere from Montauk to Cape Cod. We got good government geodesic maps and found many isolated lakes that could not be reached by road. It was great fun. We packed in Friday nights and spent all day Saturday and some Sunday mornings fishing before driving back to Queens. We carried an inflatable rubber boat along. We found a remote freshwater lake near Montauk Point that had good fishing. The most amazing discovery was that Fort Pond located on the main road in Montauk was a freshwater bass fisherman's paradise. Everyone there was wrapped up in salt water fishing. No one ever fished that lake, or as far as I could discover, ever thought about it. I remember when Jack and I caught 26 largemouth bass, up to five pounds, one fabulous day at this lake. Our favorite spot was the Mill Pond in Patchogue on Long Island. One year Jack got a seven pound bass there. The next year I got one better than six pounds. The yellow perch fishing was great. From time to time we would see a gigantic snapping turtle. It would have been a tight fit in a large wash tub. I imagine by now it must be large enough to eat a row boat. He took our baits two or three times a year and pulled us around the lake until he got loose. We found three good remote lakes on Cape Cod. The best freshwater bass lake was north of Provincetown. It has since been reclaimed by the sea. The other two lakes were a pickerel fisherman's dream. We mounted the largest we ever caught. It just made it to four pounds.

Jack Pearlman was an engineer. In the early 1950s when things were winding down at Sweet Life he accepted an offer to become chief engineer for the Hudson Pulp and Paper Company in Palatka, Florida and moved south.

After my mother died in 1951 my father lost interest in business. It did not come as any surprise when I made it clear I had no interest in taking over the family's grocery businesses. My father offered me twenty of his supermarkets if I would stay in New York. It didn't tempt me for an instant. I spent less and less time in the grocery business and more and more time with tropical fish. Dad remarried, a pretty blue-haired buxom lady, named Rosalyn who gave him affection and fed him well.

General Aquatic was born in 1952 and kept me sane. I was having great difficulty trying to be content in crowded and polluted New York, working in the grocery business. A new type of pet business "Tropical Paradise" had been started in 1950 by a certain Murray Director. Director had a small advertising agency. My father knew him as he had done some small jobs for our Thos. Roulston grocery store chain (Sweet Life operated the Thos. Roulston stores at that time). Director was very bright and was very strange. He was the person who conceived the franchise plan for pet shops. This idea was later perfected by Milton and Norman Doktor from Philadelphia. Director went bankrupt trying to get his franchise concept started. The financial disaster that finished him was the bankruptcy of one of his only two franchise holders. That franchise had been owned by Milton Doktor. Director's Tropical Paradise operation followed some months later. The Doktor brothers later used Murray Director's franchising ideas and were very successful. They did again get into financial trouble, but the name and the idea survived their ownership. The idea was just too good to disappear. An imaginative Boston financier named Vincent Ryan took control and saved the Doktor chain. Tropical Paradise operated one store that had been built to showcase Director's franchise plan. This was in a three story building under the elevated subway on Broadway in Queens near the Brooklyn border. Coincidentally this store (Tropical Paradise) was only four or five blocks from the old Herman Rabinow store on Myrtle Avenue that I had visited as a child. Rabinow was one of the early pioneer tropical fish retailers who had started dealing in tropical fish about 1905.

My father knew most of the auctioneers in the area. All of the auctioneers were members of the same loose guild. The auctioneer who was to sell the store and contents knew my father. He was a beefy, well-dressed man about fifty who talked very loud. I knew of the sale and had decided to attend and try to buy any bargains. My dad called Mr. Fleisher and asked him to help me, as I had no idea what I was doing. I had never even been to an auction. I got to the store early the day of the auction. There was a lot of inventory on the third floor, a fully equipped office, and still more inventory on the second floor. The ground floor was a fully stocked retail store. I found out later that about ninety percent of the upstairs inventory was composed of ceramic ornaments that Director had imported from Hong Kong. I never managed to sell even half of them. The business had operated until the day before the auction. There was still a good inventory of live fish. I spoke with the manager who was anxious to keep his job. He filled me in on some of the details. The landlord was there. He made it known that he would honor the existing lease if the new owner wanted to continue to operate the shop. I was warming to a fuzzy idea that should I get a bargain, I might try to operate the store. I made myself known to the auctioneer who instructed me to bid very low on every lot, and he would do the rest. There were about a dozen people present. Only four turned out to be active bidders. An announcement was made that anyone could make a bulk bid, and then Mr. Fleisher started auctioning at a very rapid pace. I had no idea what this meant. I later learned that if a bulk bid exceeded the totals of all the individual bids that bid would prevail. No one made a bulk bid. I had a great time bidding in some tremendous bargains. Mr. Fleisher, the auctioneer, (it took me a while to realize that he was manipulating the sales) would let one after another of the bidders buy bargains. He loved everyone and we all loved each other and Mr. Fleisher. If I got fifty new aquariums for sixty dollars he then would let someone else buy twenty wrought iron stands for thirty five dollars. At the end he disappeared for about five minutes. He returned and announced that he did have a bulk bid five hundred dollars higher than the total bid on the individual lots sold. I was disappointed. Mr. Fleisher asked me to stay. Only then did I find out that I was the bulk bidder. I had bought the entire store's contents for six thousand dollars including the auctioneer's commission. I was in the tropical fish business for myself. Wow! What excitement! I was in a real business dealing with tropical fish. I had no idea what I was doing. I was having the best time of my life. It kept getting better for the next forty years. Many times as the years have gone by I have been stunned, when I stopped running long enough to take stock of my life, and realized that I was actually doing something I loved and making money at it. I would gladly have paid for the privilege. I have gone to bed every night, anxiously waiting for the next day to start so I could keep on raising, studying, and breeding tropical fish. I have been so fortunate. I have always mourned the fate of the vast majority of people that spend lives working at jobs they do not enjoy. I did exactly that for nine years at "Sweet Life". I've been conscious of the wonder of being my own boss and doing exactly what I wanted. I know I have been good at it, and the reason was that I loved every minute of it. I was not a good business man. I did not enjoy handling people. I tended to want to do it all myself. At this late date I've finally realized that I did not have to do it that way. In fact it was pretty stupid. I now know that I ran off some wonderful and talented people who would have been great assets for the business. I also hired some real crazies. My problem was in not letting people think for themselves. They did not get a chance to demonstrate their abilities. Early on I realized that there were better educated people competing with me. It was easy to remedy. I was perfectly happy working longer and harder then they did. It worked.

Years ago my father made me memorize a little poem that says it all: "Early to bed and early to rise. Work like hell and advertise".

I certainly taught our children how to work. They are all overachievers. None are fish farmers or ever seriously considered it. Loise and I had them work at the farm as kids for their spending money. It amazes me now to know that they all love me in spite of my authoritarian behavior. I am a loving father, but have not always been a smart one.

General Aquatic Supply was born the day of the auction and lived for almost four years. I hired the existing crew for starters. This consisted of the manager whose name has disappeared from my memory. Thinking about him now makes me think of the old saying "He rose from mediocrity to obscurity". He lasted just a few weeks. I was trained by my father to supervise retail grocery store operations and I learned the most common behavior patterns of thieves. I could and did spot this type of manipulative artistry. I had been well trained watching some real artists in the grocery business. This guy was a bad amateur and he quickly became history. I hired Ed Buschell, a super hobbyist, as my manager. He did a good job. In fact, Ed later relocated to Florida and worked for me for several more years. His assistant was a certain Murray Weiner. Murray was the stereotype New Yorker. Most often Murray had his mouth in gear before his brain. His honesty, energy, and loyalty more than made up for this. He moved and spoke fast. A wonderful and gigantic (6'7") native Bajun (from Barbados) completed the regular crew. Maurice (Slim) Graves had an appetite to match his size. We had breakfast together Saturday mornings. He always ordered eggs. Slim would stop, pose, ponder, and then say, "Mon, dis be a seben egg day" and proceed to order seven fried eggs. The number always varied. I recall one special eleven egg day. Last crew member was a very bright, pudgy, sixteen year old named Stanley Levy. He was the part timer. He seemed to be there all the time. I put the business through three phases in the next few years casting around and learning—strictly retail, and then a retail/wholesale combination, and finally only wholesale livestock. I got to General Aquatic from Sweet Life (where I had been since 7 AM) about 3 PM every day during the week. I stayed two or three hours. I handled all of the night time arrivals of live fish shipments. It was fascinating and I kept learning. I spent every Saturday at General Aquatic and often also on Sunday. We started as only a retail business and I used the advertising methods my dad had perfected in the supermarket business. "How does he do it" and "Why pay more" now sold tropical fish instead of groceries. The average grocery shopper knows the prices on less than twenty items. Prices on such staple items as sugar, Maxwell House Coffee, Mortons Salt, Pillsbury Flour, Ivory Soap, apples, Heinz Catsup, potatoes, onions would be remembered, seldom anything else. Low prices on the items where the buyer knows the prices, and then enough of a mark up on the balance of the stock would average out profitably. In the retail pet shop the items became Longlife fish food, ten gallon tanks, neon tetras, zebra danios, parakeets, unsexed canaries, vibrator pumps, etc. I had no problem turning on the volume. In a very few months we even showed some small profits. Parakeets came from a shipper named Baty in New Braunfels, Texas. He made a living driving through Texas and Oklahoma picking up birds from farmers who he had set up and taught to breed parakeets. It worked. He also had people collecting horned toads and prairie dogs. We sold them all. Quality was not great. The prices were. Canaries came from Japan. The item bought was offered as "unsexed" canaries and which were always females that will not sing. If anyone ever got a "singer" (male) from the "unsexed" canaries I never heard about it. The Japanese were turning out vibrator pumps for less than $2.00 each. We did considerable business. In order to improve profits I had to buy to advantage. I found this a lot easier in the pet trade than in the grocery business. Paying cash really did wonders. I could send a truck to Mr. Hermann's Metaframe Aquarium Company in New Jersey, and take a full load of aquariums at special prices for pick up and payment in cash. I could sell a stainless steel fifty gallon tank for $30.00, and almost cover the cost. The fish were still the most interesting part, and the reason behind my entry into the business. I had to try to buy fish direct from the countries of origin, and not from wholesalers (Roosevelt, Henry's, Favors, Paramount). My first contact was with a Mr. Sutton in Trinidad. I was able to buy *Plecostomus*, *Corydoras aneus*, Rosaceus, and *Pristella* from there. The basement at General Aquatic could not be entered. It was full of galvanized metal fish cans. I did get some good addresses from the labels but no one wanted the cans. I eventually paid thirty five dollars to have them taken (two truck loads) to the dump. I found Mr. Sutton's name on one of these cans. Occasionally fish would come to Mr. Sutton in Trinidad from British Guiana. He would mark them up and resell them to me. There was no connection then to get the wonderful Guianese fish directly. I had had just two shipments of fish in German fish cans when shipping fish in metal cans became history. Even today the older buyers order a can of this and a can of that meaning, of course, a plastic bag full of fish. I am sure some of the newer hobbyists have heard "a can of" and not realized what it meant (I still put groceries in the "ice box"). The innovative use of a plastic bag to hold both fish and water had arrived. It revolutionized the industry.

I met a wholesaler from Baltimore several times when he came to New York to pick up fish. I think I met him first when we both were at Rabaut's place in Brooklyn buying some of his newly arrived Far Eastern fish. This was Merrill Cohen. He was more experienced than I and brighter (he still is), an extraordinarily farsighted and imaginative person. He also is unassuming and quiet. Merrill and I became friends then (1953) and remain friends today. Merrill Cohen was the person who first started using plastic bags to transport fish. I am delighted to give him the credit due him for this idea. As far as I know this credit is also the only thing he ever got out of it.

Merrill's father, a police sergeant, was an avid hobbyist. Merrill was hooked on tropical fish early. He obviously inherited these good genes. After graduating from college with degrees in Education and Biological Science, he had started the Aquarium Service Company (1944) while still completing his schooling. He married his wife Helen in 1948, and in order to keep eating also worked for his new father-in-law. This was Morris Dubow who was in the packaging business. This is where he got the inspiration to use plastic bags to transport fish. There were all sorts of problems before he made his idea work. Bags leaked or bags burst when sealed tightly. What thickness made both the product secure and the cost low? In 1948 he contacted the Bemis Bag Company for help. They made various sizes and weights of plastic bags that Merrill had tried (his father-in-law was a good Bemis customer). They suggested he try a newly developed process (electronic sealing through water). This solved the leakage problems. It was a great success from the start.

The first party he got to try them (other than Merrill himself) was Dr. Thomas of the Three Springs Fisheries in Lilypons, Maryland. At first Thomas would only use the plastic bags on truck deliveries. Inside of a year Lilypons was using the new sealed plastic bags in cardboard cartons to ship all of their goldfish by rail.

The first tropical fish shipper to use plastic bags in air shipments was Bill Sternke from Sunnyland Fish Farm in Florida. Sternke was Merrill Cohen's major supplier. To be safe Sternke put the plastic bags inside of metal fish cans. After three trial shipments without problem Sternke was convinced. He left the cans behind on all future shipments. Elsberry Fish Farms south of Tampa was the next convert. The ball was starting to roll. Merrill Cohen's plastic bag revolution started slowly. The old German fish can was dead and gone by 1953.

His next step was to open a retail store in Baltimore (1948). He also was wholesaling out the back door. Dow-Corning had just developed (in the late 1940s) a new product called Silastic (it was only black then) and Merrill read about it in the new product section of Modern Mechanics magazine. He ordered some and then made the first all-glass aquariums. It worked. One of his customers in Baltimore was Joe Cooley who had started manufacturing conventional galvanized metal "marble" aquariums. Cooley agreed to make the newly designed all glass aquariums for Merrill Cohen who sold them in his retail store. Cooley later moved to Florida where he manufactured almost all of the aquariums used by the Florida tropical fish farming industry. Dow themselves became interested in this unforeseen use of their Silastic. They exhibited their Silastic at the Jay Winters N.A.P.I. trade show in New York. They exhibited in Merrill Cohen's Aquarium Products booth and demonstrated the new product making all glass aquariums. They also showed how Silastic could be used to enhance the decorating of aquariums by bonding ceramics, wood, and rocks together. This made much more effective aquatic displays.

The Pan American airline cargo representative told us in 1954 that a direct flight from British Guiana to New York would be coming within the next year. That was really exciting. British Guiana meant headstanders, hatchet fish, four kinds of pencil fish, *Anostomus*, *Leporinus fasciatus*, *Otocinclus*, various species of *Corydoras*, banjo and talking catfish, *Geophagus* and keyhole cichlids, Hoplo catfish, Arowana, gold tetras, dwarf cichlids, *Anableps*, and piranha. I determined to visit British Guiana to arrange for a decent shipper when the fish became available. The opportunity to see my first wild tropical fish in the tropics was a life long dream. I would make a stop in Trinidad on the way and visit Mr. Sutton. The only two real shippers in British Guiana at the time were Louis Chung and Leonard Rafferty. Neither would sell to me. They supplied Paramount (Fred Cochu). Fred was the dominant figure in the business. He was a big and well established buyer. He was bringing in almost all of these fish and using his own airplane. A brilliant idea! He had made it work for years. He would not sell to me as I competed directly with Paramount's operation in New York City. He was absolutely right. There were several other small, newly established dealers in Georgetown, British Guiana. I had some correspondence with a Sam Persaud and one attempt at a shipment via Trinidad that was a disaster. The trip seemed a must. This was the first of at least fifty collecting trips I made south into Latin America in the next forty years. I think this was the only trip where I did not enter the jungle to personally collect fish.

Murray Director, who had operated the defunct Tropical Paradise business (that I had bought at the auction), surfaced again in (of all places) British Guiana. A really strange coincidence. He now was in the gold and diamond business. He even had persuaded my father to invest money in his newest scheme. Director knew I was in the tropical fish business, and had bought his defunct Tropical Paradise location at auction. He wrote me about six months before my trip. He was expanding his operation and would be entering the fish export business. I wrote him that I was coming for a visit, and I would see him there. By the time I got to British Guiana he was mostly in the fish business. The diamond and gold ventures were not working out (not surprisingly my dad lost his entire investment).

I spent only two days in Trinidad. I had scheduled five days. I was the first customer who had ever visited Sam Sutton. I felt very uncomfortable in Trinidad. I soon picked up on a strong degree of discomfort on Mr. Sutton's part. The strict racial separation that the British established in their colony was the cause. Mr. Sutton was black. He was very uncomfortable (and unwelcome) visiting in the hotel where I was staying. He was not permitted in the restaurants. He was a real gentleman and an excellent supplier for many years until his death. I cut the stay short as I was very aware of Mr. Sutton's discomfort and did not know any other way to handle it. Sutton took me out to see *Plecostomus* being collected. I was amazed to see them taken out of deep holes they had made in the banks. I did not realize they could grow to 15 inches in length. He gifted me a unique albino *Plecostomus*. It was a beautiful animal and I wondered then if anyone would ever be able to breed *Plecostomus* commercially and if an albino strain would ever be established.

A new friend named Jimmy Atz (later Dr. James Atz), who worked at the Museum of Natural History taught me that pronunciation of a Latin name was often only a question of who said it first, with the most authority. Latin as a spoken language had been extinct for more than a thousand years. No one really knew how to pronounce Latin words. The Trinidad tropical fish community had little or no verbal contact with the rest of the tropical fish world. All pronounced the names as they imagined they should be said. It took me a few minutes to realize that Rowzasoos were Rosaceus and then PLEEcoSTOmus with the accent mostly on the first syllable was easy.

I stayed in British Guiana ten days. During this time I made arrangements to buy fish from both Persaud and Director. I would be able to eventually pick the best. Director had a man named Joe Jardim working for him. He ran the crew and was very capable. He supervised the keeping, packing, and shipping of the fish. I spent a lot of time with both Jardim and his assistant, a very young and very bright Harry Rambarran. It was quickly apparent to me that Director was not in it for the long haul. He was having money and personality problems in British Guiana and within the year he was expelled. We never heard about him again. His fish were very good, in spite of him, as both Jardim and Rambarran were excellent fish handlers. They both were unhappy with Director. He was having problems with the authorities. I was not surprised when, three months later, I received a letter from Joe Jardim telling me that he had left Director, and wanted to go into business for himself. He said he was writing to me first to try to find a partner who would finance him, and own half of the business. He had no money. I immediately answered. I was interested. I knew exactly what I could do if I could establish a partnership with Jardim. Jardim had nothing. He knew how to buy, keep, and pack fish. I could do the selling, advertising, and select the best customers. Then as now, there were a good number of dead beats around that preyed on new shippers. I gave him the $4,000 he asked and was a 50% partner (I thought). I had not yet learned to do things formally. No papers were ever drawn.

General Aquatic could never absorb what he could supply. I knew if I could call the shots I could turn on the business. I made the price lists. The fish were properly described, named, and priced. I directed the destinations for our price lists. He now could ship directly to New York. I NEVER let anyone know that I owned half of Jardim's business. Our business took off like a rocket. It worked better than I had hoped. I sold to all my competitors without them ever knowing I was a half owner of Jardim's business (Favors, Roosevelt, Paramount, etc.). They paid good prices. They got good fish. In a matter of a very few months we were making good profits. At the end of the first year 1954 I met with Jardim in Guiana planning to formalize our agreement. I had written him repeatedly to have the papers drawn. His lack of enthusiasm was making me nervous. We had already been able to pay for all the equipment, had bought a vehicle, and had leftover a profit of almost thirty thousand dollars. This was only the beginning. I had plans for a large expansion into other countries (Colombia, Brazil, Peru, and Venezuela) and felt we would be making six figures or more in another year or two. When I met him face to face I was dumbfounded to hear from Jardim that he was not going to make a formal agreement with me. In fact he was returning my "loan". I had met and become friends with two young Guianese lawyers, Sonny Janki and Forbes Burnham. I visited them immediately. Forbes Burnham pointed out things to me that made it impossible to think of recovering the money. I learned an expensive lesson. That was the end of that learning experience. I have never quite recovered from that treacherous act.

Forbes Burnham later became the Premier of the newly independent country "Guyana" and served in that capacity until his death many years later. I never saw him again and I never returned to Guyana. Jardim never ever got back to the point he was at when he cheated me. He eventually went out of business which still makes me smile when I think about it. In the meantime Harry Rambarran was able to enter the business. I was his first customer and he and Edna have remained among my close friends. I see him from time to time. He always laughs and says, "How is my oldest living customer?" Harry Rambarran is the very best and the most honest shipper I have ever met; a gentleman to the core.

I am smiling now, thinking about the Anaconda. It was more than tense when it happened. Not in the jungles of Guyana, but at General

Aquatics in the wilds of Brooklyn. I had a note from Jardim which came weekly giving me his inventory so I could cable him our order. I paid little attention to the statement that he was sending me a "novelty" as a gift. I expected something like a rare artifact, a piece of jewelry, or a carved mask and looked forward to my present. Slim and Stanley picked up the next shipment. They staggered in with legs bowed under the weight of a huge wooden crate (my gift). Stanley said "Boss, you won't believe this ...." Jardim's "novelty" was a sixteen-foot Anaconda. It had a terrible scar on its head. It had evidently been captured by an Indian using a wire snare. This had made it mean as hell. I've never met a snake with such a vile disposition. Fortunately, we had a huge three hundred gallon aquarium made out of angle iron and plate glass that always leaked. It was almost eight feet long and large enough to keep this nightmare creature. We had no problem getting it in, keeping it in was something else. We took turns laying on the oversized wooden door we had atop it as a cover while the others scurried for concrete blocks. Soon we had enough concrete blocks piled on to contain this Godzillasnake. It was a big mistake putting the snake in the front display window where it attracted an almost immediate summons from the New York City Department of Health. I had seven days to dispose of the snake or the wrath of bureaucracy would descend to close me down and fine me a horrendous amount of money which apparently would double every few minutes. They were really serious. I needed no push to want to get rid of this gigantic headache. I had been trying and had already called everyone I could imagine. Dr. Carl Kauffield, who was then the curator of the Staten Island Zoo, was the only one interested enough to come to see it. I learned from him that no zoo would display the snake because of the scar. He wouldn't have it for a gift. My price dropped to zero. Ed Buschell, at this time, came up with a great idea. He found a copy of an article written about a teenager living on Long Island who had a large collection of snakes. Ed suggested offering the snake to this precocious juvenile herpetologist. We did. I can still remember the part of the conversation I overheard from our end. I told Ed not to try to sell it, but to give it away. Not Ed, who could sell anything. He had an excited buyer on the phone and I heard him say "about ten or twelve feet" (I could not blame him for lying about the great size) and then "How much have you got" followed by "that will be enough." "You can send the rest of it later" and finally "you must come down and take it tomorrow morning about an hour before the store opens." The boy turned up the next day as arranged. It was momentarily disconcerting when he said that he came by subway and would take the snake back that way. He was not the least shaken when he saw the huge snake. I was surprised as I had expected him to turn and run. I would have. I am sure he felt he was cheating me. Everyone knows a sixteen foot plus snake is better than a twelve foot snake. He gave Ed part of the agreed on money. I think it was less than twenty dollars as a down payment. We mobilized for action. As owner I announced that I was the boss and director of the operation. I then stationed myself part way up the stairs to the second floor where I could see everything that was happening and safely shout orders. We had saved the huge bag that the snake came in. It was some sort of a very tough burlap. The plan was simple. We would stuff it in the bag. The juvenile had told us that if we took it to the subway and helped get it on the train, he could drag it off. Then he would call for help from the platform on his end ... Sounded good to me.

I stationed the buyer at the head. He had already volunteered to grab the monster and pull it out. Slim would then grab the middle (he was by far the strongest). He had already turned down my offer to let him get the head. Bushell would handle the bag. Murray Weiner would help stuff it in the bag. Stanley would take the tail. I wish that I had used a camera. No words can describe what happened. I still can not believe it. It was total bedlam. Everyone had their instructions when we put the plan into operation. I had neglected to tell the "snake from hell", what he was supposed to do. He improvised. God, did he ever. The Anaconda was so glad to get out of the box that he shook himself like a wet puppy and splattered the walls with flying employees. Stanley pushed by me and disappeared up the stairs. The snake was free and trying to find a way back to British Guiana. I could visualize the headlines in the newspapers "GIANT SNAKE WIPES OUT PET SHOP — SIX PEOPLE HOSPITALIZED — OWNER ARRESTED".

The juvenile was either brave or stupid (I suspect both) as he shamed us all by again grabbing the head and hanging on as the huge constrictor started to encircle his body (just like in the movies). I got involved at this point mostly to try to avoid a life in jail provided that I was lucky enough to survive the next few minutes (which seemed unlikely). It took considerable doing and mostly thanks to Slim, who was almost as strong as the snake, to get it stuffed into the huge sack and then securely tied. We all carried the monster snake into our van and drove (all six of us) the three blocks to the subway. We each paid our five cents and dragged the snake forward, under the turnstile, up the stairs, and onto the platform and close to the platform's edge. A train came almost immediately. We stuffed the snake and his new owner into the train. The door closed. The train left. We stood there silently. All of us were in semi-shock. We never heard from the snake, the juvenile, or the Department of Health again. It all happened almost forty years ago and I am still worrying about it.

About this time I made two lifelong friends. All three of us were about the same age. We all were busy getting established in the Tropical Fish business. The first was Earl Kennedy from the Philippines. No one will ever touch him as a collector and shipper of marine fish and invertebrates. I was his second customer. It took, with all connections working (which did not happen very often), sixty plus hours to get a fish shipment from Earl. A young chemist, Walter Smith, who made private label products created a synthetic sea salt for us. I called this "**Seamix**". There was a salt mix on the market (Neptune) and we had used it with only fair results. Our chemist said he knew what was wrong with that product and could improve it. He did. We had a much better result with his new product. He felt certain trace elements were missing. He solved that by gathering a collection of various types of soil from different areas. He mixed them all together. He used this in the artificial salt water mix. Surprisingly it worked. His instruction was to periodically add a tea spoonful of sodium sulfathiazole to each tank. I think this did more than anything to help as it buffered the water and helped prevent bacterial infections and acidic build ups. Marine fish keeping was very primitive in the early 1950s. Only the bravest and wealthiest customers could indulge themselves in trying to keep these wonderful, newly available, marine fish. None had names. I made them up as best I could, and some of them stuck, such as the tomato and the skunk clownfish. About this time Walter Smith, our chemist friend, figured that we might use a drug called paraldehyde as a tranquilizer. This is an aldehyde of alcohol used to wean alcoholics from "real" alcohol. It satisfied an immediate craving, and then they vomited. The fear of vomiting was an important deterrent and easy to understand why it could eventually work. We had been using with some benefit things like Miltown, one of the early tranquilizers, and sodium pentothal. Paraldehyde worked and in fact still is the best tranquilizer I have ever used. I gave this "secret" to my best three suppliers Earl Kennedy, Harry Rambarran, and Pierre Brichard. We all used it with great success shipping fish. The dose in fresh water is forty drops to the gallon which is too strong for marine fish. To tranquilize marine fish use twenty-five drops to the gallon. Paraldehyde helped reduce our costs and improved results. Freight cost could be cut in half as we now could safely pack double quantities. We were still years away from jet plane service and only propeller driven planes were flying.

Earl and Gloria Kennedy are two of the brightest and most honorable people the industry has ever produced. We did not meet for many years. They made Loise and me God-parents, by proxy, of their first child (Gaylene). It was more than fifteen years later that we finally met. Many of our closest friends are Chinese. They have sincere and honorable traditions in business and have all proven to be the most virtuous of suppliers. Given a free choice I would blindly buy fish from anyone who is Chinese. Imagine our surprise and delight when my Irish friend Earl Kennedy turned out to be Chinese. Earl 's father had emigrated from China to the Philippines. The immigration people had spelled his name Kennedy (it actually was something like Kenai Dai) ... shades of Ellis Island. We had a wonderful visit. Earl has a degree as an architect, and draws beautiful murals. We drank a lot of beer together one night, talked and talked, and then Earl drew a mural on the living room wall. I thought it beautiful. Gloria had other ideas. We haven't seen each other since, but keep in touch. The Kennedy's closed down their marine collecting and shipping business years ago. The Philippine collectors all started fishing with cyanide. The Philippine fish being sold were damaged. I know some of my complaints helped identify the problem. Large percentages of fish would not survive for long. Given the choice of using these drugged and weakened fish in order to stay competitive, or go out of business, Gloria and Earl closed the doors. This decision came as a surprise. This was not an easy decision for the Kennedy clan and I think unique. It was a testimonial to their character. Earl remains in the "fish" business. He has for years now raised *Macrobrachium* (the giant freshwater prawns) and milk fish. He does considerable consulting work throughout the Far East and is honored and respected by all.

The other great friend I found in 1953. He was a Belgium by the name of Pierre Brichard. He had just started shipping fish from the Belgium Congo in Africa. He had sent two sample shipments to friends of mine (Aaron Dvoskin, Bill Harsell, and Rosario LaCorte) in New Jersey. Pierre asked them to recommend another buyer. I was selected. Aaron died some years ago. He had left the industry and became a school teacher. He suffered from a strange disease that is invariably fatal to many of us in the fish business. Fortunately, I learned early on to (somewhat) discipline myself. Aaron didn't, and the disease was fatal to his business (Suburban Tropical Fish). Oh yes, the disease. It is known as "hobbyitis". It is incurable and the more serious you are about the hobby aspect of fish keeping the more dangerous the disease. It is hard to show profits when you can not get yourself to sell the best fish.

I think 1953-54 was the most exciting time in my life as that is when I received every week one of Pierre Brichard's shipments which always contained some unknown new fish. I would never let anyone else handle them. They always arrived by Pan American or Scandinavian Airlines in the middle of the night. Shipments usually were between ten and twenty large double boxes. Alone, in the fish room at General Aquatic in the middle of the night, I opened each bag and saw fish that never had been seen in America. I have never admitted it before, but most times when, all alone, unpacking these new and strange fish I found myself continuously screaming out loud in pure delight. No mind altering drugs could ever have affected me as much.

I preserved the fish that arrived dead. In order to learn what they were, I started searching for someone who could help. No reference books were available. Finally, I located a copy of the George Boulenger four volume set of "**Fresh-Water Fishes of Africa**". The set was in the library of the Museum of Natural History. I went there on a Saturday morning to try and use it. No one was working. I wandered about the almost deserted halls of the off limits 5th floor when suddenly a voice startled me. It belonged to an elderly man wearing moccasins who shuffled into the hall from a small office. I introduced myself and told him my problem. He took my arm and firmly steered me into his office. There I realized how lucky I had become. This ramrod straight, elderly, distinguished man was the famous Dr. John Treadwell Nichols, and even more exciting was that he was just delighted to help me. Before I left he gave me a gift of one of his own books. This was his report of an ichthyological expedition he had made to the Belgian Congo in the 1890s. It even had a number of good color plates. Together we then went over the Boulenger books. I learned a lot. I repeated the visit a number of times and eventually, with his help, I managed to locate a copy of the set in London and bought it.

Dr. Myron Gordon and Dr. Charles Breder also shared laboratory space on the fifth floor and had offices in the same area. Breder was then working on the newly discovered race of eyeless blind cave characins that Basil Jordan had just found in caves in Northern Mexico. Years later Dr. Breder retired to Florida in an area just south of where Gulf Fish Hatchery was located. A young Dr. Eugenie Clark was then (1953) working for Dr. Gordon doing research on the reproduction of live bearing fishes. She will, of course, be remembered for her book "**Lady with a Spear**", but her pioneer work on livebearer reproduction added greatly to our knowledge. Time marched on and Eugenie became the Director of the Cape Haze Marine Laboratory, again in the same area of Florida. So after many years I had Dr. Breder and Dr. Clark again as neighbors. I enjoyed the friendship and advice of both of these remarkable people. Dr. Myron Gordon and I had a lot in common and I was happy to be able to help his projects by supplying fish he could not otherwise get. The fish he wanted had little to no commercial value and the average dealer was not interested in trying to get the fish. I was flattered by Dr. Gordon's friendship and delighted to help him. This included the little known *Micropoecilia* from British Guiana and, more important, living specimens of *Tomurus gracilis*. *Tomurus* were not hard to catch, but just hell to keep alive long enough to send to me. Myron Gordon had a terrible time trying to keep them alive. He kept at it and we made a number of different trials before good results were obtained. The fish is so transparent that it becomes invisible in its natural habitat. It lives in midstream of the Demerara River in British Guiana. It was easy to collect. His interest in the fish was stimulated because *Tomurus* is an egg laying fish with many characteristics of livebearing fishes. It lays fertile adhesive eggs (singly) that were already coming to term, and the egg hatches in a very few days. I do not remember ever billing Myron Gordon for fish. I eagerly accepted his offer to trade for his

Telephone
STagg 2-0300

Cable
GENAQUA

GENERAL AQUATIC SUPPLY CORP.
714 Broadway
Brooklyn, N. Y.

NEWS LETTER - REPORT ON NEW ARRIVALS - SOME SPECIALS WHILE THEY LAST....

FAR EAST- Some new and welcome arrivals including clown loaches $2.50, Flying foxes(Epal.Kallopterus) $3.00, Chocolate Gourami $2.00, large Kuhlii Loaches 28 or 24 per 100, Rasbora Heteromorpha 28 or 24 per 100, Scissortails 30 or 27 per 100, Scats large $2.00, smaller $1.50, Monos, red tail and black sharks are available, also large bumble bees 55 or 45¢ per 50, should have next week Botia Pulchripinnis $2.50, and the tiger Botia Hymenophysa $2.00, also Barbus Schwanfelti $1.75 and Hexazona.

SOUTH AMERICANS- received our second direct shipment of Discus. I made a mistake and only ordered small and the next size larger as I didn't think I'd be able to move all of the jumbos and mediums but they've all been sold, so this month only small and a little larger $3.00 and $4.00 and they are bigger average than you're used to getting. Piranahs on hand small $1.00, 2"-$2.00, 3-4"-$3.50, larger $10.00. Wild angels, mediums $1.00, 4" plus $2.00, these are P.Altum as illustrated in Tropical Fish Hobbyist March-April Issue. Red spots and bull dog nose..Neons 18½¢ in bag lots 15¢ per 100, marble hatchets 18 and silvers 20, mettynis 45, Marginatus pencils 14, and unifasciatus 22, silver tets 15 and 13 in 100's, gold tets 17, Roascaius, Pristilla 17, Head and tails 19, Anostomus 85, Chilodus Punctatus small 65 large 75. Wild oscars from Peru 1½" 50, G.Jurupari 75, large knife fish 8-10" $2.50, melanistius cats 18, leopardus 24, julii 26, large arcuatus 26, rabauti 30, whiptails 30, otocinclus 23, hastatus 22, plecostomus 25, if less than 100's on the cats add 2¢ per fish- Tetra Perez, the bleeding heart tetra large and beautiful 45¢, mixed unidentified and rare South American cats $3.50 per dozen.

From EUROPE glo lites 25, sumatranis barbs 20, black ruby 23, gold 24, oligolipus 24, T's 26, cherry 23, filimentosa 45, clowns 25, Badis badis 35, german bettas 65, females 37, Telmaterini Ladegisi 85, Panchax Chaperi and Linneatus 45, Australe 65, and all the rest..

AFRICANS moving just fine and receipts are steady-if you haven't tried these yet you're missing a sure thing. As they're expensive they don't all sell like guppies but they are here to stay and it's a real chance to have something different and attract the real hobbyists- snakeheads $3.00, featherfin lungs $3.00, Dist Affinis $1.25, D.Lussosso $6.00 & small $4.00, Jimmy Durante Mormyrids $7.00 other varieties $2.50 and $3.50, puffers $1.50, red puffers $2.00, spiny nosed eels $3.50, Upside down cats $1.25, 25 lots $1.00, buffalo headed dwarf cichlids $2.50, copper nosed barilius $1.50, golden sharks $4.00, african black sharks $3.00, unidentified grab bag of african sharks $25.00 per dozen, grab bag of weird african catfish $17.50 per dozen and for those who are unfamiliar with Africans an assortment to introduce you with, worth much more than the $20.00 per dozen we charge..african knife fish $1.75, cognatum and other african panchax 75¢, Electric catfish $5.00 and $10.00 for large. Pantodons $5.00, Shovel nosed cats $2.50, and many, many more...

We're doing a wonderful job on pacific marine fish and if you are interested we'll send you all the information. Prices are kept down to the point where anyone can purchase as for example small clowns $2.45. We have our own salt mix that works like a charm. If you want to give it a try I'll send some of it to you.

Incidentally don't get the idea this is all we have to sell as we have many 100's of other fish in stock at all times-priced-right-in fact to my knowledge we have the greatest variety of fish ever offered by one source- all the florida bred fish, too... We're sending out a lot of these news letters to new customers and if you want to continue to receive them you must write and ask to be put on our regular mailing list(old customers will keep getting it whether they like it or not). If you haven't our complete catalog write for it. $100.00 minimum order. Call us collect if you want and ask for Ed or Ross- Cash with Order. Shipments made within 48 hours.

Brass Valves - 2 way or 3 way...22¢ per 100
5" Daphnia nets.............11.00 per dozen
3" Goldfish nets............ 6.00 per 100
All Dry Goods.....Corals....Brine Shrimp Food

March 15, 1956

SUMMER NEWS LETTER AND SOME "HOT SPECIALS"

Just completed arrangements with the best shipper in England of Asiatic fishes, to handle his sales for the U.S.A. Bag lots only, special price list for terms, etc. on request. (Rasboras-Bees-Kuhlii-Sharks-Botia-etc.) Have shipped directly to Florida this week without losses--so it looks good for our wholesale accounts.

We are now exclusive representatives for Vavasseur Trading for their Ceylonese fishes. First shipment came in this morning. "Wow" Six inch Belontia Signata, Crimson Red in color, Wild Cherry Barbs (Red as Serpae) at .50--Panchax Dayi at .65--Barbus Binotatus and NEW SALT WATER FISHES that take your Breath away.

Selling lots more MARINES than ever before now that our customers are learning that they can keep them alive indefinitely with our Synthetic Salt Mix. -- Getting unsolicited Testimonials every day -- Prices are lower than ever and an additional 10% off if you take 25 or more assorted Marines. INTRODUCTORY SPECIAL

Enough Salt for a 10 Gallon Aquarium-Hydrometer- 2 Clown Fish for $6.50.

Most EXCITING Fish of the Month is RED BEAKED and Full Beaked half-beaks that Earl Kennedy shipped us from the Palowan Islands in the Phillippines. The Red Beaked one grows to five inches. All sold out quickly, but more on the way.

Archer fish at 2.25 and Scats (1.50 med. 2.00 Large 2.50 Ex-Large) are moving out fast. Our Scats are clean and healthy and in pure fresh water. The secret with Scats is Hard Water and the best way to give it to them is to crush a purifier block (Plaster of Paris) and throw it into their tank.

All of the South Americans with the exception of Discus are coming in and the Discus should be here by the time you receive this letter. Limited quantities of Chalceus, Wild Severum .55, Farlowella 1.00, Buenocephalis Catfish .85, besides the old standbys. Melanistius Cats .18 in 100 lots, Plecistomus 25.00 per 100, Marble hatchets .17 and silver .19, God Tetra .18, Rosaceus and Pristella .16, Marginatus Pencils .16, Unifasciatus .22, Auratus and Trifasciatus .25, Mettynis .55, Anostomus .85, Headstanders .75, Loricara Parvia .40, Silver Tetra .15, Buenos Aires Tets .15, Black Tets .15, Wild Angels, Piranah, Festivum .35, Otocinclus .22, Arcuatis Catfish .28.

Some New Africans coming through in good quantities--A. Myersii .50, A. Cognatus .75, A. Sexfasciatus .75, P. Interruptus in 50 Lots .75, Upside Down Catfish .80 in 50 Lots, 1.00 in 25 Lots, Ctenopoma Ansorgi 1.00, Leopard and Chocolate Ctenopoma 2.00, Red Puffers 2.00, Green Puffers 1.50, Both are 100% Fresh Water, Featherfin Lung Fish 3.00, Snakeheads 3.00, Underwater Frogs (Fully Aquatic) 1.00 Anew Barbus - B. Hulstaerti-Very Pretty, N. Nudiceps 1.25-Breeders 2.50, Spiny nosed Eels 2.50.

Our German Breeders are shipping us regularly all of the Barbus--Clown.27-Golds.25-Black Ruby.26-Cherry.25-sumatranus.21-olegolipus.25-andBadis-Badis .35, Glolites .26, Monkhoesia Pitteria .40, Bettas .75, Chaetedon (Black Banded Sunfish) .45, Panchax Linneatus .45, Chaperii .45, Australe (Lyretail) .60.

Asiatics on hand include---Black Sharks & Clown Loach, Rasbora H. .24 in 100 Lots, Scissortail Rasbora .30--.26 in 100 Lots, Bumble Bees .55--25 for .45, Glass Cats .55, Kihlii Loach .28--.24 in 100 Lots, Orandas 3.00.

We are set up to start manufacturing PLASTIC TANKS this Summer, but want to know who would be interested-- Write us and we will give you an idea of prices (which we know will be real cheap) Jobbing set up, etc. It looks real good.

Call Collect to place orders ask for Ross or Ed. Not less than 100.00 unless we know you.

GENERAL AQUATIC SUPPLY CORP., 714 BROADWAY, BROOKLYN 6, NEW YORK
STagg 2-0300, 2-0301, 2-0302, 2-5083

Emilio Saiz (left) checking fish shipment.

Dr. Joanne Norton lecturing at F.T.F.F.A. meeting.

Pierre Brichard

Rosario LaCorte with the author

Crescent's Efficient Service works so smoothly that few people realize the large extent of CRESCENT'S operations !

Here are a few statistics:

807 Ponds . . . . . 4x8x15 . . . . in New Orleans
1 Hothouse . . . 48x124 . . . . in New Orleans
1 Hothouse . . . 27x124 . . . . in New Orleans

6700 . . . ½ Gallon Bowls for Bettas and live bearers
300 . . . 12 Gallon Aquariums
300 . . . 5 Gallon Aquariums
28 . . . 80 Gallon Aquariums

At Slidell . . . 6 acres (out of 28) entirely covered by ponds.

Number of fish shipped in 1937 (actual from invoices) 632,744.

Gross receipts in 1937 — $34,920.00.
(We will let you try to figure the net)

Number of Employees: 14.

With the above figures, is it any surprise to you that we ship practically every jobber and a great part of all the pet shops in the country?

If in a Hurry — wire CRESCENT.
YOU ARE ASSURED OF SATISFACTION

CRESCENT FISH FARM

1624 Mandeville St. New Orlenas, La.

April 1938

CRESCENT FISH FARM

LARGEST PLANT IN THE UNITED STATES DEVOTED TO THE RAISING OF ORNAMENTAL AND EXOTIC FISH.

115 PONDS. MOST OF THEM 3½ BY 7. SOME LARGER. 44 OF THESE UNDER GLASS. 150 TEN GALLON AQUARIUMS CONSTANTLY IN USE. OUTPUT 20.000 TO 25.000 TROPICAL FISH PER YEAR. WE SHIP PRACTICALLY TO ALL STATES IN THE UNION.

SUMMER SPECIALS

MOLLIENISIA SPHENOPS

THIS IS UNDOUBTEDLY ONE OF THE MOST ATTRACTIVE AND SATISFACTORY FISH FOR THE AQUARIUM, JET BLACK, CONSTANTLY ON THE MOVE, EATING ANY FOOD THAT OTHER TROPICALS EAT AND LIVING IN HARMONY WITH THEM AND ARE BREEDING 90 TO 100 PERCENT TRUE TO COLOR. BREEDING SIZE FISH

$5.00 PER TRIO.

SPHENOPS—Meaning wedge shaped. The male of the species has a smaller dorsal fin than most of the well known Mollienisia family, and it has a peculiar wedge shape.

These are not collected fish. All are raised in small ponds and aquariums on our farm. The perfection in color, etc. is due to years of watchful care and selection from original stock. Mr. Geo. S. Myers, in his description of Sphenops in "The Aquarium and Its Denizens," published by the Hudson Aquarium Society in 1922, says: "A perfectly black pair is very pretty and highly prized." We have them, male and female, jet black.

RED HELLERI

LARGE FEMALES 2½ to 3 INCHES LONG. $1.00 EACH.

HYBRIDS, HELLERI-RUBRA

LARGE FEMALES. $1.00 EACH

PARADISE FISH

LARGE. $4.00 and $5.00 PER DOZEN.

CLIMBING PERCH

YOUNG. $1.00 AND $1.50 EACH.

DANIO RERIO, SWORD TAIL, GUPPYS, MOUTH BREEDERS, DANIO MALABARICUS, GOLD PLATYS.

ALL BREEDING SIZES. SEE OUR FRONT PAGE AD.

Shipping Cans 35 Cents Each.

VALLISNERIA SPIRALIS

THE BEST ALL AROUND AQUARIUM PLANT (WORKS ON BOTH ENDS) TOP OXYGENATES BETTER THAN MOST AQUARIUM PLANTS AND THE ROOTS REACHING FOR NOURISHMENT KEEPS SAND AND BOTTOM OF AQUARIUMS CLEAN., PRICE

$1.50 PER 100 POSTPAID.

OUR GROUND SHRIMP IS ALL THAT WE CLAIM FOR IT. PURE SHRIMP (NO SHELLS), FINE FOR BOTH TROPICALS AND GOLDFISH. PER POUND IN 10 LB. LOTS, 35c.; 25 LBS. 32½c.; 50 LBS. 30c. AND 25 c. PER POUND IN 100 LB. LOTS, F. O. B. NEW ORLEANS.

A CORDIAL INVITATION IS EXTENDED TO OUR FRIENDS AND CUSTOMERS WHEN VISITING THE SOUTH THIS FALL AND WINTER TO LET US SHOW YOU OVER THE "FARM."

1624 MANDEVILLE ST., NEW ORLEANS, LA.

May 1925

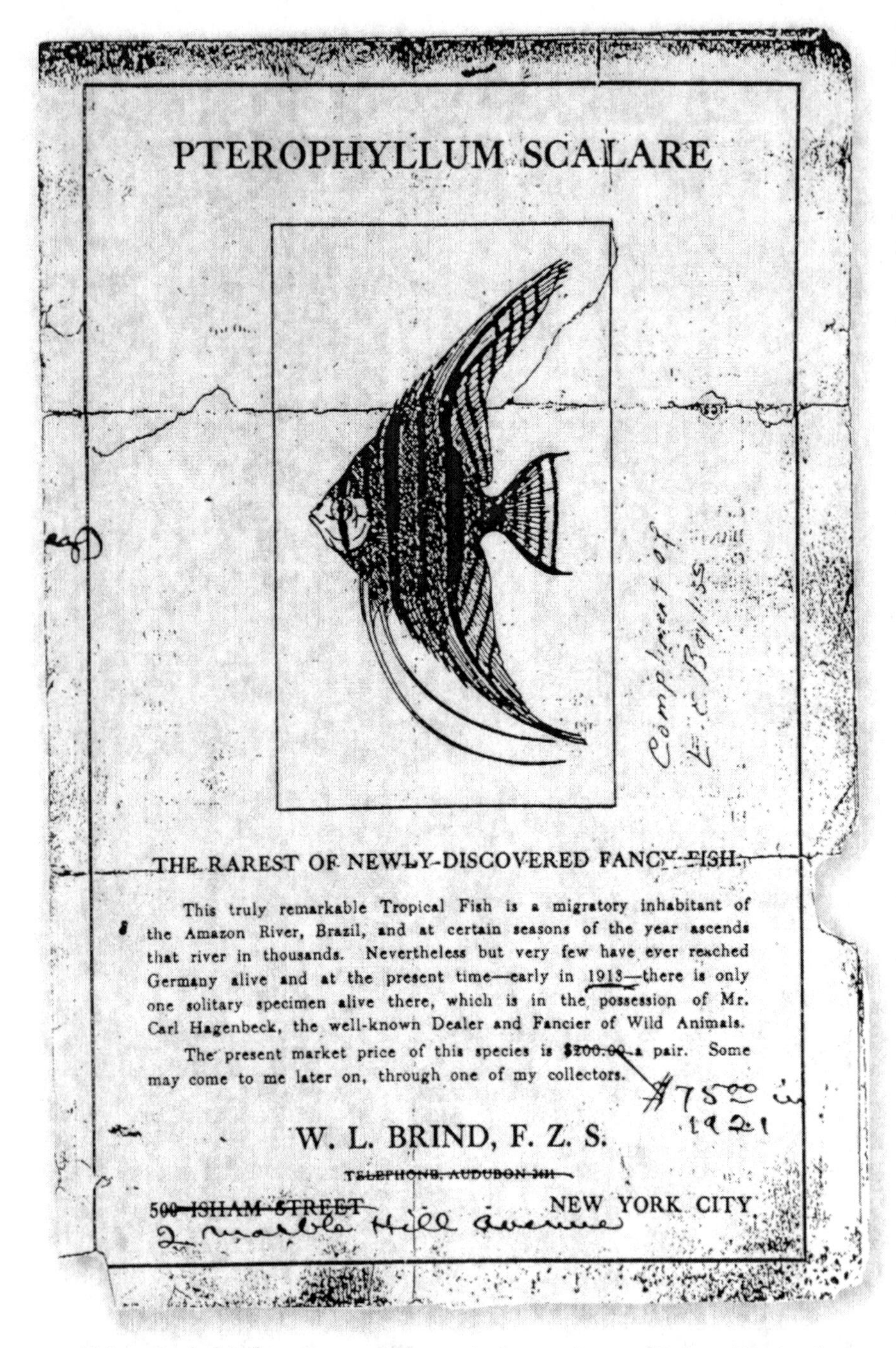

PTEROPHYLLUM SCALARE

THE RAREST OF NEWLY-DISCOVERED FANCY FISH.

This truly remarkable Tropical Fish is a migratory inhabitant of the Amazon River, Brazil, and at certain seasons of the year ascends that river in thousands. Nevertheless but very few have ever reached Germany alive and at the present time—early in 1913—there is only one solitary specimen alive there, which is in the possession of Mr. Carl Hagenbeck, the well-known Dealer and Fancier of Wild Animals.

The present market price of this species is ~~$200.00~~ a pair. Some may come to me later on, through one of my collectors. $75.00 in 1921

W. L. BRIND, F. Z. S.

~~TELEPHONE, AUDUBON 3611~~

~~500 ISHAM STREET~~ NEW YORK CITY
2 Marble Hill Avenue

Compliment of E. C. Bayliss

This remarkable four-page catalogue is the property of Robert Harris of Scarborough, Ontario, Canada. I thank him for permission to reprint it and also the letter from Dr. Innes to Bayliss.

W. L. BRIND, F. Z. S: Aquarist, 500 Isham St., cor. [illegible]
New York City, N. Y., U. S. A.

PRICE-LIST OF RARE AND BEAUTIFUL AQUARIUM FISHES.

TOOTH-CARP GROUP:—EGG-LAYING FISHES

FUNDULUS FAMILY—(KILLIFISHES)	Price Per Pair
Red and Blue Spotted Fundulus, F. Chrysotus	$2.00
Blunt-headed Fundulus, F. Heteroclitus	1.50
Rainwater Fundulus, Lucania Parva	1.00
Gold-spotted Fundulus, F, Dispar	2.00
Black-striped Fundulus, F, Notatus	2.00

TOOTH-CARP GROUP:—LIVE-BEARING [illegible]ES

Holbrook's Gambuse, Gambusia Holbrooki	1.00 to 2.50
Nicaragua Gambuse, Gambusia Nicaraguensis	2.00 to 3.00
Two-spotted Gambuse, G. Caudimaculata	2.00
Red-finned Gambuse, G. Rubropinna	2.50 and 3.00
Ten-spotted Gambuse, G. Decem-maculata	3.50
Spotted Girardinus, G. Reticulatus	2.50
Rainbow Girardinus, G. Guppyi (Poecilioides)	2.00
Flag-fin, Mollienesia Latipinna	2.00 to 5.00
Sword-tail, Xiphophorus Helleri	2.00 to 5.00
Jalapa Sword-tail, Xiphophorus Jalapae	3.00 to 5.00
Double-striped Sword-tail, X. Brevis	5.00
Rachow's Sword-tail, X. Rachowi	6.00
Ruby Moonfish, Platypoecilia Rubra	2.00 and 3.00
Black Moonfish, P. Nigra	2.00 and 3.00
Spotted Moonfish, P. Reticulata	2.00 and 3.00
Blue Moonfish, P. Maculata	2.00 and 3.00

LABYRINTH FISHES:—BUBBLE-NEST BUILDERS

Paradise Fish, Macropodus Viridi-Auratus	1.00 to 2.50
Red and Blue tailed Polyacanthus, P. Dayi	3.00
Point-tailed Dwarf Paradise Fish, P. Cupanus	2.50
Red Fighting Fish, Betta Rubra	4.00
Resplendent Fighting Fish, B. Splendens	5.00
Striped Gurami, Trichogaster Fasciatus	3.00
Dwarf Gurami, Trichogaster Lalius	3.00
Spotted Gurami, Osphromenus Trichopterus	4.00
Ocellated Snakehead, Ophiocephalus Ocellatus (Brindi)	5.00

MISCELLANEOUS FANCY FISHES

Mesogonisteus Chaetodon, Banded Sunfish	1.00 to 2.00
Soldier Fish, Etheostoma Coeruleum	2.00 to 3.00
Fantailed Darter, Etheostoma Flabellare	2.00 to 3.00
Diamond Bass, Apomotis Gloriosus	2.00
Peacock Bass, Centrarchus Macropterus	2.50
Indian Catfish, Saccobranchus Fossilis	3.00
Panther Fish, Callichthys Fasciatus	3.00
Weather Fish, Misgurnus Fossilis	3.00

NOTE:- Prices subject to change without notice.

W. L. BRIND, F. Z. S; Aquarist, ~~500 Isham St., cor. Sherman Ave.~~
New York City, N. Y., U. S. A.

PRICE LIST OF RARE AND BEAUTIFUL AQUARIUM FISHES

GOLD FISH VARIETIES

		Price Per Pair
Tiger Fish, Veil-tailed High-Fin		$5.00 to $100.00
Tiger Fish, Ditto, Telescope Eyes		5.00 to 100.00
Tiger Fish, Ditto, young specimens	each	.50 up in season
Fringetail Japanese Goldfish	"	1.00 to 10.00
Fantail Japanese Goldfish	"	.35 to 5.00
Telescope Chinese Goldfish	"	1.00 to 10.00
Comet Goldfish	"	.25 to 3.00
Common Goldfish	"	.10 to 1.00

BARBUS GROUP:—EGG-DROPPING FISHES

	Price Per Pair
Golden Ide or Golden Orfe, Leuciscus Idus	$2.00
Bitterling, Rhodeus Amarus	2.00
Copper-striped Dace, Notropis Metallicus	2.00
Black-nosed Dace, Rhinichthys Atronasus	.50
Red-bellied Dace, Chrosomus Erythrogaster	2.00
Rosy-sided Dace, Leuciscus Vandoisulus	2.00
Golden Dace, Abramis Crysoleucas	2.00
Giant Danio, Danio Malabaricus	3.00
Zebra Danio, Danio Rerio	2.00
Spotted Danio, Danio Analipunctatus	3.00
Red-breasted Barbus, Barbus Conchonius	3.00
Banded Barbus, Barbus Semifasciolatus	3.50
Red-finned Rasbora, Rasbora Heteromorpha	5.00
Blue-striped Rasbora, Rasbora Cephalotaenia	4.00
Gold-striped Rasbora, Rasbora Leptosoma	4.00
Barbu[illegible] species, from China	5.00
Yang-Tse-Kiang Barbus, new species	5.00

TOOTH-CARP GROUP:—EGG-LAYING FISHES

HAPLOCHILUS FAMILY:—	Price Per Pair
Red-spotted, Gold-Green Haplochilus, (H. Rubrostigma)	$3.00
Red-Chinned Haplochilus, H. Chaperi	2.50
Blue Haplochilus, H. Spilauchen	3.00
Red-Tail Haplochilus, H. Panchax (var.)	3.00
Gorgeous Haplochilus, H. Calliurus or Elegans	8.00
Six-striped Haplochilus, H. Sexfasciatus	3.00
RIVULUS FAMILY:—	
Bahia Rivulus, R. Bahiaensis (Brindi)	3.00
Painted Rivulus, R. Flabellicauda	4.00
Spotted Rivulus, R. Ocellatus	3.00

NOTE:- Prices subject to change without notice.

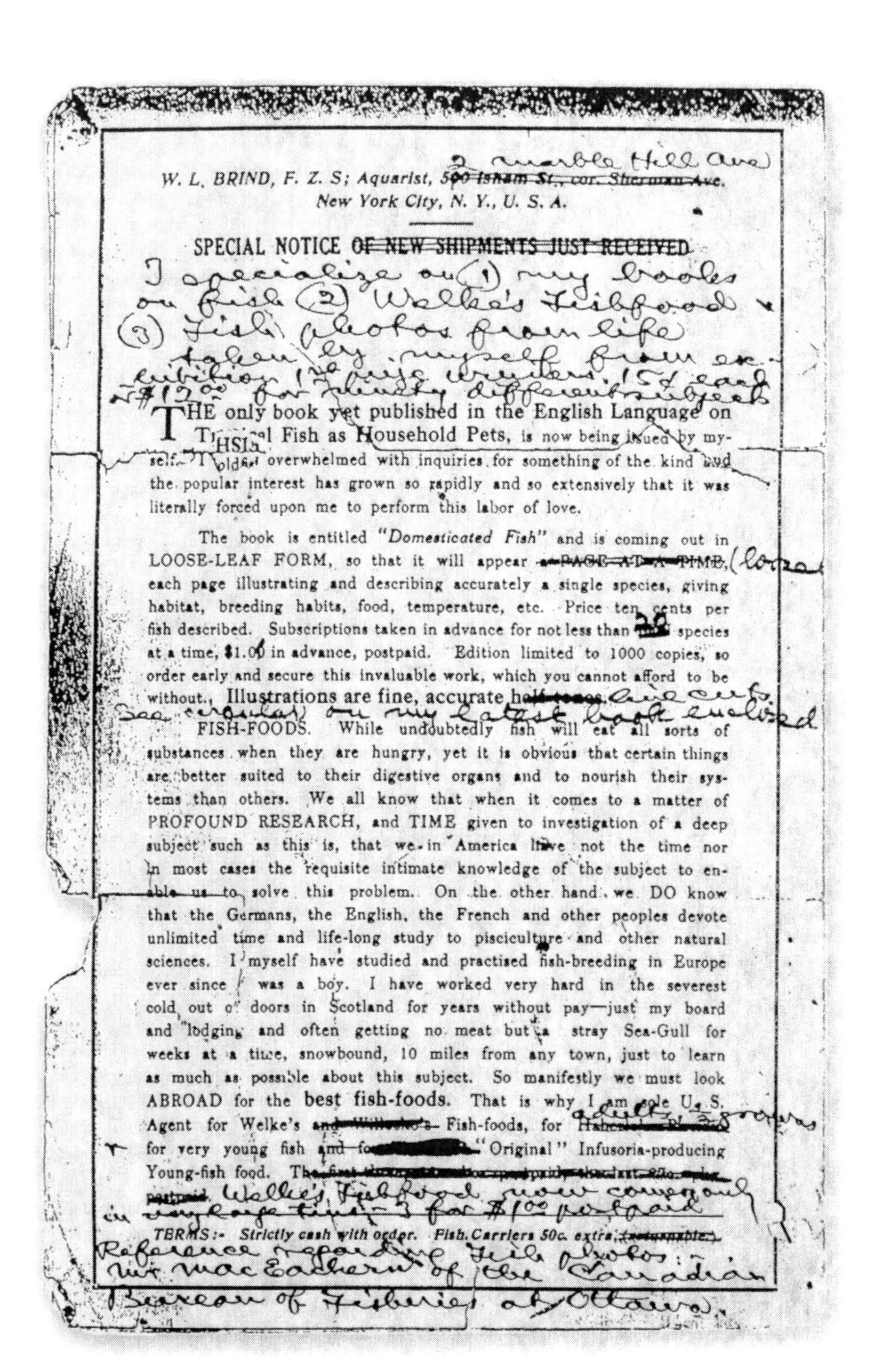
W. L. BRIND, F. Z. S; Aquarist, ~~500 Isham St., cor. Sherman Ave.~~ 2 Marble Hill Ave
New York City, N. Y., U. S. A.

SPECIAL NOTICE ~~OF NEW SHIPMENTS JUST RECEIVED~~

I specialize on (1) my books on fish (2) Welke's Fishfood & (3) Fish photos from life taken by myself from exhibition prize winners! 15¢ each $12.00 for hundred different subjects

THE only book yet published in the English Language on Tropical Fish as Household Pets, is now being issued by myself. I [am] overwhelmed with inquiries for something of the kind and the popular interest has grown so rapidly and so extensively that it was literally forced upon me to perform this labor of love.

The book is entitled "*Domesticated Fish*" and is coming out in LOOSE-LEAF FORM, so that it will appear ~~a PAGE AT A TIME~~, (loose leaf) each page illustrating and describing accurately a single species, giving habitat, breeding habits, food, temperature, etc. Price ten cents per fish described. Subscriptions taken in advance for not less than 20 species at a time, $1.00 in advance, postpaid. Edition limited to 1000 copies, so order early and secure this invaluable work, which you cannot afford to be without. Illustrations are fine, accurate ~~half-tones~~ line cuts.

See circular on my latest book enclosed

FISH-FOODS. While undoubtedly fish will eat all sorts of substances when they are hungry, yet it is obvious that certain things are better suited to their digestive organs and to nourish their systems than others. We all know that when it comes to a matter of PROFOUND RESEARCH, and TIME given to investigation of a deep subject such as this is, that we in America have not the time nor in most cases the requisite intimate knowledge of the subject to enable us to solve this problem. On the other hand, we DO know that the Germans, the English, the French and other peoples devote unlimited time and life-long study to pisciculture and other natural sciences. I myself have studied and practised fish-breeding in Europe ever since I was a boy. I have worked very hard in the severest cold out of doors in Scotland for years without pay—just my board and lodging and often getting no meat but a stray Sea-Gull for weeks at a time, snowbound, 10 miles from any town, just to learn as much as possible about this subject. So manifestly we must look ABROAD for the best fish-foods. That is why I am sole U. S. Agent for Welke's ~~and Willecke's~~ Fish-foods, for ~~Half-grown~~ adult & ½ grown for very young fish ~~and for [illegible]~~ "Original" Infusoria-producing Young-fish food. ~~The first [illegible] postpaid [illegible] 25c. each postpaid~~ Welke's Fishfood now conveniently in ~~very large tins~~ 3 for $1.00 postpaid

TERMS:- Strictly cash with order. Fish Carriers 50c. extra, ~~(returnable)~~.

Reference regarding fish photos: Mr. MacEachern of the Canadian Bureau of Fisheries at Ottawa.

Would you eat sea gulls to learn about fish?

INNES PUBLISHING COMPANY

Aquarium Literature

12TH STREET AT CHERRY

PHILADELPHIA 7

12/25/56

Dear Mr. Bayliss -

It was a pleasant surprise hearing from you. Thanks! You seem to continue vigorous.

Frank Barrett is living but in a nursing home. I think he is about 87. I am nearly 83. I will never forget coming back from Toronto with him. The conductor had passed and Frank thought the coast clear, so he pulled out a bottle of whiskey and took a swig. Right in the back of the conductor was the customs officer. He arrested Barrett, took him off the train at Niagara, where he was fined $20 and the rest of the whiskey confiscated. Besides he had to stay another day at Niagara in a hotel!!

I had a quart under the seat which they didn't find!

Innes

"EXOTIC AQUARIUM FISHES." The standard work of reference on tropicals. 542 pages, many color plates. $8.75 mailed. Foreign, $9.00.

"THE AQUARIUM," an illustrated monthly magazine. $3.00 yearly in U.S. and So. America (except Guianas). Foreign, $3.50.

"GOLDFISH VARIETIES & WATER GARDENS." Complete book. Many beautiful pictures. 386 pages, $5.50 mailed. Foreign, $5.75.

"AQUARIUM HIGHLIGHTS"—A complete, well illustrated, 520 page book of selected reprints of articles, editorials and "Correspondence" from "The Aquarium." $5.50 mailed. Foreign, $5.75.

"THE MODERN AQUARIUM."—Contains the best points for the beginner, condensed from our two larger books. $1.

"YOUR AQUARIUM," an attractive and clearly written Primer for Beginners. 25c from dealers, or 30c mailed direct by us.

Loise and Carlos Prentis holding almost four-foot *Plecostomus* —Iquitos, Peru (1961)

wonderful large *Cryptocoryne* plants. These were grown in his many, many aquariums. These housed the very large fish inventory of his ongoing genetic work on inheritance of the Melanoma cancers found in Platys and Swordtails. The pet industry benefitted enormously as the residue of his research included the fixing of wonderful new red and wagtail strains of Platys and Swordtails. He was a very warm, friendly, and helpful man who died at a very young age not too many years later. His star research assistant was Dr. Donn Rosen. Donn later helped me locate a very rare Guatemalan livebearer (*Xenodexia ctenolepus*) which I collected with Jaap de Greef in 1989.

While still in New York City I spent as much time as I could at the American Museum of Natural History with all of these wonderful and helpful people whose company I enjoyed. They all gave freely of their time, and taught me many things I did not know and wanted to know.

Late one Saturday I found a few hours free and called Dr. Gordon and arranged a visit. I was late and he waited for me. He left me reading as he had to get home. He told me I was the last one there and that the elevator would be shut off soon as the museum was closing for the weekend. If I missed the elevator I could go down the stairs. About twenty minutes later I finished reading and started for home. The elevator had stopped running. The place was deserted as I flipped off the last lights in the area. I found the stair well and headed down. I tried to get out at the 4th floor and it was locked. The third floor was locked. The second floor door was locked. The last flight down to the first floor increased my anxiety. I was horrified to find that door also locked. I rapidly retraced my steps planning to exit on the fifth floor as I had entered there and almost panicked when I discovered that door had locked behind me. I spent the next two hours walking up and down the stairwells visiting the five locked doors and becoming more and more aware of the quiet. The darkened halls got darker. The lack of any noises became more apparent. The lack of any response to my shouts kept me on the edge of total panic. I also realized that no one had any idea that I was at the museum, much less imprisoned in a stairwell. It was Saturday evening late. I could only envision a wait until the museum reopened on Monday morning. I was delighted after being imprisoned for over two hours to rouse a watchman whose existence I had doubted. He was convinced I was a thief who had caught himself. He detained me (arrested?) until he could find Dr. Gordon at home who convinced him

I was not a robber. I have never since been able to get myself to enter a stairwell with the door locked behind me. This confession will explain to a lot of people why they have found doors in stairwells jammed with folded pieces of paper preventing door locks from catching.

Today, when we think of elephant nosed Mormyrids we think of *Gnathonemus petersi* as that is just about all one sees. I had at least twenty different types of mormyrids that first year from Pierre Brichard. He found he could collect the excessively rare and beautiful *Synodontis angelicus* catfish at night near a spot where rusted out automobiles had been dumped in the Stanley Pool near Leopoldville (now Kinshasa). Neither of us ever figured out why, but only there could he get full boxes of them and nowhere else. The items that were easiest to sell, as they were easiest to collect, were *Distichodus affinis*, the small aquatic frog (*Hymenochirus boulengeri*), Congo tetras (*Phenacogrammus interruptus*), and the "hottest" item of all the "upside-down catfish" (*Synodontis nigriventris*). This last still has not been bred commercially. An occasional spawning is reported. Every good commercial breeder has tried and failed. The varieties of Synodontid catfish seemed endless. One more beautiful than the other. It took Pierre more than a year to find the rare *Barbus hulstaerti*. It looked more like a *Rasbora* than a barb. It was located in an area tough to reach and shipments were infrequent. None have been seen for the past 30 or 35 years.

One of the most unpleasant experiences I ever had occurred with a big shipment of fish from Pierre. You get used to disasters caused by weather, airline stupidities, and things beyond anyone's control. What you do not get used to is pure unbridled malice. About ten one night I had an expected call from Pan American confirming the arrival of fifteen double bag boxes of Congo fish. It was just then being unloaded. As it was valued far in excess of the $250 that marked the break off point where you could clear the fish informally I had to call my custom broker to clear it. I then headed for the Pan American cargo department. The Congo fish shipment should be cleared and ready for pick up by the time I arrived. It was ready and I then was escorted into the strictly off limits area where all merchandise was stored that had arrived "in bond". There was my large pallet load of fish boxes. It was an unbelievable stomach wrenching sight. I had heard stories about this type of an outrage, but until I actually saw it I had dismissed the stories as nonsense. People just were not that mean and destructive. I was wrong. The entire shipment had been sabotaged. The boxes had all been riddled with something like fifty stabs by (more than likely) an ice pick. Almost all the bags were leaking; fish were dead, and dying. The boxes were collapsing on top of each other. Water was everywhere. Judging from the leakage it could not have been done more than thirty minutes before my arrival. I had Pan American load the mess into my Station Wagon. I raced back to General Aquatic. I salvaged what I could. It was a disaster. I called Pan American Airlines and raised hell as soon as they were open in the morning. I demanded to know who had been allowed entry unsupervised into the bonded area. This was a violation of U.S. Customs Department rules and regulations. I was told to sit tight. They would be back to me quickly. Quickly meant an almost immediate visit in person from the Cargo Manager. He could not have been nicer (which was unusual for Pan American). I found out who was the competitor, and the name of the employee who did it. I also realized there was nothing I could do to punish the guilty party. I could prove nothing. The owner of the business, who I must assume directed or permitted the act, died that year. The actual perpetrator I have tracked all his life and unbeknownst to him I have repeatedly burned him. As an Italian friend told me years ago "I don't get mad, I get even". If I had gone to the police I could prove nothing and all I would be doing then was to put Pan American in serious trouble. Nothing was ever done about it and Pan American hand delivered a check before the week was out for payment in full for the cost of our loss.

The strangest wholesale customer General Aquatic ever had was a pet shop owner and part time jazz drummer (maybe it was the other way around) named Rip Murray who usually was referred to as "The Ripper". Rip had a high volume shop somewhere in Manhattan. He was a cartoon character that came to life. He not only acted bizarre, but looked the part. He squinted constantly, and blinked his eyes a lot. None of his clothes ever matched. He had a huge (really) chain about his waist that terminated in a stout handmade leather zippered pouch. This all was secured to his body by a combination numbered padlock. If you wanted his money you would have to take him with you. He only operated for cash. His wad of money looked enormous. I always suspected it was mostly singles on the inside and big bills on the outside. It certainly looked good. I am sure every supplier (including me) wanted to get his share of it. Rip's buying pattern was unique. At the time I also thought really stupid. Now, looking back forty years, I am not sure I was right. He bought the less important items in a normal way. When it came to the bulk of his order it was a piscatorial game show. The game went like this.... "How mutch for dat tankafish". I would reply those zebra Danio will be nine cents each. Then as though talking to a moron he explained "I wanum all; how mutch". That was the game. He thought he knew better than you did how many were there, and he may have been right, as I never got to count any of the many tankfuls he bought from me and after he bought them we put them uncounted in a bag. I put the price on the tank as it stood and he bought or passed. It was fun and I like to think I always was the winner but...??? The last I heard was that he had moved to New Orleans and gone into the wholesale business there.

Rosario LaCorte and I have been good friends since the early 1950s. His brilliance as a breeder was showing even then. He haunted my place, and I saved choice material for him to try to breed. No one before or after "Za" LaCorte has had such phenomenal success with the reproduction of a truly amazing variety of rare fish. Lots of people breed rare fish, but no one that I have ever run across has been able to reproduce the amazing spectrum of varieties he has successfully spawned. He got several spawnings of *Barbus hulstaerti*, but no eggs ever hatched. If you think his results were from luck I have a bridge to sell you. "Za" has made many collecting trips to Brazil and over the years has taught himself to speak Portuguese. This has helped him a lot. He has discovered a number of new varieties that have been named in his honor.

Protopterus lungfishes were an easy sale and we had three species in all sizes. I had two albino lungfish from Pierre Brichard about a year apart. One went to the San Antonio Zoo and the other to the Shedd Aquarium. Occasionally we would get a juvenile tiger fish (*Hydrocynus goliath*) and these always went to the public aquariums.

After a couple of years, Brichard came on his first visit to the United States. I still get a laugh when I recall the story he told me later about our visit to his first Chinese Restaurant. Pierre did not know Chinese Food at all and this was something new. He loved the food. We passed each different dish around to sample. In those days you ordered by the numbers. His favorite was the item we ordered as number 10. When he got to Chicago he went to the first Chinese restaurant he could find. He ordered #10. Naturally it was something else. He admitted he had done it again in Los Angeles with still another dish served. About then he figured out that each Chinese restaurant had a different system.

I always cultivated relationships with public aquarium directors, and I went out of my way to offer them all of the really interesting and rare fish. Pierre sent me the first two live *Monodactylus sebae* seen in the USA since the 1930s when some were brought to New York City by an enterprising sailor. We gifted ours to the New York Public Aquarium which was just then opening in Coney Island. I had supplied all of the small Pacific marine fish they had on display. These, of course, came from Earl Kennedy and included the "first ever" live stonefish displayed in the United States. I knew I had arrived when Dr. Ross Nigrelli, New York Aquarium's pathologist called me. Dr. Nigrelli asked me about a fungus he thought he saw on the back of his stonefish. He wanted to know my formula for "bright copper pennies". That is how we first treated with copper. I forget now how many to the gallon. It worked too. Later we switched to "chore girl" copper sponges which were easier to use as it was hard to find pennies that were shiny bright and not yet oxidized. We had to get new ones at the bank. About that time Brichard made arrangements to get fish, from his cousin who was the airport manager in Stanleyville, near Lake Tanganyika in the Belgian Congo. This was almost one thousand miles from Leopoldville. The Germans had managed, in 1959, to get a few Lake Tanganyika fish alive to Hamburg. The outstanding fish they collected was *Tropheus moorii*. This was the fish Pierre was after. He managed to send me two small shipments of Tanganyika fish before the Congo exploded in a terrible, bloody, and primitive revolution. I had just relocated in Florida. I had received from Pierre the first live *Julidochromis ornatus* and *Lamprologus leleupi* (I also had *Tropheus* that arrived dead). I had five or six live adult specimens of each. I gave them to newly hired Henrik Hansen to try to breed. He bred both of them that winter. Spawns were small. We had almost one hundred of each by early spring. Tanganyika fish exist in very hard and alkaline water and should be ideal candidates for natural reproduction in Florida, or so we thought. No one knew we had them, and we had also bred them. I was ready to make a killing.

That spring I set aside two perfect ponds for them. They were located almost adjacent to the hatchery and as a result better protected than the average pond. The proximity to traffic kept potential predation down. I expected to pay off the mortgage with these fish. I got nervous when the Belgium Congo War apparently was going to continue for a very long time. The entire inventory outside of Africa was in these ponds. Most white residents left the Congo. The atrocities committed by the natives were unimaginably cruel. Many, many non-native people were slain and frequently eaten. Quickly, the vast collecting network Brichard had built in the previous six years came apart. Many of his collectors were killed in the remote bush country. The exodus of non-native people was almost total. Brichard was one of the very few white people who remained. He had finally gotten to the point where his debts were paid, and his business had been getting better all the time. You had to know this tough Belgian to understand that he did not know how to retreat. It was not part of his personality. His toughness had been well developed. He had spent the greater part of World War Two as a Belgian resistance fighter. The Germans knew him well. He was never taken. Brussels, where his family lived, and where he had grown up was just was too tame for him. He left Belgium after the war, to seek his fortune in the Congo. He went into the marine supply business in Leopoldville. He called his business Congo Marine. It had nothing at all to do with fish. This outboard motor and small boat business was not making it for him. As a tropical fish hobbyist he was fascinated by the local fish he found in the Stanley Pool. He went to Europe and found a few people who agreed to take sample shipments (1952). From that point on the hobby was never the same. Brichard opened Africa to the rest of the tropical fish world. Never before had so many new, interesting, bizarre, and beautiful freshwater fish been seen. Now with the Congo in violent civil war he had a much reduced supply of fish. The remote areas were not accessible so the rarest fish disappeared. I had one shipment of the still rare *Pelmatochromis dimidiatus* just then, and never had another, but still the wonderful Stanley Pool fish were available. The trick to stay in business was to stay alive. That was not easy. Twice during that period I sent Pierre a huge crate, by air, with a reconditioned outboard motor inside and identified it as such on the airway bill. What actually was concealed in each crate was a shipment of armaments. I sent guns, bullets, and mace. I tried to get hand grenades, but never could.

Somewhere he had gotten a submachine gun which he mounted on the landing of the second floor of his home. This gun was manned twenty four hours a day for all those years. When daughter Mireille went to school the machine gun was mounted on the jeep that took her back and forth. Pierre let everyone know he was well armed and, incredibly, he lived through the entire revolution. The rest of the family left the Congo and spent years away in Belgium while Pierre Brichard held the business and home compound secure. When the war was over he knew that the Congo would not recover for many, many years. Time has proven him correct. He managed to sell his home for a very good price to a member of the new government. He left the Congo which was now Zaire. The people who bought his fish business never got it off the ground. Brichard and family relocated in the Republic of Burundi on the other side of Lake Tanganyika. Brichard received an exclusive fishing right from the Government of Burundi. The family still operates the business. Pierre died in 1989. The business now is run by Mireille Brichard. Mireille is a trained biologist and ichthyologist. She is raising almost as many fish in the hatcheries and ponds they built as the wild fish captured in the lake.

I want to reproduce here something that Pierre wrote about one of his fishermen. It explains a lot about a part of the tropical fish world seldom described.

One *Cyphotilapia frontosa*

by Pierre Brichard
Republic of Burundi

I don't suppose anyone would have called him bright, if being bright means being well known or making money. A peasant, like so many others on the hills of the African bush close to the shores of Lake Tanganyika. How could he be making money? With barely an education, what could he hope for in poor and overcrowded Burundi, but to spend all his life tending a banana grove or a tiny field, raising a few chickens and a goat or two. Perhaps, if he were lucky or thrifty, he would eventually acquire a Watusi cow, the ultimate status symbol in this cattle-raising country. He would then grow old, respected, and envied by his neighbors until his last day, after which he would be quickly forgotten, one who sinks beneath the surface of Mother Earth without a ripple.

Meanwhile, he and his wife did not earn much, just the ten dollars a year which is the annual average per capita earning in this country. But they did not starve with the beans and bananas they grew...if the dry season wasn't too long nor the rains too heavy. Altogether, from day to day, they had a peaceful life, found in what the experts of international organizations call "subsistence economy". They had few needs, few worries, fewer hopes, and no dreams.

They were "hill people", and although they had spent their lives near the shores of Lake Tanganyika, they seldom got near it. They never fish, never swim or wade in the water, leaving this to the "water people", the fishermen who earn their living with net and line and do not belong to the same tribe. It is like this over all of Central Africa. On the one hand, the bush or forest people who tend their fields or raise cattle, and on the other hand, the water people. The former sedentary and the latter semi-nomadic, independent and perhaps smarter, having been in contact with more people and seen more of the outside world,

One day our man happened to overhear a bunch of fishermen as they were sitting and mending their nets. What he heard made him stop and hear more of the story. It seemed as if a few days before, a foreigner, a white man, had come and asked for inedible and very tiny fish; he wanted them alive and in very good health.

The price he wanted to pay for such "junk" was incredible. One of the fishermen said "Ridiculous! The guy is stupid. Why he paid at least ten times more for them then I would have asked?"

"But" cut in the man from the hills, "what does he do with such fish?"

"I heard that he is sending them to Europe by plane, in boxes with water. But that is not the point. What is important is that I make extra profit on an easy catch. Look at those fish there, in the pebbles ... they're a gold mine for me."

"I wish I could fish them too", said the peasant.

"Go ahead, said the fisherman, "but you know nothing about fishing. Why don't you try to sell him your goats?" And everyone burst into laughter.

He got hold of a small second hand net which the fishermen

were quite willing to get rid of at a profit (nothing is given free between people of different tribes). He put the shreds together and started to fish. His days were now spent wading in the shallows with his younger brothers, whom he had enrolled as helpers.

My God!; how hard it was and how meager the catch at the end of a day's work. At sunset one could see him by the roadside, waiting in the dusk for the white man's truck to pass. Sometimes he stood there for hours before he could bring forth the small pot in which some of the fish had already died and suffocated from heat and pollution. Most of them, anyhow, were useless. The fisherman had not told him exactly which fish the man would buy, and his catch usually wound up wriggling in the dust. He received a few coins to bring back home, shivering from cold and exhaustion.

Other hill people had also tried their luck at collecting fish, but it wasn't worth all the trouble or the sarcasm from the fishermen. But he kept observing the fishermen and the fish they brought to the foreigner. Their names he didn't know. That didn't matter much. What mattered was that his fishing was becoming more selective and the pay greater now from day to day. He buried his money in his hut from fear of thieves. He was earning now in a week as much as he earned all the previous year. All his unfulfilled wishes came back to him, more intensely, as they were now within his grasp. His priorities were now to first buy a bicycle, then a transistor radio, fancy clothes, a sewing machine for his wife, and cases of beer. As a rich man should he think about entertaining his neighbors?

These were his thoughts when he explored the lake shores for better fishing grounds or when he ventured in open waters as he daily improved his fishing. "The fishermen are not laughing at me any more. I am as good as they are", he thought. "The white man knows it too; he gave me goggles and fins to improve my fishing, and this equipment he only gives to the very best".

One day as the white man was picking up the day's yield, one of the fishermen produced a splendid fish, azure blue with deep blue vertical stripes.

"So, you got one" said the white man with a deep smile. "Congratulations, man! You get the prize that I promised, although the fish will most certainly die. You brought him up too fast. How deep did you catch him?"

"Very, very deep boss," said the fisherman, and the fish-buyer started to explain why the fish was dying and how to bring them up. Of course, it was easy for the foreigner to be talking like this. He went down into the lake with bottles of compressed air on his back. He could stay under as long as he wished, hunting the fish for hours if need be. But what a fantastic price he paid for a fish like that!

"I will get some", the peasant promised.

"No you won't", answered the buyer. "You don't know enough about diving, and it is dangerous work, it's too much for you."

Next day a few of these fish, which the man called Ngumu Ngumu were found and there were many happy faces.

"You see, you are still not a fisherman", said one.

Our man of the hills started diving deeper and deeper toward the steep slopes where the blue fish live. Sometimes he happened to sight their bright shapes silhouetted against the dark background of scary depths. His eardrums ached intolerably, but each time he managed to stay a few seconds longer, to learn a bit more about the fish and their ways, before having to paddle back up to the surface desperately in need of air and his head buzzing with pain. His young brothers on the beach were afraid and begged him to come back.

"You are losing a day's fishing," they said. But next day he would be at it again, swimming in the depths. The fishermen had a trick which they kept between themselves, of course ... if you have a pot of gold you do not tell where you keep it.

He was all by himself in the deep, and he couldn't have possibly brought up a fish alive. He was going down to depths of eight to ten meters, several hours in a row, and one morning he caught one Ngumu Ngumu. Very probably it is almost impossible to imagine the amount of dedication, sheer courage and physical endurance which was needed to get that first fish. How many fruitless dives to sight but one fish, and to isolate it on favorable ground within that dark and hostile world? So many desperate struggles back to the surface to dive again, to trap the fish in the net, up again, then down, to free the net from the rocky snags and then, as often as not, to discover that the fish had found an opening in the net and escaped to safety. That morning the fish died and similarly all the others, which he collected during the following days.

The white man gently said, "I know how you feel, but you can not do it by yourself. It needs teamwork, and you are alone. Do not dive too deep and never dive alone. This is an absolute safety rule."

The peasant had a contrite smile on his lips and did not answer. If the fishermen can do it so can I, he thought. He could earn in one day what he earned during a year's work in the banana grove and the fields. One Friday this past August he did not come up. His brothers waited on the beach until evening.... (end of story)

Pierre, along with his wife Marie Louise, had one last adventure. Pierre went to the far end of the lake to see what he could discover in Zambia. He collected and shipped for two years. He discovered many new varieties. The compound could not exist as a viable business because of the lack of dependable air transport. The preliminary work has been done, and when and if Zambian Airlines gets its act together more wonderful new fish will be available. No one during my lifetime ever discovered as many new species. Many have been named to honor him. He was very ill the last years before his death. We had corresponded for almost forty years. Our letters never had much to do with fish. We were both interested in politics and history. We argued back and forth for many years. I never admitted it to him then, but I will now. He was usually right. He always was much more perceptive then I. He suffered from emphysema. He had a heart attack. He had a stroke. Any one of these would have killed a lesser man. He fought his way out of it. He called me from Bujumbura, Burundi, a week before he died to talk. He had just received a beautiful award from the American Cichlid Association that I had mailed to him. It had taken almost six months to get there and had just arrived. A beautiful set of brass book ends suitably engraved for his contribution to the hobby. It was the only such award ever given by the A.C.A. We talked for over an hour. I miss him a lot and I am sitting here crying as I think of him.

That fall we pumped the *Lamprologus leleupi* pond and then I pumped the *Julidochromis ornatus* pond. I never got a single fish back, did not see either again for another eight years. This pattern has been repeated over and over again. Lake Tanganyika fish do not pool breed in Florida, and many do not even survive.

General Aquatic Supply was a great learning experience. My grandfather Joseph had taught me two things, and I thank him for insisting I remember them. Firstly, it is more important to know what not to do then to know what to do. Secondly, to always trust your first impression. I can do that now. Then, my instincts were all wrong. My very first order from my very first advertisement was to a buyer in California. He sent me the order and a check for $200. As he wanted the very rarest of the Africans I could only send him about $50.00 worth of fish. I enclosed a rebate check for $150 with the air shipment of fish that I sent. I was proud of the fact that I had made the shipment the same day I had gotten the order. You guessed it. His check bounced and mine cleared. When I finally caught up with him he was already in jail for other more serious crimes. Another new customer from Chicago continued my education in the fish business. His name was Al Wechsler. He ran a large wholesale/retail house called Suwannee Water Gardens in Chicago. He bought a huge order of Mr. Sutton's Trinidad *Plecostomus*. I sent it to him open account as he told me everyone sold him that way. I figured he was reliable, as I had seen the large advertisements he ran in the trade magazines. After I had shipped his order I learned he had a very bad reputation. I waited and waited for my check. I called. I was told it had just been mailed. I waited some more, and called again. They apologized for the new girl. By now five months had passed. I never could get him to the phone. "Check was going out that day". I finally got a check for about ten percent of what I had invoiced (after he got a letter from my lawyer) with an almost undecipherable note telling me that the fish were sick and I should be ashamed of myself for sending out such garbage and P. S. they had mostly died. I fumed, threatened, and naturally took a bad beating. I was out of my league with Al Wechsler. He was a beautiful piece of work. I think of him now as the Picasso of deadbeats. I never did get an explanation as to why he did not report a problem with the shipment. I was learning fast. I learned that everyone else in the business knew that buyer and that scam. I was certainly stuck, but fortunately a quick learner. It was a good and cheap lesson in the long run. No one is completely useless—Al Wechsler did well when used as a bad example.

The years that I was in business in New York I met some of the most terrible scoundrels, and also some really wonderful "normal" people. Many of these remain friends. Jerry Rosen from Penn Plax had a retail store (Amazon Aquarium) not far away. Earl Schneider had one in Manhattan. Wardley had just started. Ed Levey, the owner, would come by every month to take our orders. His son, Allen Levey and I are still very close friends. Irving Galt and Sy Bergen were known as Gro-well Fish Aid then, Harding and Alan Willinger had a retail store in Manhattan.

One real nut case was the famous "Kockamamie Kid". He grew up to be Stanley Druse, and was one of my favorite people. He sold decalcomania that were to be affixed to the backs of aquariums and supposedly depict a natural underwater world. His business operated from the back seat of his car and only he knew what was there even if he could never find it. Stanley got these decals from god knows where. They were Olympic quality ugly. They depicted wonderful "aquatic" scenes like Jesse James holding up a train, sunsets in Nevada, the bombing of Pearl Harbor. There is a definite lunatic percentile in our population. These are the people who buy the "uglies" at county fairs and flea markets. With a hypnotic personality Stanley could push all the right buttons. When I first met him I was convinced he was a potentially dangerous mad man and as a result I always was polite. His main selling point for these irresistible pictorial abortions was price. They were really cheap and potential profits enormous. You only had to sell a small fraction of the purchase to break even. That is the best anyone ever did. I never did. More important he would always tell me how many Jerry Rosen at Amazon Tropicals or Earl Schneider at Aquarium Stock Company had been selling. It was always a great surprise to me when some one bought one from us. I wasn't surprised often.

A certain Martin Alernick had gone into the tropical fish import business in Manhattan in the early 1950s. This business imported great amounts of foreign fish, and had many major disasters which were not unusual then. Alernick imported Brazilian fish from Belem, which at that time was the only exporting center in Brazil. I had been having remarkable success with some new antibiotic and antibacterial medications. His problem fish gave me an opportunity to experiment. I tried to cure his terminally sick discus and other fish. I would buy (and they were delighted to sell) apparently doomed discus at a fraction of their worth. To my great delight I managed to save a worthwhile percentage of these fish. I was sad when they quit importing them because he was my source for discus. I learned a lot about handling imports from this experience. At times I did stupid things. The ultimate results of this practical trial and error method helped me a lot in future years. Most problems are secondary infections. These will quickly kill fish that have had their resistance lowered (almost all imports). The most important lesson is to be sure that you do not compound the problem by putting the stressed fish into an environment that will further stress (weaken) them. Use good clean water that is as close to the fishes' natural water as you can determine. Water must be tempered, and should never have contained fish. Dose the tank with medication, and leave them alone for the next 36 hours. Do not attempt to feed them, and then when you do live food is very important (daphnia, *Tubifex*, adult brine shrimp). Realize that wild fish have never seen commercial dry foods. They must learn to eat them. They will learn fast enough when they are feeling better. A "dither" fish works wonders. This is a fish that already feeds well from your existing stock. Quickly, the wild fish will emulate its feeding habits. This becomes very important when live food is not available. Change all or most of the water after 36 hours, and then decide whether the fish need to be re-medicated. The only thing you must do from the start is to remove all dead fish, and siphon as needed. A dirty tank soaks up medication fast, defeating your purpose. An elevated temperature works against you. Seventy two to 76 °F will work the best. The most effective drugs I used then always included Tetracycline Hydrochloride plus (depending on what I could see) Acriflavine or Malachite Green. Methylene Blue, salt, and copper sulfate are useful additional and proven medications. I made up a mixture to be used with antibiotics that we called "cocktail". It works well and although I tried many other medications never found anything as effective. It was a combination of copper (in solution), Acriflavine, and Methylene Blue. Learn how to use a microscope. It is an essential investment that will pay unbelievable dividends. Just remember that "stress" is the real killer. You will seldom see a specific problem as few shippers will send obviously sick fish. Notice that I said few. When you see a specific problem, treat specifically and if not, treat to prevent the problem. Most shippers and importers are scared to death of the fish they are holding for shipment. As a result they send them out as fast as they can regardless of their condition. Avoid these beauties like the plague. I was honored by visits from Dr. William Innes who twice came by to see the new African fish we were importing. The editor of his Aquarium Magazine then was Alan Fletcher. Alan and I were good friends. We helped each other whenever we could with information that would help the hobby.

I bought a lot of locally bred fish at General Aquatic. Paul Hahnel, who lived in the Bronx, brought me guppies. He also sold me excess water sprite that he raised in his guppy tanks. He claimed water sprite kept his water perfectly conditioned for his beautiful guppies. I think he was right. A breeder from Camden, New Jersey, named Tom Schubert, brought a good variety of fish. He had developed a new Golden Barb that sold well that he called Barbus Shuberti (which was not a valid name).

A fellow named Bill Parker bred fish in Nyack, NY. He made deliveries two or three times a month. He had a partner named Fred Leidecker, who I never met. Leidecker had decided he could break the virtual total monopoly that Fred Cochu had on neon tetras. Cochu brought his neons in from his own collecting station in South America with his own plane. We all bought them from him. No one else had them. Leidecker arranged a huge shipment of neon tetras directly from Colombia to New York. The price was great and I, and all the rest of the New York dealers, ordered a bunch. Payment was to be made when live delivery was accomplished. That it did not work would be putting it mildly. The huge shipment of neon tetras arrived C.O.D. with freight collect and very dead. The shipment was his, and he had to pay for it. Leidecker offered a check which the airline would not take until it had been certified. The story that I had been told, and which I believe is true, was that Leidecker then left the airport, went to the bank, and drew out all the partnership's money. Putting the cash in his pocket he returned to the airport. This time he did not go to the cargo department to pay for the hundreds of boxes of dead fish. He passed the cargo area and got on a plane. He flew off to Bogotá, Colombia. He left wife, family, and partner. Bill Parker quickly learned that he no longer had a partner, and was ruined financially. Parker was a really nice guy and a talented breeder. He had to go out of business. Eventually, he suffered so much from this emotional holocaust that he ended up confined in a mental hospital. One day, more than 35 years ago, Bill walked out of the institution. He has not been seen since. Leidecker was now settled in Colombia. He had remarried to the daughter of the man who ran the Customs Department at Vanguardia airport in Bogotá. He used his father in New York as his agent, salesman, and money collector. He shipped up very good fish. Everyone was aware of the neon tetra deal. No one would ever trust him again. No one had to trust him again as his dear old dad would deliver Leidecker's Colombian fish that you had ordered to you. You would then open the boxes. If all was in order you paid for the fish. They were invariably good fish.

By the mid 1950s we were all using plastic bags with oxygen. Fish could survive for long periods of time. Freight costs were lower. The few remaining monopolies were rapidly coming undone. Fred Cochu still did very well. He was brighter than any of us. Fred had been smart enough to serve his big buyers honestly and well. He did not now have the big profits, but he did keep his customers. Cochu, in early 1956, brought in a wonderful new fish. He had it all alone. This he named the Cardinal Tetra. The cardinal tetra was twice as large as the neon, and an even more spectacular fish.

I had started corresponding with Gene Wolfsheimer, a California fish breeder. Gene was then the most accomplished fish photographer in the United States. Gene and his wife Bert became our good friends. No one could breed discus in those days. A woman named Lois Sophian in St. Louis was breeding a few. Gene traded fish with her, and she sent him seven of her baby discus. He raised them, and got three breeding pairs. That was mind boggling in those days as even an infertile spawn was news. Discus fish had probably not been bred by more than 25 people in the 35 years since they made their first appearance. Gene Wolfsheimer bred many. He made it seem easy. He discovered that apparently the first food for free swimming discus fry came from the slime on the parents bodies. His remarkable photographs, and lengthy article showing this phenomenon, graced an issue of National Geographic Magazine. It was a big boost for the hobby. Each month Gene went to Catalina Island to collect spectacular and hardy Catalina marine gobies. I took all he collected plus much of his wonderful home grown fish. He died much too young.

I started importing amphibians and reptiles from Africa. A South African supplier, named John Woods, sent me young *Xenopus laevis*. This aquatic toad (that everyone calls a frog) had been used for years as a laboratory animal to determine pregnancy in women. The young were an interesting, hardy, and fast selling novelty item. They also ate anything they could get their mouth around. I took as many as ten thousand at a time when they were available. Air transport from Africa remained hazardous, but even with unexpected delays these hardy animals always arrived alive.

An albino form turned up in Russia many years later. Loise figured out how to commercially reproduce these more attractive *Xenopus* "frogs". She was very successful. She raised many by inducing spawns with the use of chorionic gonadotropin in amounts that worked when injected properly.

There was a good retail market for fancy guppies. Paul Hahnel, who supplied us with truly beautiful fish, never had enough. General Aquatic was without top quality stock more often than with stock. Casting around for another source of supply I heard about a fellow named Bill Sternke who operated a business called Sunnyland Fish Farm near Miami. He had wonderful fancy guppies for us. They were equal to those from Paul Hahnel. Sternke also had limited amounts of the new Ramirezi dwarf cichlids. His were large and sold themselves on sight. His Rams stimulated my appreciation of these jewel-like fish. I have always raised Rams. They are my favorite fish. The quality of all of his fish was exceptional.

I never was able to buy much else from Mr. Sternke. The cost of raising fish in concrete vats in Miami as against the less costly dirt pool production in the Tampa area was forcing a transition in the operations of the Miami fish breeders. Hatcheries in Miami had to charge more for the same fish than the Tampa operators were. This was the reason why, in the next ten years, the Miami concrete vat operations were either forced out of business, or became specialists raising fish in vats that did not do well in dirt ponds, or increased production of aquatic plants, or switched to importing fish from South America.

A number of marginal Miami hatcheries made their owners rich as the Miami real estate business boomed. A lot of breeders, who had done little more than eke out a living raising fish, now found themselves rich as they were offered, and then accepted, great gobs of money for their properties.

I spent time with Bill Sternke in 1953-55 on two different occasions when he came to visit his customers in New York. He was born in Berlin in August of 1892. His father had died and his mother had then remarried. His stepfather was a stern and difficult man who made Sternke constantly unhappy. The only positive thing that Bill Sternke remembered from this marriage was that his stepfather was a successful fish breeder, and aquatic plant cultivator. Bill Sternke learned his craft from this man and for that we all owe him a debt. In exchange for the work he did in the hatchery he was allowed to sit in on the frequent "get-togethers" at his home with other commercial fish breeders. He liked these men. He listened and learned and developed his lifelong addiction to fish keeping.

Bill Sternke immigrated to the United States in 1908 when he was just sixteen years old. He could not get along with his stepfather. This was the driving force that made him decide to strike out on his own. Many, many years later when he told me his story he got emotional when he recalled that as his stepfather said good bye he had slipped an envelope into his jacket. This envelope he discovered later that day after the ship had left Germany. Inside was a gift of one thousand marks which was greatly appreciated and badly needed. He worked at a variety of jobs in and around New York City. He eventually settled in Cleveland, Ohio. His Uncle, who had emigrated earlier, lived there, and he got Bill a good job. His English was good and he did well working for a real estate company. He also was making extra money breeding tropical fish. He did well and saved his money. He joined at once, and then became active in, the newly formed Aquarium Society of Cleveland. In 1922 he became vice president. In 1923-24 he was the president of the society. He had saved enough money to relocate the next year to Florida. He had a burning desire to utilize the warmer southern climate where he knew he could best capitalize on his skills to commercially breed tropical fish. He had enough money to build a hatchery and stay alive until he had some product to sell. He knew how to raise a wide variety of tropical fish. Bill Sternke in 1925 was in business in a place called Seabreeze Station at 215 Orange Ave. in Daytona Beach, Florida. He was the first tropical fish breeder in Florida. Many years ago Clara (Mrs. William Sternke) gave me photographs of the original hatchery asking me to let the world know more about her husband Bill. I am glad to oblige at this time. He named the new business Sunnyland. In big black letters he painted the legend "Sunnyland Fish Farm, Inc. - Ornamental and Tropical Fish Hatchery". If you examine the picture closely you can see that he had painted and then blocked out "Admission 10 cents". Either no one would pay 10 cents to see this marvel or he later intended to raise (or lower) the price. I suspect the former. In 1925 there were no other ornamental fish breeding operation in the State of

Florida and, in fact, none until 1930 when Albert Greenberg arrived in Tampa. The closest anyone could come to a tropical fish hatchery before Sternke's "Sunnyland" hatchery were a very few people catching and shipping fish and plants that were collected from the wild. Jack Beater who operated the Florida Fish Farm in Fort Myers was the most successful. Green Sailfin Mollies were the most important item. In his first years in Florida Bill Sternke also caught and sold wild fish. Sternke ran his first advertisement in Aquatic Life Magazine in May of 1926 and offered Sailfin Mollies, *Heterandria formosa*, Pygmy Sunfish, *Fundulus chrysotus*, Florida Flag fish, and *Lucania omnata*. These he priced at $1.00 per pair. A legend appeared at the bottom of the advertisement reading "Will trade any of the above varieties — What have you got??"

In 1927 the one inch ad had grown to one third of a page in size. He now had his own produced fish to offer. He offered guppies for $2.00 a dozen, gold or blue Platys for $1.25 a pair, black swordtails for $2.50 a pair, red paradise fish for $1.25 a pair, giant snails 35 cents, and small alligators for $2.00 each.

Sternke made a trip back to Germany in the summer of 1927. He carried with him a quantity of wild fish. The most popular item, and the one that commanded the highest price, was the selected gigantic wild Florida Green Sailfin Molly (*P. latipinna*). He spent all the monies he received for his fish on varieties of fish not available in the United States. He told me that he had enough money from the Sailfin Mollies alone to make the trip a success. He returned with Giant and Thick Lipped Gourami, Festivum, new barbs and characins such as Von Rio's, Buenos Aires Tets, and Head and Taillights all of which he bred and was selling in 1928. In 1929 he had managed to get some Velifera Sailfin Mollies (*P. velifera*) from the Yucatan in Mexico and offered them for $2.50 a pair.

In Slidell, Louisiana, a man named Bill Schomburg ran what was then the largest tropical fish farm in the world called Crescent Fish Farm. He also caught and sold green sailfin mollies. Schomburg, along with Bill Sternke, spent many years developing an all black sailfin molly. Jack Beater in 1923-1924 in Ft. Myers (whose business was collecting and shipping wild fish) held back the rare and seldom seen few wild black blotched fish he caught. He actually did raise some mostly black mollies in aquariums and concrete vats. They were not great, but they were mostly black and they were the first black mollies.

He sold his culls to his regular customers. This did include Schomburg and probably Sternke. Jack Beater had a black sailfin molly before anyone else. At best it was "mostly black" and only a small percentage of the young grew into black fish. Sternke and Schomburg did the same thing a little later. Their strains were really black, and they produced a good percentage of black fish. By 1929 Sternke and Schomburg had well-established strains. They were beautiful fish and adults were sold at retail for as much as $25.00 a pair.

Sternke raised a wide variety of fish. He never stopped working on and improving his molly and guppy strains. He did marvelous things in the next fifty years with these two fish.

He set up and bred Angelfish (which was then a very difficult fish to reproduce), Severum, Siamese fighting fish, rosy barbs, dwarf gourami, and a variety of livebearers. He had several customers for wild plants and fish. This helped him exist while he was raising the more sophisticated egg layers for additional breeding stock and some for resale. He managed well and in the next years prospered.

Daytona Beach was a mistake for Sternke as it is too far north, and it got cooler there than expected. The available transportation north from Daytona Beach was inadequate. He relocated to the Miami area in 1931. He picked a spot in Opa-Locka, Florida, a suburb of Miami. Having learned from his experience, he built a model hatchery. He tried with some success to dig pools in the coral rock. He told me the water rose and fell with the tide. They could not be pumped dry and when he set up a new pool he had to poison the old one. Blue Stone (copper sulfate) was the chemical used and it worked. He raised a lot of mollies, platys, guppies and swordtails in these ponds. Fortune smiled on him. The checkerboard barb (*Barbus oligolepis*) is a fish that does not reproduce in Florida ponds. He had some in his outdoor ponds being raised to become breeders. They not only bred naturally, but did so consistently and by the thousands. He made more money from his ponds of checkerboard barbs than any other ponds of fish he ever produced. As often happens, no one has yet duplicated this "happening". The hatchery now was devoted to an ever increasing variety of egg layers. He won a special award for the most unusual fish when he was head judge at the Miami Aquarium Society show in 1932. He displayed the first silver hatchet fish ever seen in Florida. He wrote an article for the Pennsylvania Fish Culturist, where he advertised in

1933, describing how he reproduced and raised *Metynnis roosevelti*, the spotted silver dollar. This was a remarkable accomplishment. No one has yet been able to breed this fish in the United States with success. In the mid 1930s he started working on another black molly strain. This he named the Black Yucatan Molly. The Yucatan molly is made from wild black blotched *Sphenops* mollies and his established black sailfin strain. It is a very popular fish. Millions of Bill Sternke's Yucatan mollies are raised and sold each year. The trade off was the loss of the sailfin in the Yucatan strain. The big plus was a very prolific and very hardy black molly. Despite what is generally believed black sailfin mollies are very difficult fish to maintain and ship. This is particularly evident in the winter months when they often develop "shimmies" as they are stressed by the temperature. This invariably leads to other diseases (Ich and mouth fungus). The Yucatan molly strain solved this problem.

After World War Two, Bill Sternke concentrated on developing his fancy guppy strains. He had, in 1933, developed three unique guppy strains. This was the Bottom Sword, the Top Sword, and the Lyretail. Sometime before 1933 Bill Sternke made the first ever commercial air shipment of tropical fish from Miami. Early in the 1950s he travelled to Germany to the International Guppy Show and Competition in Berlin. Sternke won all the prizes. His Satin Black Guppies were judged the best fish in the show, and he returned to America with many trophies. In 1957 the American Guppy Association was formed. As a tribute to Bill Sternke, card #1 was issued in his name. He made a trip to the west coast of Mexico in 1955 with his friend, Carlos Bonner, to try to capture the incredible four-eyed fish (*Anableps anableps*). He knew that Greenberg, in the mid 1930s had collected a similar, but different species in Cuba, and lost it after he got them back to Tampa alive. Sternke got back with seventeen of the thirty fish he caught still alive. He kept them in a variety of conditions in concrete vats and was able to breed them. This was a first in Florida.

After Bill Sternke died Clara Sternke remained active. We remained friends. She would call every couple of months. She represented several South American fish exporters and handled the arrival and disbursement of their shipments when they arrived each week. She used to sit in a chair and wield her cane barking orders which always were promptly attended to. She had a bark that was intimidating, but no bite. If you were her friend you could do no wrong. Years beforehand I had casually remarked to Clara, who was Greek, that Loise's stepfather was also Greek. This made Loise a Greek to her. I can still hear the phone calls from Clara that always went like this: "Hello Jew, this is Clara. I'm only calling to be sure you are being good to your nice Greek wife." She was one of a kind.

The better Florida tropical fish producers (Jim Woolf, Claude Tanner, Art Whilden), whose fish I wanted, would not sell to General Aquatic. They all had established accounts in my territory. I ended up buying most of my fish from Gulf Fish Hatchery (cheap prices) and Elsberry (outstanding sized egg layers and large livebearers that fell apart immediately after arrival). In 1955 the manager of the Elsberry operation came to visit me. He had first called from Florida to tell me he was visiting all his accounts. He had a new special money saving proposition to reveal that could not be put in writing or discussed on the telephone. When he arrived he explained that the newly organized Florida Fish Farm Association had just met. All members (he was one) had agreed to establish a minimum price on the major items. This meant, for example, that blue platys would be eight cents each and no one would sell a blue platy for less. The secret that had brought him to New York was then revealed. Elsberry would sell me blue platys for eight cents each (they had been charging six cents each), BUT they would put in each bag an additional number of fish free so they could continue to undercut the market. He would bill for one hundred fifty fish and send two hundred fish. This would be done on all items. I learned later that this type of sharp, slick, and unethical (at the least) business practice permeated their entire operation. The owners (who I later met and liked) certainly did not know that their employees were running a variety of dishonest sideline businesses at their expense. The Elsberry family were absentee owners. I learned this a few years after I moved to Florida. The manager was stealing. The outside employees learned about this about the same time that the manager learned that the employees were stealing fish and selling them. The stolen fish were mostly shipped to buyers in Miami. Neither could stop the other without having their own dishonesty revealed. The amazing thing is that it went on a lot longer than anyone would expect, and then the business did fail. My personal feeling is that the actual owners, who were very successful local vegetable farmers, never had a clue as to why they could not make it in the tropical fish business. Their business, when it started, was managed by Emil Kushmer. While he was there things went well, but started down hill when he left to establish his own farm. Competing farms were burdened with cash problems, facility problems, equipment problems, and all of them eventually prospered while Elsberry operated consistently at a loss. They had all the resources the rest of us would have killed to own.

I had found two good reptile suppliers in Kenya. "Lefty" Whitehead was the first. He supplied me for years. He died about the time I left New York for Florida. Our other supplier was Jonathan Leaky, the son of Louis and Mary Leaky, the world renowned anthropologists. He sent fine, healthy animals, but did not stay in the business long. He handled a lot of poisonous snakes which is something I have always avoided. The Jackson chameleons from Kenya are one of the most interesting and bizarre of all creatures. He got us many of them. They sold well. It came as a great surprise to learn from the appearance of tiny miniatures that they were live bearing reptiles. Loise kept them as pets at home for years. Several times they had young which were not difficult to raise.

A German collector named Mueller in South Africa proved to be the best of all our reptile suppliers. One of his shipments was almost my undoing. Mueller incorrectly marked, and then the airline misread, one of our large wooden boxes (actually he used tea chests). I had three large chests as ordered, but the largest one was destined for the University in Upsala, Sweden. I got their crate and they got one of mine. I received a large crate full of Africa's most deadly animals; poisonous snakes (vipers, mambas, cobras) and poisonous insects (scorpions and spiders). As soon as I discovered what had happened I tried, without much luck, to conceal my panic. I have never allowed an employee to handle a dangerous animal. This act of supreme macho stupidity had me instantly in a cold sweat. All the hairs on my body stood straight up and my eyes glazed over. I realized that I now had not just a poisonous animal, but most of them. Mueller apparently had emptied all of South Africa to make up this shipment of nightmare goblins. I could not turn them loose. I must admit I did consider it. The youngster that had taken our giant Anaconda was suggested. Fear forced me to discard this really good idea. The Airline that carried them to America told me they would get back to me and then they must have cut their telephone lines. The next 24 hours were hairy as I explored all potential candidates for my salvation. God bless Bill Chase. Chase, an animal dealer in Miami, was just delighted to take them all and off they went. I thought it only fair to use the same airline to Miami that had brought them to us. I forget how the airway bill read. I think I described it as a shipment of "baby bunnies". I can still picture one of the gigantic baboon spiders killing a mouse using its one inch long hollow fangs. The mouse went rigid immediately. An hour later it was gone. The only evidence that a mouse had ever been in the cage was a small, wrinkled, dry leather-like wad of material. This was all that remained. The contents of the mouse's body had been liquified. All of it had been ingested by the baboon spider.

Things were going along great at General Aquatic as I continued to make mistakes and learn. I had finally gotten to the point where the mistakes were not happening faster than I was learning. We actually started to make money which was a surprise. Up until then I always had "month left at the end of my money."

The turning point was when twelve Allied Stores invited us to supply their pet departments on a weekly basis. The ones in Queens were very easy. The furthest store was in Harrisburg, Pennsylvania, and that was not easy. The only way to make deliveries was with our station wagon. We could get almost fifty boxes into it after taking out the back seats. We delivered to them sometimes twice each week. It was a hard trip. We earned our profit. Dick Majeska was then the manager of the biggest store in Queens. He was smart enough to move to Atlanta shortly after I moved to Florida.

Carl and I had gotten fish from Aquarium Stock Company when I was a child. It gave me great pleasure, in later years, to be able to sell them, as they were one of the two most prestigious accounts in New York City. The other was Macy's Department Store. This was a subsidiary of Hartz Mountain. The manager was a fast moving redhead named Claude Kissen about my age (he still is and we are still friends). They had the largest volume pet store in the world; an amazing place that is long gone. I made a special trip years later to visit the pet department in Harrods Department Store in London, reputed to be "the largest." It isn't and was not even close to what Macy's had then.

I realized about that time that my future in the tropical fish industry would always be as a primary supplier. I like people that I choose to be around. The retail business in New York did not suit me. I thought eventually I would like to move to Florida and combine my new import knowledge with the old knowledge of breeding and raising fish.

This wish came true almost immediately. I had a phone call at home late one night in the fall of 1956. The entire block that contained my General Aquatic Supply business was on fire. It was history by the time I got there. I never did find out how or where the fire started. It was a total and cataclysmic loss. I stood across the street alone that night, and watched my personal fairyland disappear in a holocaust of flame and smoke. My zany sense of humor saved me from crying, and I started to laugh. I tried to stop and couldn't. I was suddenly aware that someone would see the "owner" laughing. It would then be "obvious" to anyone that I had to be the culprit who started the fire for the insurance money. This would explain my fiendish fit of laughter in what should be a grim situation. This last only made me laugh more. Why??? I had in a flash of monumental idiocy, two weeks earlier, not renewed the major fire insurance policy. Inexcusable stupidity! This was an example of what happened to the boy who twisted the mule's tail. "He was not so good looking as he once was, but he knew more." Our lease was about over. I had thought to relocate nearer Idlewild Airport (J.F.K. now). I was saving money (right). I next thought of an eight foot African rock python that had escaped in the store two weeks before. It had not been found. We had spent the last weeks searching and searching for the snake. I had visions of headlines in the Daily News. I was sure the Health Department (with my previous record) would do something terrible to me. The vision was of the python crawling out of the flames screaming "All right, all right I give up ...." The insurance company brought me a check almost immediately. I was insured for about one third of what I lost (everything). By the time the sun came up I had decided I would rebuild the business. We would relocate near Idlewild Airport. This made sense. I started looking for a location that day as I had nothing to feed, clean, buy, or sell. I located several good spots within 24 hours and called the agents for information.

The phone call that changed everything came on Monday. I had been buying cheap Florida fish from Mary Ohms, who with her partner, Jim Briggs, operated the Gulf Fish Hatchery in Palmetto, Florida, located some 45 miles south of Tampa. Mrs. Ohms had heard about the fire and was calling to offer me an opportunity to buy a one third interest in their business. She even gave me the price ($30,000). I said I would get back to her. I had already made up my mind. I realized then how much I wanted out of New York City. I did not know why, but I had to own part of a fish farm. The time was right to leave Sweet Life Food Corporation as it was in the final phase of liquidation. My father was retiring. I had just about enough money to make the move and buy into the partnership. I was so happy fantasizing the life of my dreams that my brain slipped out of gear and then locked in neutral. If anything in my life shows that a simpleton can improve on my business acumen the story of my purchase of Gulf Fish Hatchery should do it. It was then that my father offered me twenty supermarkets to own and operate if I would stay in New York. I declined. It was years before my father and I became close again. My stepmother told people that Ross had moved to Florida to raise something called "goofies". That was the only thing funny in the early Florida years.

Quick as I could I flew to Florida, and for the first time, met Mary Ohms and Jim Briggs. I never questioned why they would want me to be their partner. Thinking back now the only explanation for my totally naive behavior was the fear that the fantasy I had created for myself might disappear. I went ahead with negotiations without questioning anything. I paid each of them $15,000 for one third of their stock. Each of us ended up owning a one third interest in the business. I agreed to take $150 a week in salary as they each did. I had been getting $400 a week in New York. I was totally unconcerned about details such as where I would live, and how I would pay for anything. All of my money was going to Ohms and Briggs. In fact I could not wait to give it to them. I had asked for a statement and a balance sheet so I could see how the company was doing. I was told by Mrs. Ohms (sweet old lady) that everything was just fine and to please call her "Mom". Mom only had a bookkeeper, and claimed not to know about formal statements. That was fine with me as who would question "Mom". The pencil figures showed that they didn't owe much. The accounts receivable looked healthy. Payables were small. My only fear then was that they would change their minds. It was a done deal. Briggs was not involved in the negotiations. He was a quiet, big, strong, handsome redhead. He had a degree from the University of Florida where he had been the star of the boxing team. I sold my home in New York quickly. I bought a beat up, but cheap frame house in nearby Bradenton for $6,500.

My first day on the job was also the day the Tampa company that had sold them the nice new truck repossessed it. I next found out why my negotiations had been kept so quiet. Things started to unravel. My brain after its prolonged hiatus slipped back into gear. No emotions at all were now replaced by terror. I had not been introduced to the employees until that first day. Mom, obviously, was afraid some one would talk to me. Now I got into the records. They owed everyone money. In a matter of days, mostly in a cold and clammy sweat, I found out how badly I had been cheated. They were hopelessly in debt. They had never operated at a profit. The accounts receivable were overstated by three or four hundred percent. The accounts payable were understated by three or four hundred percent. They had taken and then never given the Internal Revenue the monies they had withheld from the employees. Mom had gotten into the business by getting Jim Brigg's mother to give her one hundred acres of land at $100 an acre. This was a fraction of its value. Jim Briggs had been a problem for his mother. He had gone through his inheritance. He had a wife and three small children and no income. He had always been more interested in drinking, fighting, and partying then making a living. Mom took advantage of this scenario and with the financial help of Mrs. Briggs (Jim's mother) Gulf Fish Hatchery had been born. Mom next had sold half of the bargain land for more than enough money to build and equip a hatchery and dig and stock one hundred and fifty pools. Mrs. Ohms handled the inside and Jim Briggs the outside. A very capable man by the name of Homer Turner was the assistant field manager, and he was the only thing that saved them from absolute ruin. Three years later they were mired in debt. I had brilliantly figured out how to own one third of it. I had done well with certain of their fish as they were cheap. It was not until then that I found out you could not make a profit offering fish at Gulf's bargain prices. All of the better and more sophisticated fish they had sold to me they had bought and mostly traded dollars. I knew just how Custer felt. I looked around me and all I could see were Indians. I was in big trouble. It was not possible to continue working with Mary Ohms. I demanded the return of my money. One visit to an attorney showed me that that was not going to happen. This was the lowest point in my life.

I had no choice but to stay with the deal while trying to figure out some way to get out of it. I had no option, but to try to fight out what now appeared to be an impossible task. I was embarrassed by my blindness which was probably the least serious of my emotions.

William A. Sternke shortly before his death, with author, in 1976 at 84 years.

Wm. A. Sternke

The first fish hatchery in Florida built by Bill Sternke in 1926 - (Daytona Beach).

Interior of first Florida hatchery – Note the now priceless antique aquariums - 1926

Interior of first hatchery – Bill Sternke is the man in the picture working the vat - 1926

How Do You Like Sunnyland's Special?

BLACK MOLLIENISIA SAILFINS.
MALES WITH
ORANGE-RED BORDER ON DORSAL

Limited supply like above cut. However, (Dealers note!!) WHOLESALE QUANTITIES OF EXCELLENT BLACK MOLLIENISIAS.

WE HAVE A WELL DIVERSIFIED LINE OF TROPICALS,
Among Which are Our

SUPER RED PLATYS

bigger and better than ever. Pleased to quote you on single pairs, dozens or hundred lots.

REMEMBER!
STERNKE for Quality

SUNNYLAND FISH FARM, Inc.
13 FISHERMAN STREET OPA-LOCKA, FLORIDA
(12 Miles Northwest of Miami on the S. A. L.)

Sternke of Florida Presents
An Entirely New Black Mollie

A Pioneer of The Black Mollie Now Offers You
THE PERFECT BLACK MOLLIE!

"THE BLACK YUCATAN"

We announce a new edition of an old favorite. Now here is a new Black Mollie with none of the flaws of the old. *No more special foods!* The Black Yucatan will eagerly eat any food and thrives on dry foods. *NO MORE SHIMMIES!* This new Mollie will not sicken overnight and die for no apparent reason. The Black Yucatan is hardy and lively and will remain so for a longer life span. It can easily be raised from small fry to full adulthood in the home aquarium. Will not grow big and bulky. At full growth they are the ideal aquarium size (as shown here). For 20 years Sternke has been working to produce a new and better Black Mollie. The Black Yucatan is the result.

Dealers write for price list.

DEATH TO ALGAE!

Another outstanding contribution to the aquarium world by Sternke of Florida. FORMULA X-44, THE PROVEN KILLER OF ALGAE! Hard to believe yet a fact that FORMULA X-44 will solve your algae problems. A few drops will rid your tanks of its unsightly menace and prevent the future growth of this plague to aquarists. Algae, a growth which has defied destruction since the beginning of time can now be completely wiped out with FORMULA X-44. It is absolutely harmless to fish - plants - live foods - humans. Use it with complete confidence. (Disconnect filter during treatment.) Send for a bottle by direct mail. $1.00 Postpaid.

SUNNYLAND FISH FARM
3562 N. W. 79TH STREET, MIAMI 47, FLORIDA

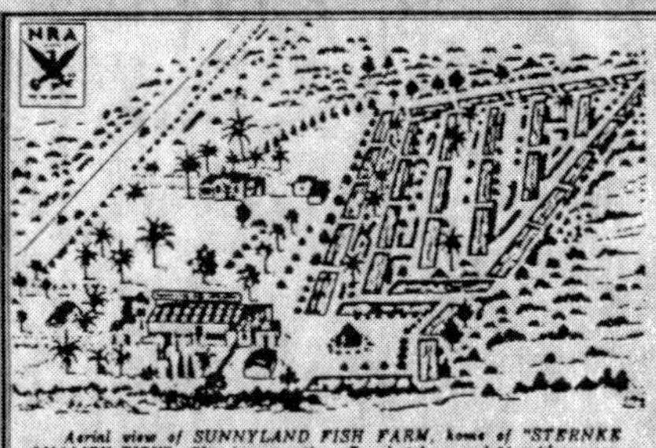

Aerial view of SUNNYLAND FISH FARM, home of "STERNKE QUALITY FISH"—Showing executive office, hatchery and 14 outdoor rearing pools, each averaging 100 feet in length.

RARE—EXTRAORDINARY—PEACEFUL

Our own importation from Yucatan—the New Scarlet Cichlid—CICHLASOMA MEEKI. Easily bred and have rare color combination of purple and red predominating.

A RARE MOLLIE

For the first time in many years we are able to offer the GENUINE MOLLIENESIA SPHENOPS with large, prominent red crescent in tails. Both plain and spotted varieties.

Bigger and better BLACK MOLLIES with orange-red bordered dorsal on male.

Full line of other Tropicals. New importations of out of the ordinary specimen received weekly.

Write for New 1934 Price List—Just Off Press.

Remember! "Sternke for Quality"

SUNNYLAND FISH FARM, Inc.
WILLIAM A. STERNKE, President
OPA-LOCKA, FLORIDA
12 Miles N. W. Miami on the Seaboard Railroad

REMEMBER!
"STERNKE For Quality"

While You May Not Be From Missouri
LET US SHOW YOU

We HAVE

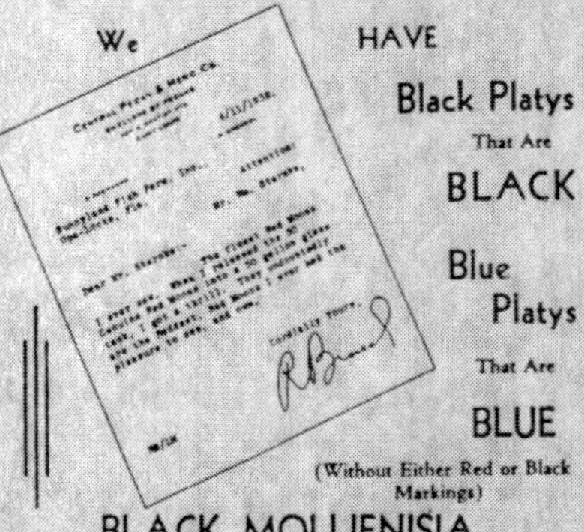

Black Platys
That Are
BLACK

Blue Platys
That Are
BLUE

(Without Either Red or Black Markings)

BLACK MOLLIENISIA
And Other Varieties

SUNNYLAND FISH FARM, Inc.
Wholesale and Retail
OPA-LOCKA Drawer H FLORIDA
12 Miles N. W. Miami on the Sea Board Rail Road
Write for Prices No Catalogue

SUNNYLAND

FISH FARM

213 Orange Ave., Daytona Beach, Fla.

I have recently returned from Europe having delivered to Dealers there a large supply of Tropical Fish raised here in the only Fish Farm located in

THE TROPICS OF the UNITED STATES.

Upon my return trip I brought with me a collection of Rare Fish, which I am offering to the American market a part as listed below:

WILLIAM A. STERNKE.

	Each		Each
Danio malabaricus	$ 1.00	Barbus semifasciolatus	$ .90
" analipunctatus	1.00	Hemigrammus ocellifer	1.00
" albolineatus	.50	Pterophyllum scalare	2.00
Trichogaster lalius	1.00	Cichlasoma aureum	2.00
" fasciatus	2.00	(A new Cichlid from Gutemala.)	
(Imported stock from Northern India)		Cichlasoma festivum	10.00
		(In mated pairs)	

Of course we offer stock as covered by our June adv. in Aquatic Life.

TERMS: CASH WITH ORDER. Shipping Cans 50c. Extra.

From Aquatic Life Magazine – September 1927

I AM OFFERING FOR SALE

GUARANTEED PAIRS

METYNNIS ROOSEVELTI

MY OWN BREEDING

(See my account of breeding this remarkable Amazon River Fish)

THE STEEL BLUE LIVEBEARER FROM YUCATAN

Both sexes deep steel blue in color. Male with two bluish-black bars in dorsal. Throat and stomach orange-yellow. Size and shape like **Limia vittata.** No special food required.

Rare — Extraordinary — Peaceful

A NEW CICHLID FROM YUCATAN

Must be seen to be appreciated. Note especially. They live peacefully with other fish.

Bigger and better BLACK MOLLIES with orange-red bordered dorsal on male.

Full line of other Tropicals. New importations of out of the ordinary specimens received weekly. Write for price list. No catalogue.

PAIRS, DOZENS, HUNDREDS OR THOUSANDS

Remember! "Sternke for Quality"

SUNNYLAND FISH FARM, Inc.

OPA-LOCKA, FLORIDA

12 Miles N. W. Miami on the Seaboard Railroad

From Aquatic Life Magazine — September 1932

"Mom" told me she would sell out to me for only $40,000. That made absolutely no sense at all as her shares in the company were worth a lot of minus dollars. I knew the only hope I had was to quickly rid myself of "Mom". I had no money, the business had a serious minus net worth, the customers were all unhappy, and the production was inadequate so I made the deal. The trade off was for time. The company bought her stock. I had three years to pay it off. I borrowed ten thousand dollars from a family trust fund, and paid interest only until I could repay it.

I had met Sheldon Moody when I first came to Bradenton. Mr. Moody was the owner and president of Manatee National Bank in Bradenton. Along with three or four other people he ran Bradenton. I called him and asked him if he would please talk to me as I needed help. I can still hear the tap, tap, tap of his pencil as he kept me at his desk for several hours feeding me questions and listening to my admitted stupidities, hopes, plans, and dreams. He was one in a million. A breed of small town banker that unfortunately is now extinct. He helped me based only on his own perception of my potential. Whatever he saw he liked. When he finally stopped tapping, he gave me the loan and said: "Ross, we had best take the interest out at the end as you sure as hell can't pay it now." He kept me alive and gave me a chance to turn the disaster into a business.

"Mom" stayed in town for several more years. She next broke several people in a local housing scheme that she promoted. Her husband, Earl Ohms, divorced her then married a younger woman, and left town. "Mom" made sure Earl got nothing from the marriage. The divorce left Earl broke, but happy. To everyone's surprise (and delight) Earl inherited almost one million dollars from his parents who had both died within the year and after the divorce. "Mom" left town shortly after this for California. I never saw or heard from her again. I was now a member of an informal club that consisted of five people in town who had dealt with "Mom" and gotten cheated. "Dave" Davidson, one of the members, became one of my close friends and he tells about his experience in Mrs. Ohmes plantain chip business as I relate my experience in her tropical fish business.

Jim Briggs was still my partner and seemed happy with what I had been doing. We talked. He quickly agreed to let me run the show. "Mom" was history. He promised to do what he could to help. He gave me many anxious moments, but no real problems as we left each other pretty much alone. He never carried his weight. He was totally unreliable. He would disappear for days. One time when he showed up after being gone for three or four days he was unwashed, smelled of booze, and had badly bruised knuckles. He told me he had no idea where he had been. He thought he might have killed someone. I put up with him for lots of unimportant reasons. The only important reason was that I could not afford to do anything about it. The end came when Verna Robertson, our secretary, came to me with a recently uncrumbled handwritten cash invoice Jim had thrown in the waste basket after selling some fish for cash. She had recovered the bill. He had pocketed the cash. He wasn't even a smart enough thief to destroy the evidence. I waited for several days giving him every opportunity to tell me about it. He didn't. Two days later I asked him to stay after we closed down for the day. I had already discussed the problem with the company's attorney. He was standing by as I had told him I had to disassociate myself from Briggs even though I could not afford it. I confronted Briggs. He did not deny the theft. I did all the talking. I told him we were finished. He either bought me out or he sold out to me. Neither of us had any money. I asked him for time until the end of the week to try to give him ten thousand dollars cash and a note for two years for another ten thousand dollars. He agreed. I called my father for help that night. I explained the situation. He arranged to get me another ten thousand dollars from the family trust fund. Next morning I met Briggs at the attorney's office where we signed the papers.

The lawyer told me he wanted me to wait after Jim Briggs left. He had something to talk to me about. The lawyer (who I later learned had a shady reputation) told me gleefully that he had not given Briggs a copy of the signed agreement. I think I was supposed to be happy about this deceit. I made a copy of mine and sent it to Briggs. Then I went down the street to a certain Frank Arpaia and asked him to be my lawyer. That was one of my lucky days. Frank Arpaia was and still is a brilliant, honest, and effective lawyer. We have been good friends and occasional business partners ever since.

A couple of years after this Frank ran for and was elected Justice of the Peace and the Judge of the Small Claims Court. He held court at night and pretty soon the word got out that his courtroom was the best "act in town". Fair, fast, and funny describes the scene. Loise and I went down to watch Frank conduct the proceedings. His lectures to the defendants and his frequent wry comments were far more meaningful than anything that has appeared on commercial television. He must have been the inspiration for Judge Wapner.

A lot had happened to me in little more than a year. I was now the 100% owner of the Gulf Fish Hatchery. I had managed to turn the business around after the first year and we even made a few dollars in profit. The direction was clear to me. I was getting up at 3 AM every day and staying until 4 PM. I then would head home. Loise always knew I was heading home as the phone started to ring. At home every evening I took orders and sold fish. Four hours of sleep kept me going. I had inherited two fish breeders. Claude Gladden, the more experienced of the two, left shortly after I bought the business to try raising fish himself. He was one of the earliest and best of Florida's commercial fish breeders. He is a talented fish breeder and was hard to replace. The breeding department now consisted of a crusty old West Virginian with a lot of potential who worked hard developing his skills. He had little experience, good imagination, and listened to me. This was Ellis Horn and he raised a lot of angelfish, white clouds, dwarf gouramis, Leeri, Kissers and several items (new for Florida) that I pushed on him such as Nudiceps, Kribensis, chocolate cichlids, bumble bees, and even a few of the new Lake Nyasa (now Malawi) cichlids such as *Pseudotropheus zebra* and *tropheops*. These were the first that got to Florida. I had bought and sold fish to Dr. Walther Griem, the owner of Aquarium Hamburg, when operating General Aquatic in New York. Griem was the first one in Europe to get the new Lake Nyasa (Malawi) cichlids, and he sent me the first ones to come to the United States.

I badly needed to upgrade the quality of Gulf Fish Hatchery's livebearer strains. They were not quite good enough to be graded terrible. I had done considerable business with Elsberry Fish Farms. They were the logical ones to ask and they could not have been more helpful. I had ponds prepared and about six new strains to stock. I handled this personally. I opened the first bag at the pond site. I started to slip the fish into the pond. I took a quick glance at handsome velvet red swords and noticed a bonus in the form of new babies. At the very last second the fact that the babies were grey and not gold (as velvet sword babies are at birth) registered. I saved myself a lot of time and trouble by stopping that instant. The babies were newly born *Gambusia*.

Examining all of the bags carefully revealed the same contaminant. I could have understood if my request for good breeding stock had been refused. This was just inexcusable behavior. The *Gambusia* would have taken over the pool and eaten all the swordtail babies. I could not let it pass, and as soon as I got myself under control I called the manager and reported what I had found. I was told it could only have been an accident. That statement reminded me of the woman who "accidentally" shot her cheating husband six times. After this lesson I learned how to improve strains, and seldom had to obtain fish from outside sources. When I did I always traded.

I had dealt with Albert Greenberg and went to visit his Everglades Aquatic Nurseries in Tampa. He did provide me with good breeding stock and would not take payment. Everything he gave me was very helpful. We became lifelong friends. He retired in the late 1960s. I made it my business to visit each year. He died in November of 1993 just weeks before his 97th birthday. I called him in late November that year to wish him a happy birthday. I got his sister on the phone who explained to me that the next day they were putting Albert in a rest home. She told me he would not know me as he had become senile. I have had some experience with things like this and asked her to talk to him the first thing in the morning and tell him I had called to wish him a happy birthday. I was surprised and delighted when he called me early the next morning. He knew me. We had a good last talk. I did not expect him to last the eleven months that he did in the rest home. Rest homes are the wrong place for independent free roaming spirits like Albert Greenberg. He was something very special and was one of the two men who laid the foundations for the Florida tropical fish industry (the other was William A. Sternke).

Albert Greenberg was born aboard an English freighter, in the port of Odessa, Russia where his mother had gone to settle her father's estate. Her father had been a wheat broker in Russia. Albert was registered as a U.S. citizen at the American Embassy as his parents were U.S. citizens. He always wondered if he might also be a British citizen. The entire family had previously settled in Oak Park a suburb of Chicago, Illinois. The stimulus for his lifelong interest in aquatic plants and tropical fish came from his green-thumbed grandmother and an uncle (M. Dagobert) who operated a large ornamental plant nursery where the teenaged Greenberg worked for spending money.

I am not sure I believed him, but he did tell me that as a youngster he had walked ten miles to the nearest place where he could buy fish. This in 1903 when he was only seven years old. He could get two "imported" livebearing fish for five cents. These were Gambusia. There always were tropical fish in his Chicago home. Angelfish were newly arrived from Germany. They arrived there in 1913 and were priced at $200 a pair. After World War One angelfish imported from Germany were still priced at $75 each. By 1922 they were selling for $15 each in Chicago. His dream eventually came true. The dream was to be able to afford a pair of angelfish and breed them, sell the young, and then have all the money there was. This almost all came true in later years. Unfortunately by that time angelfish were being bred without difficulty, and he had to make his fortune with other items. He left the University of Chicago after his freshman year. The United States entered the First World War and Albert Greenberg enlisted in the United States Navy. His naval career almost ended before he saw his first ship. He was by then a badly addicted cigarette smoker. It was against the rules to smoke in the barracks. He broke the rules as did most of the others. His smoking led to big trouble. Greenberg was arrested. He ended up in the brig after he accidentally burned down the entire barracks. He had dropped his cigarette atop a pile of rags that looked like garbage. The rags had been saturated with gasoline. It caused a big fire fast. He served some time in the brig, and swore off smoking forever. Then for almost three years he was aboard ships in the Far East.

After he was discharged he went to work for the Enterprise Chemical Company. He sold chemicals on the road for the next ten years and saved his money. In 1929 he had enough money saved to consider going into business for himself. He knew just what he wanted to try. The United States was now entering the depression and he found his inadequate savings now had unexpected and welcome buying power. He had fallen in love with Florida. In 1929 he quit his job and bought land in Tampa. He relocated in early 1930. He had the Everglades Aquatic Nurseries open for business late in 1930. Red *Ludwigia* was the item that convinced his to move to Florida. The wild plants in Florida were free for the picking and were many times better than the ones that were on the market imported from Germany. The imported red *Ludwigia* were sold for 40 cents each. He couldn't wait to collect and market *Ludwigia* and the many other similar native Floridian aquatic plants.

His first, and for some time, only customer was Vaughan's Seed in Chicago. His second customer was Walter Chute of the Shedd Aquarium who bought large amounts of native Florida plants and fish. He put out his first catalogue in February of 1932. He always sold fish and plants.

Greenberg was the first person to raise tropical fish in dirt ponds. His first dirt ponds were dug by hand using spades and wheel barrows. The first ponds were eight feet wide and fifteen feet long. Wages were $1.00 per day. It took ten young men one entire day to make that first pond. These first ponds were little more than three feet deep in the center. The natural springs and shallow wells provided water with no problems. The very first fish raised commercially in a dirt pond in Florida were zebra danio. By the end of 1931 pool digging men were partly replaced. The addition of two mules pulling a "drag" moved dirt a lot faster.

Albert was always more botanist than ichthyologist. He was honored by having a pink hybrid water lily named "The Albert Greenberg".

In 1932 he hired a man named Al Wechsler, who he knew from Chicago, to manage the tropical fish part of the business. This did not work out. He described that association to me in these words: "He made me crazy." That story is discussed in detail in the section done on H. Woolf and Son as Herb Woolf inherited Wechsler. He turned out to be the same person who was my second customer at General Aquatic. He helped my education a lot (what not to do).

The first employees, remarkably, stayed with him until they died of old age or outlived Greenberg's ownership of the business. Donald, the very first employee, and Norton Jennings were given the business when Albert Greenberg retired. Donald Jennings was on the very first pool digging crew. Roy Bass and Johnny Gallo were two other original, valuable, and loyal employees. These four people helped Everglades grow to become an institution known worldwide that possessed an enviable reputation for excellence.

His first catalogue (five mimeographed pages) offered 34 varieties of aquatic plants which included the still rare Madagascar lace plant (*Aponogeton fenestralis*) and no Cryptocorynes which later became his specialty. Bunch plants were sold at three and a half cents per bunch. *Sagittaria* and *Valisneria* were three or four dollars for one hundred plants depending on the species. The sleeper was the water hyacinth. You could have all you wanted for two cents each.

Everglades offered a good variety of pond-raised fish including all the then popular livebearers and some egg layers. Included in the list were Texas cichlids (*C. cyanoguttatum*) which were being sold at $1.65 each for small and $2.50 each for young adults. He also pond raised red paradise, Buenos Aires tetras, zebra danio, and rosy barbs. Indoors he raised Siamese fighting fish, and both dwarf and thick-lipped gouramis.

The bulk of what Greenberg sold in the first years were plants and fish that were collected from the abundant wilderness areas near Tampa. He would find promising habitats in promising looking remote areas and then he planted aquatic plants. This idea worked out very well and some seeded spots remained fruitful for many years. I suspect he also seeded a few spots to see if they would provide a harvest of exotic fish as they did with the plants. There are established populations of Texas cichlids in the Alafia River and *Plecostomus* in Seven Mile Creek both near Tampa, Florida. His best selling item was the local freshwater flounder (*Achirus fasciatus*). These Al Greenberg described in his catalogue as aeroplane fish and it read: "The new rarity that is our largest seller, and the fish that has made the greatest success. These fish swim on their side and are very different and only sixty-five cents each." Fifty years later they are priced at 25 cents each.

The business grew, and additional room for dirt ponds was required. Greenberg hunted for months for good land and good water near Tampa. The original hatchery rapidly was being engulfed by new residents as Tampa grew. When he found what he wanted, the only thing he could think of was "Eureka, I have found it" which he explained to me was Greek. It had been cried out by Archimedes when he discovered a method to detect the amount of alloy in gold. Greenberg bought the land, and named it Eureka Springs. The name stuck and that is what the area is called today. The almost eighty acres in Eureka Springs had everything. There were eleven free flowing natural springs on the property with wonderful water from the Floridian aquifer. He kept half of the land for his home site and the remainder for more dirt ponds and large buildings where he could also grow plants in concrete vats under shade cloth.

His home site was developed over the years into a wonderland of exotic plants. Greenberg brought back, from his many collecting trips, rare and exotic plants. These he planted on the property. Eventually he transformed the land into a fairyland rainforest. His green thumb had worked a botanical miracle. In 1967 he gifted his home site and the botanical parkland he had created to Hillsborough County. He stipulated that he would live in his home until his death, the park could never be sold, and that entrance would always be free. His cremated remains are there now with a suitable marker. There is now a half mile boardwalk through the natural bog areas. Look sharp and you can find Asiatic Cryptocorynes that are firmly established where Al Greenberg planted them more than 65 years ago.

In 1932 a close childhood friend, George Moreno, who had lived in Oak Park, Illinois, but was from Spanish Honduras asked Albert to come to Spanish Honduras to be the best man at his wedding. George's uncle was the President of Spanish Honduras and his aunt an avid tropical fish keeper. This was his first collecting trip. He took down to Spanish Honduras, as gifts, some of his best Siamese fighting fish and also new hybrid livebearers. The gift fishes opened up all sorts of magic doors. He had all the help he needed to collect fish and move around the country. He returned to Florida with some new cichlids, merry widow livebearers (*P. amates*), several new livebearers, and best of all the pure freshwater sailfin mollies (*Poecilia petenensis*) which he collected on the way home in Northern Belize. All fish breeders know that the native Florida green sailfin mollies (*P. latipinna*) are about the most difficult fish to ship and to keep in freshwater. For years Everglades bred and sent out Petenensis sailfins without ever telling anyone they were not natives. They were so much better. Everyone wanted to know and never found out the secret conditioning method that kept Everglades sailfins mollies from getting "shimmies".

His most exciting adventure was a trip to Madagascar in late 1946 to collect plants. This was the trip he dreamed about all of his life. He made a wonderful collection of new and rare aquatic plants. He stayed for five months. The boat, on the return voyage, ran into a terrible storm which resulted in the loss of almost all his specimens.

He went to Cuba in 1934 at the invitation of Dr. Masnauta, director of the Havana Public Aquarium. The reason for the trip was an attempt to locate an interesting cave fish. This turned out to be an all white, blind Brotulid less than six inches in length. The fish was also a livebearer and had evidently managed to survive and convert itself in the cave while losing its eyes from a marine fish into a freshwater one. Quite a trick. He brought back living specimens which he put in a concrete vat with some all white blind cave crawfish. The crawfish killed the blind Brotulids. He had collected the cave crawfish near Homasassa Springs in Florida from a place called "Bat Cave". As far as I know no one has ever been back to Cuba to try again. Masnauta also lost his fish. I suspect it is on the Endangered List now (or should be).

The very first kissing gouramis to come to Florida arrived at Everglades in 1935. The last survivor of the original lot died when it was 22 years old. Albert showed me the just expired fish on my first visit to him in 1957.

Loise and I miss our visits to Al Greenberg. Every time Loise and I went she would cook him one of the special Jewish dishes he had eaten as a boy. He really looked forward to seeing Loise more than seeing me.

In 1961 I visited Europe. This was my first, of many, trips. The trip was a gift from one of the Scandinavian airlines. I had been a good customer as they had handled my considerable freight from Brichard in the Congo. I spent several days with Dr. Griem at Aquarium Hamburg. I learned a lot. He had continued to raise fish all through World War Two. He had been forced to operate without aeration (undependable or no electricity) and did so well that in 1961 he still was not using electricity to aerate the water. He had many, many hundreds of very large glass aquariums. These were more than one hundred and less than two hundred gallons each. These aquariums were used to grow out the newly hatched egg layers. The amazing thing was the quantities of fish growing fat, fast, and healthy in these containers with no aeration. There was no secret other than controlled feeding (a lot of live food), well timed daily siphoning of the bottoms and then large daily water replacement.

The Malawi cichlids Aquarium Hamburg sent me, arrived mixed, torn up, mean, dead, and dying. It took time to figure out which female went with what male. No one had a clue in 1957. Next problem was to learn how to breed them. The first spawn I had was with P. zebra. This came after I first found out how to feed them. I remember my shock discovering that they wouldn't touch baby guppies. They did well on my paste foods, beef heart, and adult brine shrimp. They were mouth brooders. I counted the days for release of the eggs (21 days that first time). I had paired them in a forty gallon tank. It worked. Later I found that they did better in a dirt pond as they beat each other up terribly when paired to breed. Still later we learned that colonial spawning (one male and five to eight females) was the most practical method to breed these fish. In Germany, I also visited Hans Schmidt who ran Tropiquarium in Frankfurt. Hans and I had sold fish back and forth for years. He took me to visit his brother, Dr. Edward Schmidt-Focke, who then was mostly interested in Siamese fighting fish, and just getting into discus. Edward had actually reversed sexes on Siamese fighting fish by surgically removing and transplanting reproductive organs.

The two Sidoli brothers in Paris were anxious to try some Florida fish. The sales manager and buyer for Sidoli was a retired French Major named Roule. His English was perfect, and we did well together. Importing Florida livebearers would not make any sense unless we could somehow reduce the freight costs. The answer was obviously to tranquilize the fish. I sent him an order as soon as I returned to Florida. I was very unsure of the dosage of paraldehyde and think I used too much. Either that or the fish were frozen en route, which was a common occurrence in those days. I awaited results anxiously. I shortly had a letter from friend Roule. He said that the "shipment arrived perfect—fish all look good. However, it has been almost a week and the fish have not yet come out of the tranquilizer." It took a re-read to realize he was telling me the fish had all arrived dead. I finally stopped laughing and felt like crying. Afterwards we sent many thousands of fish with good success to Europe. Eventually that business dried up. Even with the tranquilizers the high freight costs prevented anyone from profitably importing Florida livebearers into Europe.

We sold Europe a lot of native Florida fish. These we bought from the wild plant and fish collectors the fish farmers always referred to as "swamp rats". These people collected plant material for the various live plant shippers, who then bunched it, and sold it for three cents a bunch. Many were fierce and all were tough people. More than once terrible battles erupted when one would poach on another's territory.

From the start the "swamp rats" all seeded secret patches with aquarium plants. In a year or so they could return, and harvest their crop. This is where the problems started. One collector would trail another to try to discover a secret aquatic garden. There was one murder, and almost certainly another. That particular collector just "disappeared". No body was ever found. He has not been seen for the past 40 years. I doubt anyone still expects him to turn up.

They collected pygmy sunfish (*Elassoma evergladei*), swamp killies (*Leptolucania omnata*), bluefin killi (*Lucania goodei*), golden ears (*Fundulus chrysotus*), red-line dace (*Notropis hypselopterus*), diamond sunfish (*Eneacanthus gloriosa*), various small turtles, freshwater flounders (*Achirus fasciatus*), Adinia (*A. xenica*), flag fish (*Jordanella floridae*), gigantic sailfin mollies (*Poecilia latipinna*) and Congo eels (*Amphiuma means*), an amphibian also called a "Siren". The Congo eels grew to over three feet in length. Early on I learned that they have a terrible bite. We took as many small freshwater garfish as we could get as they sold fast. The garfish were a particularly profitable business. They are almost impossible to kill. The only problem was getting them small enough. It got harder and harder to obtain wild fish to fill orders. As years passed the available collecting areas grew people instead of wild creatures. I liked it much better in the earlier years.

Many times I went to pick up shipments in Tampa that arrived in the middle of the night, and could not safely be left until morning. On my very first trip late in 1956 I returned from Tampa in a terrible rain storm. Turning down the dirt road to the farm I blindly inched the truck ahead. The visibility was terrible. I hit the brakes fast when I saw the grandfather of all Florida alligators (he had the right of way) resting astride the road. He was not ten feet in front of me. He seemed to reach from one side of the road to the other (twenty feet wide there). I left the head lights on and then opened the door to see how close a look I could get. I was about five feet away when the monster decided I was close enough. He reared up, showed me a mouth full of teeth, hissed at me so loudly that I leaped backward, and was seated and closing the car door before my feet again hit a solid surface. The huge gator then regally walked into the gloom. I passed that spot thousands of times in later years and always looked, but never saw him again.

Shortly after this trip I had another scary experience. I had picked up a shipment of marine fish that Earl Kennedy had sent to me. I brought it back to the farm just past midnight. I had a bag of Plotosid marine catfish. Each fish was about three inches long. I carelessly allowed myself to get "stung" in my thumb. I was in terrible pain, but I did not know what a fierce and dangerous sting these marine catfish could inflict. I searched through reference books I had in my office at the farm. I learned I would be in pain (I already knew that) and would live (which was good news). I knew then that I was lucky this was a juvenile catfish and not a fully armed adult. Adults have killed people. I must have passed out then (Pain? Relief? Fright?) as I did not remember lying down on the sofa in my office. I did not come back to life until the next morning. The bad dream was replaced by a look at a badly swollen, mostly blackened thumb. Innocuous catfish (like all *Corydoras* species) can "sting", and until you have stepped on one in bare feet catching the erect dorsal spine in the sole of your foot, you probably will not believe me. Then you will not forget.

Another day one of the commercial mullet fisherman who lived down the road from our Gulf Fish Hatchery burst into the office looking for me. He was very excited and announced that he had one of my "dragons" in his tree, and would I please get it before it poisoned someone. It wasn't easy, but we did recover an eighteen inch Basilisk from the tree. I tried to explain to the tree owner that it wasn't a dragon or poisonous. I know he did not believe me. Its months of freedom had turned it into a really prime specimen. I love Basilisk lizards. They are amazing animals. I always look forward to seeing the first of these "Jesus Christ" lizards when I visit South or Central America. Every time I see the trip's first Basilisk lizard running down the road in front of our vehicle with its body erect and its hind legs pumping away and its arms outstretched, I give an audible gasp. Evidently one's perspective gets seriously out of kilter trying to focus on such a scene. Always the first appearance is viewed as a smallish man running down the road in front of the car. The eventual recognition of what you are seeing never diminishes the experience. Not a bit. How often can you see a lizard running like a man? In fact, when they encounter a stream of water they don't break stride. They run right over it, never slowing and never sinking. That is where the nickname of "Jesus Christ" lizard comes from.

In 1961 the Florida fish farmers tried (and succeeded) in resurrecting the previous failed attempt to organize a viable association. I went to that first meeting which was very successful and very encouraging. The one thing everyone agreed on was that we would never again get involved in the price a member put on his fish. "Mac" Entel from Sumac Tropicals spearheaded the meeting and was elected the first president. The Florida Tropical Fish Farmers Association (F.T.F.F.A.) gets better every year. The second president was Fred Cochu. Colonel John Hanan, who with his wife Fran ran the wonderful Sunlan Aquatic Plant business in Miami was the third president. John was a retired marine, and all business. In later years his steady, firm hand got us through some bad years. He got to be president three or four more times, whenever things got bad. The one event at that first meeting (in Fort Myers) that still exists as a sharp mental picture, was when the discussion turned to customers that systematically cheated in reporting loses. A big customer who paid promptly was a thing of beauty and one that we all coveted. That meant we would do most anything to keep them (or get them). Mac Entel described in detail how he had closely monitored a big customer of his in St. Louis named Martin Vick. He told everyone how he had taken the time to check other customers who had gotten identical fish from identical holding vats the same day without any problems while Vick consistently claimed all sorts of losses on what other customers reported as good fish. As a valuable customer he was given credit for the claimed losses. Mac Entel reported that over a period of time this turned out to be almost thirty percent of the original billing prices, and he gave him up. At that moment Mac Entel converted me into becoming a life long supporter of the fellowship of other fish farmers. I had just that week realized I was taking consistent losses from that same customer and was wondering what to do. The advantages received by frank communication to each other were clearly revealed to all of us. The close relationship amongst the farmers is to be envied by most other business associations. It has become an unwritten rule that when one farmer needs breeding stock another farmer will supply it. No one ever charges for these fish. We all share and we all benefit. Every industry has a percentage of bad actors amongst its membership. In the Florida fish farming fraternity it is a rare thing to find scheming and greedy people.

I was privileged to be included in a group of industry leaders in 1971 that included Art Hopkins, Allen Levey, Ken Blaising, Jules Swimmer, Greg Judge and several others that formed P.I.J.A.C. (Pet Industry Joint Advisory Committee). At this first meeting, which also was attended by Dr. John Gratzek, we agreed to make an initial research grant to him and the University of Georgia. Jack Gratzek, over the years, almost single handedly brought the fish farming community into the scientific fish world. His contribution to our understanding of fish pathogens has made the previously unknown microscope a tool almost as important as a fish net. He also is a great guy. I was appointed by the Florida tropical fish farmers to represent them. I served on the very first PIJAC Board of Directors, and for a good number of years afterwards.

The macho thing in Florida was for an outlander to be able to drink well water, smile, and tell everyone it is good. It isn't. In fact it is a vile and disgusting potion. It comes up deep with no oxygen at all. The water has sulfur gas in it. This unbelievable stench takes about 24 hours to gas off. The nasty stuff then tastes like water. Drinking it from the tap is nauseating. Not only does it tastes bad but it smells like an unlimed privy on a hot day. The best way I can describe it is to ask you to imagine drinking and smelling liquid stockyard odors. Getting past the smell was even worse than the nasty taste. After surviving the nauseating initial drinking rites I too made all guests sample our "wonder water". I learned how to hoot and y'all like a real Cracker drawling out that this was fine water. This obviously was the stuff Ponce De Leon was looking for in Florida. The story goes that he died from the wounds the Indians inflicted, but we insiders know it really was from the water. There was an old second hand refrigerator in the hatchery that five or six of us used for the real water that we brought from home.

Jim Briggs was convinced that Ellis Horn, our fish breeder, was drinking his water. He brooded over this for months and planned and plotted as to how he could catch him. He told me one day that he had gotten (from a drug store owner he went to school with) some "powders" that were tasteless and colorless. Mixed with water it would make you urinate purple. He planned to trap Ellis for sure. He only hoped Horn did not die of fright when he first viewed his stream of psychedelic urine, because he was our best and only fish breeder. The only problem was that Jim had to drink cokes while the trap remained baited. He was so pleased with his trap that he told everyone (except Ellis Horn). I am sure someone told Ellis what was coming. I would see Briggs lurking around comers waiting for the happy moment when the trap would get sprung. After three uneventful weeks Jim Briggs forgot one day and drank his water himself. It worked... Surprised everyone.

Henrik (Hank) Hansen, after he retired from his sea-going career, came to work for me at Gulf Fish Hatchery as our chief breeder. Ellis Horn remained breeding a separate and easier group of fish. I loved to listen to Hansen's fish stories. Tales of his travels during the 1930s and 1940s, when he was employed as the head chef on various steamship lines, and also transporting wild exotic fish were spellbinding. Hank traveled the world, and collected fish everywhere. His culinary talents were so great that he could demand, and always received, an extra cabin for his tropical fish. He introduced many varieties (lemon tetras, *Nothobranchius*, African glass catfish, etc) I know from personal experience that he was a great chef. He made lunch for Jack Pearlman and me for years. This was the result of an inspiration (trade off) one day, after he had been at Gulf for a year, when we discussed an increase in his wages. He had not only transported fish on the boats, but kept and bred many for his own pleasure. All this while at sea. He was a skilled fish breeder. He bred many fish commercially before anyone else did. *Metynnis*, *Leporinus*, *Copeina guttata*, glass catfish, leaf fish, pencil fish, headstanders, and Congo tetras come to mind now. I even remember seeing infertile eggs from a one time only spawning of marble hatchet fish. His greatest frustration was his inability to breed bleeding heart tetras. This was particularly devastating because they look "easy" and should be easy. All of the similar looking characoids that come from the Amazon basin were bred easy enough.

On a trip to Iquitos, Peru I went to the Rio Napo where they were collected, and I tested the water. It was a lot more acid then expected (about pH 5.8). This information did not help. In later years I supplied all of the professional breeders in Florida with many healthy mature bleeding heart tets knowing one of them would certainly breed them. I was wrong. I wanted the "pick of the litter" when they succeeded. The trick in breeding most wild fish is to get the first spawn. Breeding from tank raised fish has always proven to be a lot easier. The history of the spawning of wild angelfish and discus is important information and it clearly illustrates this truth. The first angelfish came to Germany in 1913. These sold for the absolutely incredible price of $200 a pair. As late as 1922 they were selling for $75 each. The breeding of angelfish was an almost impossible task for many, many years. After they had been bred for three or four generations in the 1920s they got easier and easier. Angelfish were still considered "tough" fish in the early 1930s. By the late 1940s they were easily bred with little effort. Sloppy fish keepers, who would never have been able to breed an angelfish twenty years earlier, now had no difficulty. They were selling (with bodies the size of a nickel) for ten cents each by 1950. The same exact story, with nothing but the dates changed, has happened with discus. The first ones came to the United States in 1932. Discus are found together in the wild with angelfish. Discus are an even more "plastic" fish and the hybridization of colors is mind boggling. It wasn't until the 1980s that the breeding of discus became easy. Now they breed like angelfish.

I do not know of anyone ever breeding bleeding hearts. A few people have claimed success. On investigation the bleeding heart tetra spawnings could not be substantiated. Usually it would be another fish or very suspect reporting.

Hank Hansen had never learned to drive. He had retired a year earlier and located himself in Lakeland, Florida. He paid some one to drive him to his customers, and that is how we met. I taught him to drive, and he got rid of his bicycle. He bought a new Nash Rambler and kept it forever. I bought him a trailer and he lived on the farm. He could check his fish anytime he wanted. He learned that one species of African glass catfish would only breed on a full moon. Later he thought he improved spawnings by adding urine from a pregnant woman to each breeding tank. During that time he would stay up all night as the glass catfish ate their eggs almost as fast as they fertilized them. He had very good results.

He was an incredible slob. He seldom bathed and shaved about half as often as he bathed. His mouth was home for a big cigar that was seldom lit. It just sat there and slowly dissolved to slobber. He had never in his life been to a dentist and he often said that he never would. He never did. He didn't brush his teeth (ever). His theory postulated that if left undisturbed the brown hairy growths on teeth could not be attacked by bacteria. Evidently he was right as he kept them all as incredible as that seems. He was not a beauty, but he had great talent. His disposition was for the most part cheery. You had to be able to rise above his horrible prejudices. I must say that he was not selective. He hated Jews and all religious people. He had a special dislike for Negroes. As a Jew, his friend, and his employer I tried to understand his anti-Semitism. The closest I could come was his claim that it was genetic. That was the way his people all felt. He liked me and said I wasn't really a Jew. I still have not been able to figure that out either.

Hank never drank during the week. Weekends were something else. He started drinking Friday night and kept drinking until he

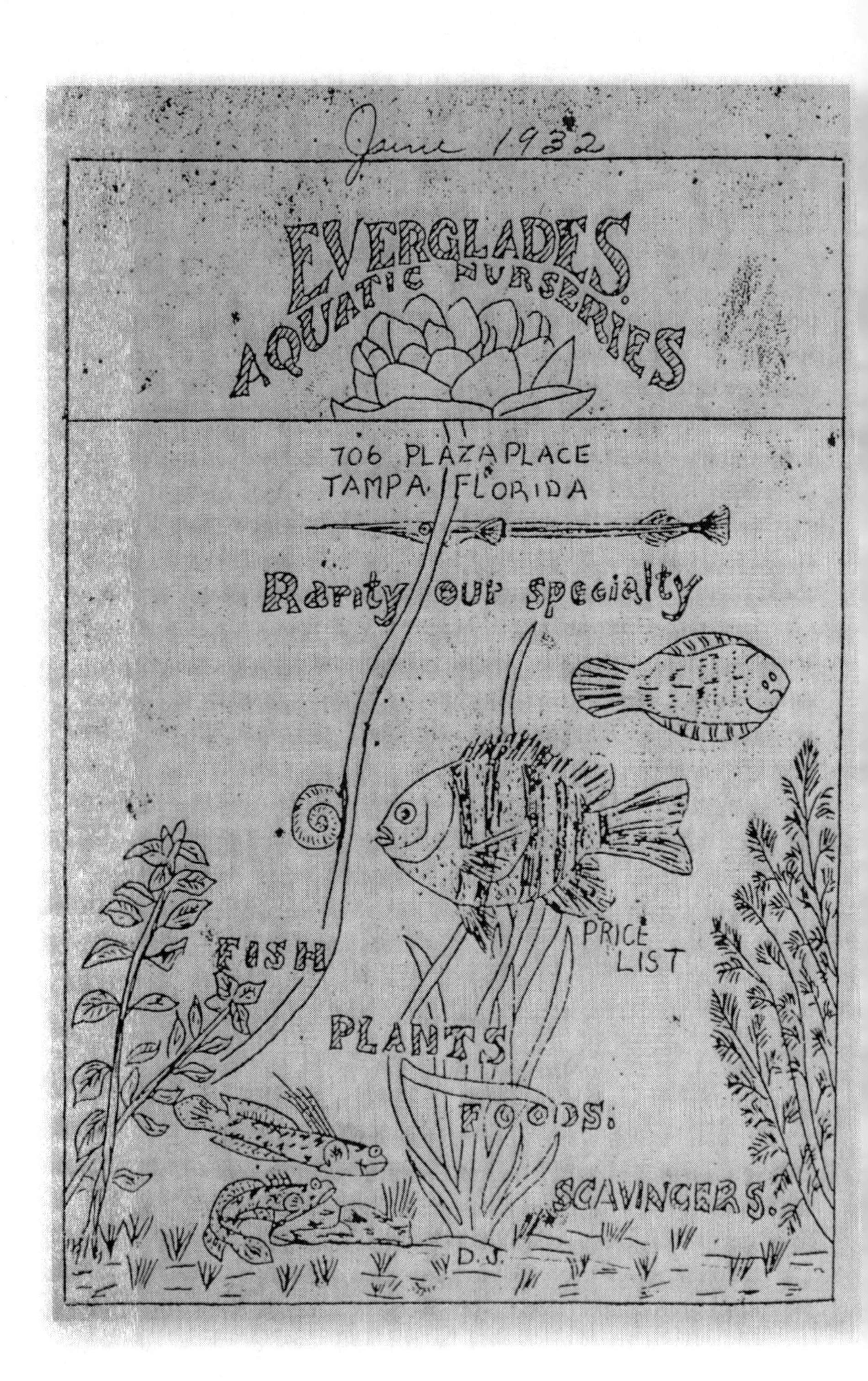
June 1932
EVERGLADES
AQUATIC NURSERIES
706 PLAZA PLACE
TAMPA FLORIDA
Rarity our specialty
FISH
PRICE LIST
PLANTS
FOODS.
SCAVINGERS.
D.J.

FLORIDA TROPICAL FISH CONT'D. — Per 100

	Per 100
Chriopeops Goodei (Beautiful) Males have blue dorsal. - -	$ 20.00
Elassoma Evergladi (Beautiful Pigmy Sunfish)- - - - - - -	15.00
Dormitator Maculatus (Odd Rarity) - - - - - - - - - - - -	40.00
Sand Darters -	25.00
Florida Catfish (Often change color from red to black) --	50.00

	Per Doz.
Large Veiltail "Show Stock" Breeding Size Fighting Fish, Green, Red-Green, Red and Blue. - - - - -	$ 15.00

RARE FISH

APOGON SPEC. - A new interesting intelligent appearing fish of a beautiful silver sheen and a black barred dorsal. See Bilderatlas.

Per Pair $3.00 Per Dozen $12.00

MEXICAN CICHLID - (Neetroplus Carpintus) The beautiful new Blue Spotted Cichlid from the Mexican Border, which has been recently bred for the first time.

BREEDING STOCK

Per Pair $5.00 Per Dozen $20.00

AEROPLANE FISH - (Fresh Water Flounders) The new rarity that is our largest seller and the fish that has made the greatest success. These fish swim on their side and are very different from all other varieties of fish. Our best seller.

Per Dozen - - - - - - - $6.00
In lots of 25 - Each - .40 each
In lots of 50 and 100 - .75 each

DWARF NEEDLE FISH - The newest oddity in the aquarium world. These little fish are long and thin, averaging from 2" to 4" in length and are exceptionally pretty, as well as odd in their movements. They are harmless to other fish and will draw anybodys attention when first seen.

Per Dozen - - - - - - - ~~$6.00~~ 8.00
In lots of 25 - - - - - ~~.40~~ each .60
In lots of 50 and 100 - ~~.75~~ each .50

ABUDEFDUF SAXATILIS (The Convict Fish)- The newest, as well as among the most beautiful, barred fish. This new addition is one of the most graceful and interesting fishes that we know of. The bars on these fish are very wide and are of a Blue-Black shade. These colors do not fade out and during the breeding season, there is nothing more beautiful than these fish. This fish is our pride and we recommend same to all Aquarists for something new and distinct.

Per Pair $3.50 Per Doz. $15.00 Per 100 $75.00

Everglades price list — June 1932

Donald Jennings and Albert Greenberg (1939)

Bunching wild aquatic plants at Everglades Aquatic Nurseries in mid 1930s.

Ross Socolof and Al Greenberg – 1982

Al Greenberg, John Hanan, Clara Sternke, Ross Socolof,
Bill Rice, and Ralph Meyer –1980

ended up in jail or someone drove him back to the farm. Palmetto and Bradenton were still small towns, and had great police chiefs. I cultivated relationships with them, and always generously donated to their campaigns. Generous in those days was $25.00. It was important to keep Hansen productive and not jailed. Our local police chief even arranged a charge account for me, and we did business by phone. I often got calls from the jail. They usually concerned a certain Henrik Hansen who they were holding in the drunk tank and "did I want him?" Talk about mixed emotions. More than once Hank had claimed to be Ross Socolof. I never could figure that one out either. This kept happening. Bradenton was a small town in those days and now writing this I remember one time about 2 AM going down to the jail to collect Hank. I captured a huge armadillo that I found rooting around on the courthouse lawn. I put the armadillo in the trunk and Hansen in the car. I liberated both (Hank and the armadillo) at the farm and then went back home to sleep.

Hank Hansen was a big help with our business, and not just as a fish breeder. We often had guests from foreign countries. He was fluent in eight languages. This really helped. Heiko Bleher (who as a seventeen year old was working for me at this time) is the only other friend who is as linguistically gifted as Hansen. We would get Hansen shaved, bathed, cologned and into his (only) brown pin-striped suit. He was a wonderful story teller and always a help. Our guests were "fish people" (his kind), and they delighted in his company. He and Loise always compared recipes. His praise for her ability in the kitchen was sincere.

It was one Saturday night about this time that Hank found a girlfriend. They met in a Bradenton bar. Hank discovered that she was separated from her husband and lonely. That was his cue and he promptly fell in love. She lived in a trailer park and invited him home. About 2 AM a hysterical and raging husband burst in on them. Apparently the "separated" wife had neglected to tell her husband they had separated and he returned early from a trip. He informed Hank that he was going to kill him, and then gathered up all of Hank's clothes and ran out of the trailer. His last message as he left was that he would be right back as he was only going to his truck to get his gun. He correctly figured that a naked Hansen would be there when he returned. Some weeks later (when Hank was talking to me again) he told me that he didn't really believe him. He thought things like that only happened in the movies. He got out from under the bed and then a blast from a shot gun riddled the trailer and his theory. Hank realized he had made a big mistake, and he wasn't at the movies. No more shots followed. By this time Hank was under the bed again with his friend. They stayed there for about three hours afraid to move. He did not know what else to do so he reached for the telephone cord and pulled the phone down to him under the bed. He woke me up and told me that he was calling from under a bed, and if I wanted to keep the world's greatest fish breeder alive it would be a good idea for me to rescue him. As I also wanted to keep myself alive I politely declined, put the phone back in its cradle, and tried to get back to sleep. Now I was awake and decided I really should try to rescue him as he truly was a fantastic fish breeder. I had no idea where he was and waited for another phone call. This never came. He was at work the next day. He didn't talk to me for more than a week.

Hank wanted a dog. Loise had a Weimaraner named Amber. I am smiling as I write this recalling the time Loise hired a new baby sitter who arrived and was introduced to Amber. She was a prim, slight, elderly lady. She had never seen a Weimaraner before and the crazy colored eyes that all Weimaraners have completely unglued her. Five hours later when we returned home Amber was sitting in the little lady's lap. The sitter had been too terrified to move (for five hours). Amber spent most of her time in the house and needed space to run. It made sense to give Amber to Hank who wanted a dog. She could live at the farm, and run as much as she wanted. About a year later Hank bred Amber to a supposedly American Kennel Club registered Weimaraner. That union produced the strangest dog ever born. Max was a Great Dane in a Weimaraner costume. He was gigantic, he was sweet, and he loved to eat cats. An old man lived down the road from the farm who had cats. He really had cats. He paid no real attention to them. They overran my farm. I know there were more than 25 cats headquartered at his shack. He never fed his cats. They cleaned out all the wild baby rabbits, and just about all the quail at Gulf Fish Hatchery. When Amber presented baby Max to Hank the balance turned toward us. The baby rabbits and the baby birds had a champion and a fighting chance for survival. As soon as Max was weaned he started eating kittens as hors d'oeuvres. As he grew and grew, he graduated to cats. He had emergency surgery about a year later. He apparently was dying.

X-rays showed a great amount of undigested bones and skulls blocking his digestive system. Hank Richter, our veterinarian, later estimated that he removed parts from at least a dozen cats.

Most days I got to the farm about 4 AM and supervised the packing out of that day's orders. These orders would make the early flights from Tampa. Everyone took a break after pack-out. I then walked the farm with a shot gun and Max making notes for work schedules. At first light one morning Max spooked a huge male Florida bobcat. This animal was as big as they get. Max and the cat entered into a battle to the death. I am sure that Max thought this gigantic cat had been sent by all the cats in the world to get even. After it was over I realized I had the gun in my hands. I never thought to use it. They ranged in and out of fish ponds. Max tried to keep the big bobcat in the water where he had an advantage. The cat wanted dry land to use his claws for cutting rather than for swimming. After about twenty minutes the bobcat wanted to be gone. The fight lasted another ten minutes until Max finally drowned the big bobcat. I got a badly wounded and bleeding Max back to Hank Richter, the veterinarian, to patch him up. Max had serious wounds, but was back hunting and eating cats the next day.

In 1963 I sold my Gulf Fish Hatchery business (another story). Hank Hansen at the same time fell in love with a lovely lady named Annie who he married. She finally got him housebroken. After Hank spent some time with the new owner of Gulf Fish Hatchery he decided he could never work for him. He gave a fair notice, and bought a piece of property about three miles away. He put up his own small hatchery. He raised great fish for many years. He satisfied many local fish farmers who passed on his fine fish to satisfied customers all over the globe. His little farm and property increased in value so that when he died he left an adequate estate for Annie. He sold his farm to a bright Canadian named Barry Milks. Barry got a priceless bonus. He and his wife, Barbara, lived next door to Hank and Annie. Hank was on hand to teach Barry, who was a quick study, a lot of things that do not appear in books. I spent many hours with Hank in the hospital when he was dying (cancer). We were a really strange mix, but bottom line was that we were friends. I have fond memories of Hank Hansen. He was certainly the most imaginative and colorful of all the fish breeders that worked for me over the years. He was a unique character, a great talent, and a legend now.

Gulf Fish Hatchery was on the move. At the end of the second year (1957) we had managed to make a good profit. At the end of the third year I paid off the bank and the trust fund. I was working fifteen hours a day, as happy as could be. I loved what I was doing. At times my brains would turn to oatmeal from pure fatigue. It was too much for me to continue to do it alone. I had no one there with any sort of executive ability. My very best friend, Jack Pearlman, was in Palatka, Florida, then as chief engineer for the Hudson Pulp and Paper Company. Jack knew what I was doing as he had visited me a couple of times. He was delighted to give up his job and come to work with me. Our understanding was that we would do everything as partners. I would still be the sole owner, but we would share all. We drew the same wages and we took the same "perks". We shared the work, and there was plenty of it. Jack was a genius. No one who I have ever met could solve work problems like Jack. Time and Motion studies were his field. He held many original patents. In very short order Gulf was innovating in ways I could never have imagined or predicted. He worked for months and built a huge "still". His still could take our terrible hard and alkaline water and make from it water that was dead soft and neutral (pH 7.0). Among other things he solved was the problem of keeping sensitive fish alive outside during the winter cold in an affordable manner. In the next years (1958-1960) Jack Pearlman designed, and we then built, five or six different types of plastic coverings for dirt pools. The first was a free balloon of plastic kept up with small air blowers (a hair dryer will work) and this certainly is the cheapest way, but a strong wind makes it into a gigantic sail. It worked best when partially supported by a wooden framework. This increased the cost considerably. Flat covering proved the least expensive, and also worked. We used both telephone poles, and rough hewed twelve by twelve lumber. These (four or five) logs were spaced horizontally. The plastic sheet was affixed with screen lath. Getting into the pond which had little clearance was a major pain. Jack ended up building up one end and leaving the rest flat. This was the most practical for us. You could get in to trap fish and even drag a seine if needed. This innovation, of Jack Pearlman's, has over the years made a major difference in the Florida fish farmers' ability to safely store inventory and breeding stock in even the most severe winter freezes. On average a covered pond will give you ten degrees more temperature than an uncovered pond.

Shipping problems lessened with the use of Jiffy insulation. Jack designed a double box inside a master which improved heat retention still further. Changing bag sizes (and lowering costs) gave more air surface. Jack helped build and design the first Styrofoam box plant and Gulf made the first custom boxes to ship tropical fishes. Some years later Roy Hardy bought that business from Gulf and he made most of the industry's boxes for a long time. Today, almost forty years later the basic design remains unchanged.

Gulf Fish Hatchery badly needed more room to hold fish. The import end of the business was booming. We had to expand. Gulf was deeply committed to imported wild fish. I applied for and eventually got (a nightmare of paper work) a three percent Small Business Administration loan for $75,000. Manatee County where Gulf was located, had high unemployment. This cheap money was available to any small business that could employ people. What Jack Pearlman did with the $75,000 was incredible. He used many clever designs to save money and give us maximum space for concrete vats and glass aquariums. The slab for the main building was 60 feet wide and 125 feet long. The building was designed to take the largest wooden trusses available. The entire slab was covered with concrete vats. Each vat had a removable stand pipe to drain dry. The building and the vats were pitched so that all the water on the floor and in the vats moved unimpeded out of the building. Water was carried off with a gutter designed to keep the floors dry. Where vats were built back to back the common 27 inch high wall held a three-tier stand that would take two of the special low forty gallon hatchery tanks back to back. These were designed by Joe Cooley, who was then building almost one hundred percent of the aquariums used by the fish farming industry in Florida. Tens of thousands of "Cooley tanks" have been built in the last forty years. The only design change he ever made was when he dropped the galvanized metal frame and went to an all glass construction. The size remained the same (36 inches long, 18 inches wide and 14 inches high). The maximum water surface available made it easier and safer to crowd fish.

I remember one spring during the silly season when Joe was delivering Gulf a load of his tanks. He approached me and asked what I was doing. Actually, what I was doing was flipping dry goat feces in the air to pass time while he walked up. I said I was eating some newly acquired Arabian candy. I gave him a few which he promptly ate. He told me it was awful and tasted like dung. I said that was a very good guess. Amazing thing is that we remained good friends.

I dug a few more ponds. I did not have the funds to do more before the Small Business Administration loan became a reality and I had some cash. Billy Gibbs was the man who had dug the few ponds we could afford the year before. I spoke to him first now that we could afford to dig more ponds. Billy ended up selling me his old Insley dragline for $6,000, and then coming to work for me on a piece basis. He worked from dawn to dusk digging one hundred foot ponds at his suggested and our agreed upon price of $19.00 for each pond. He had also agreed to do all the maintenance work on the dragline. He dug three hundred more ponds for us. This filled up all 52 available acres of the Gulf Fish Hatchery. I got a great bonus as Manatee County needed shell and marl for road construction. The northeast corner of the farm had almost three acres of it. Billy dug seven big, deep shell pits and we loaded the empty county trucks for months and months. When the material in the shell pits (we had seven of them) was depleted we had huge deep empty ponds. I had owned the dragline for a year. The project was finished and I had it for sale. It was not beautiful, and most major parts needed replacing. We were happy to get $1500 for it and retire from the dragline business. The empty shell pits, by the next year, became great lunch hour recreational spots for Jack and me. We had stocked them with thousands of baby mullet we had snared while seining for wild sailfin mollies in brackish water. Mullet are perfectly happy in freshwater. Homer Turner had told us that mullet change their eating regimen completely when living in freshwater. In their normal marine environment they are totally herbivorous. In freshwater they become omnivorous. Our mullet would attack live bait. We fished for mullet with light tackle and fairy shrimp. They eventually grew much larger than five pounds and provided great sport and good eating.

The Amazon river port of Leticia in Colombia was where almost all of the wonderful Amazonian fish originated. Iquitos, Peru did not start shipping similar fish until the early 1960s. A trip to Leticia in 1956 revealed that everything about the location was perfect for the storage and shipment of fish, but with just enough tough problems to discourage most people. Mike Tsalikes and Trudy Jerkins owned a business called Tarpon Zoo in Tarpon Springs, Florida. Mike ran their Colombian operation. He was basically an animal dealer and he lived permanently in Leticia. He also dealt in tropical fish. Mike had been helped by Fred Cochu from Paramount, who first took him to Leticia (the only other presence there). Cochu had for years shipped quantities of fish without competition. Mike agreed he would go into the animal business in Leticia while Fred would continue with fish. Fred Cochu had an exclusive arrangement with a reclusive man who he had set up years earlier. This compound was remote from Leticia (about forty miles up river near Loretto). I never met the man. No one knew anything about him. He was called Senor Wandurraga in Leticia. Sounded like a corruption of Von Derager. I was convinced that he must be an ex-Nazi hiding out. I later learned I had been totally wrong, and that he was a native Columbian. By the time I arrived in Leticia, Cochu and Tsalikes were enemies. Mike had broken his promise and gone into the fish business competing with Cochu. Fred never forgave him.

I met a Captain Emilio Saiz on my first trip to Leticia. Emilio was a career officer in the Colombian army. He was second in command at this jungle outpost, and he was retiring in the next weeks. We hit it off immediately. Our partnership and friendship was cemented in days, and lasted for many years until his death. He liked Leticia and I was at that time looking for a business there. Our timing was perfect. We never had a serious problem. Emilio Saiz was well educated and bright. He made arrangements with the Colombian government to "homestead" an island called Ronda about four miles up river from Leticia. It was two square miles in area. Our compound was built on Ronda Island. We moved in several families to live at the compound. They maintained the property. Saiz was there every day. He and his wife, Claudia, lived in Leticia. He had seven children. Maria Claudia, the oldest girl, is our goddaughter, and we remain close today. Saiz also had a home, wife, and two children in Bogotá. This always made Loise and I nervous as we were afraid we might inadvertently reveal secrets. We did learn years later that this was not an uncommon practice in Colombia where divorce is something that just does not happen. Both families knew about each other. Claudia and Emilio eventually could and did get married after he obtained a divorce in Panama. The compound took shape quickly. Construction was made from trees and plants that were growing on Ronda Island. Fish were kept in half drums. A half drum is a fifty five gallon steel gasoline drum that has been bisected lengthwise. These halves were then coated with a non toxic black paint and these half drums kept fish well. The gentle slopes make them easy to siphon and keep clean. Partial water changes were frequently made. There was no electricity so we had no electric lights, pumps, filters, telephones, or refrigeration. Gasoline motors and generators supplied power when needed.

Leticia was then, and still is, a center for an illicit smuggling business from Brazil. Mike Tsalikes was always rumored to be involved in it. I had no opinion then. I do now. Subsequent events proved it. There was no scheduled air service to Leticia. The air field (dirt) was an adequate landing strip without a tower. Mike was the airport manager. He moved his freight out with chartered planes that flew from St. Petersburg, Florida to Leticia. The round trip (usually a DC3) at first cost $2,200. We elected to use the same service. Cochu used his own plane. He made stops in British Guiana and Brazil, and picked up more fish each trip.

Our great day finally arrived and we were ready to make our first shipment from the Ronda Island compound. A date was set, the plane was chartered, and I took off from Florida to work the first load with Saiz. I planned to be in Leticia for a week or more before the plane arrived. I would return with the fish shipment.

There was a small plane from Bogotá twice a week (usually). I got to Bogotá late at night and checked into the Taquendama Hotel. I planned to leave early for Leticia. I was ready by six and called for a taxi. While waiting out front I heard fireworks(?). I saw no display. The noise got louder and closer. I realized then that the noise had to be rifle fire. Almost at once a bunch of people ran down the road in front of the hotel closely followed by tiny soldiers wildly shouting and shooting huge guns. The rifle fire was now joined by machine gun fire. My firework theory evaporated. I ran inside the hotel for safety and to try to learn what was happening. The clerk had no idea. Another guest Ralph Simpson was also going to the airport.

The road outside cleared. When the taxi arrived we jumped in and headed for Vanguardia airport. We learned from the driver that there was a revolution in progress. Heading out of town seemed a smart move. I learned then that Ralph was an animal dealer. He was heading for a place called Villavicencio, Colombia. Villavicencio is the jump off place for the Columbian Llanos (plains country) and located at the foothills of the eastern slope of the Andes. Villavicencio was also the last airport before you flew out over the jungle to Leticia some six hundred miles away. That was where the airplanes filled their gas tanks. If you fly to Leticia and miss it you must return. There was no other place to set down. Twelve hundred miles is a long way. You always fly considerably west of Leticia and find the Amazon River. Then you take a left and fly down river until you see Leticia. Sam Poole, our pilot, had only one bad experience. Visibility was obscured by a terrible rain and the river was not to be seen. He made it back to Villavicencio on gas fumes. You do not want to run out of gas. There was no place to set down and this included anything remotely like an emergency empty flat field. There are now.

Things now were heating up more in Bogotá. We heard much small arms fire close by, and booming artillery fire in the distance. At the airport we learned that the city was surrounded by the rebel army troops. The airport had been closed. The rebels (which included the Colombian Air Force) now had aircraft flying above the airport. Everyone expected bombs to start falling. They didn't. Everything just stopped for the next twenty four hours. The airport was full of people. Nothing moved. I called the U.S. Embassy. They knew less than we did and didn't seem concerned about Ralph and me. It seemed the safest place so we just waited it out in the airport, calling the embassy from time to time to try to interest them in rescuing us with no luck. The next day the rebel junta took over the country, and things started moving again. We got on the first plane that left Bogotá. It took us to Villavicencio. No one there knew when a plane would go to Leticia so I checked into the Hotel Meta. Things at the moment were quiet in Villavicencio. Six months earlier the radical bandits who then and still today terrorize the llanos area took over the town. They captured all of the policemen (six) and executed them in the town square. This was the time when Castro was actively exporting violence. Remember "Che"? The Meta was the best hotel in Villavicencio. It also was the only real hotel. I stayed there many, many times in future years. At the Hotel Meta I was introduced to Colombian "Bifstek". I stayed for two days before I could go on to Leticia. I ate "Bifstek" every meal. It was a huge thin slab of fresh beef. So large it always was folded double to fit on a large dinner plate. It is served with a dried fried egg on top. Fried plantain, fried potatoes, refried beans, and terrible Colombian beer made up each meal. The water was suspect. The "Gasiosa" (soda pop) tasted like its name only worse. I always drank beer as bad beer is better than no beer. I liked the town a lot. I even got to collect some new looking fish which I preserved. Later I turned the collection over to Dr. Jacques Géry who found three new species amongst them.

Saiz knew I was coming as I could and did send radio messages. I realized later that Mike Tsalikes also knew I was coming, as he got the messages first.

The next week was probably the most traumatic in my life. Emilio had everything set on the Island when I arrived to pack the fish for the plane. We had almost eight hundred boxes. More than half would be neon tetras. He had a working network of Indians catching fish for us. The price paid for each neon was one third of a penny. Most of the other fish were costing us one penny each. A few were as high as three cents each and there were not many of them. Items such as leaf fish, small arowana, puffers, red hook *Metynnis*, small Pacu, and the freshwater barracuda (*Acestrorhynchus microlepis*), *Abramites*, and *Leporinus fasciatus* were on the list of premium fish. There was no shortage of labor. Saiz had all the boats available to get the packed fish back to the airport to load the plane. The collectors were the labor force and all of them were there. They now were our fish packers. When we knew the plane was leaving Villavicencio we would start packing. Mike got that message to us. One unanticipated fact that later slowed us down, was that both Emilio and I forgot that we were the only people that could count.

Just as we were about to return to Ronda Island to get started I got arrested. I was arrested by the Leticia commandant (Mike Tsalikes's friend and, as I learned later, business partner). I was arrested for working in Colombia with only a tourist visa. As there was no jail I was allowed to go free. I was told I would not be allowed out of the country until my case was settled. It was funny. I laughed (big mistake). I could not believe it. Saiz believed it as this man had been his commander and bad news. He convinced me I was in big trouble.

Back on the island we got the packing operation started. I was doing eight hundred neons to the bag. We quickly realized it was not possible to count anything and keep the line moving. There was a severe shortage of counters (none). Emilio and I decided we had to estimate the neons. As the night wore on everything got estimated. I did all of that. I put the fish in the bags and I put in as many as I thought looked safe. The bugs were incredible. I welted up fast from mosquitoes and whatevers. I kept busy trying to see and speak with my mouth, nose, and eyes full of bugs. Warm beer did help, but not much. We all went back to Leticia with the last load of packed fish.

Our plane was there with some 25 armed soldiers (all about five feet tall and with much bigger guns) surrounding it. The colonel was not there. Saiz learned quickly that the plane could go. The troops were only there to shoot me if I tried to get on the plane. We got the loading started and then went to find the colonel. I had a stupid idea he would be bought off with some small "Mordida" (bribe). I tracked him down in a dirt floored hut that was occupied by the Peruvian consul. I charged into the hut and tried to be polite. The colonel was ready for me. He was almost hysterical. Inadvertently I had broken a sacred law by trying to talk Columbian business on Peruvian soil. That was when I learned the hut was officially Peruvian, and not Colombian. He took my passport. He was busy with international business and would see me the next morning. He also told me that he was then arranging with the Peruvian consul to deport me to Peru. I laughed again another big mistake as Peruvian territory was virgin jungle across the river. Nothing for hundreds of miles in every direction. I finally realized this was no joke and I had big trouble. I sent a message to Briggs at Gulf, and watched the plane leave without me. I knew (and so did Mike Tsalikes) that I was a critical part of the receiving crew. I knew how to handle the fish, medicate the fish, and where to put the fish. I was instead standing in a muddy field in Leticia scratching insect bites watching my first planeload of fish leave without me. The shipment arrived on time in Sarasota, Florida. My worst fears came true. The results were disastrous.

Mike Tsalikes had done a real number on me. I learned several good lessons. I again went looking for the colonel who was not available. I was told he would find us later. Iquitos, Peru, was three hundred miles upstream, and the closest point where I could get a plane to home. Our boat could make it. It would be a long, tough trip. We set it up as an emergency plan. Emilio and I then collapsed. We were completely exhausted. Our adrenalin had been all used up. The damage had been done. There was no hurry now for anything, but sleep. Nothing happened for the next two days other than repeatedly being told that my case would be decided soon. On the third day the colonel found me and told me he had decided to drop the charges and deport me. I did not laugh this time. He then informed me that a cargo plane was then coming into Leticia bound for Bogotá. I could get on it and go. I didn't have time to collect all my gear or clothes. I had on a pair of dirty cutoffs and a smelly skivvy shirt when Emilio Saiz boosted me up and into the cargo area. It was a full load of gumbo (big balls of raw rubber). The colonel was there to see me off. He treated me like his best friend. I clutched my passport which the colonel had confiscated, and now had returned. I kept my mouth shut and we were off. The pilot and the copilot were up front with oxygen tubes to get them over the Andes (twenty plus thousand feet high) and into Bogotá. I thought I would die before we landed. It was a toss up to see if the cold or the lack of oxygen would get me first. I got on the first outbound plane to Miami. It was a gaudily painted Braniff airplane and it was a lot prettier looking than I was. The plane was full and I remember feeling guilty sitting next to an immaculately dressed tourist. Then I fainted from a mixture of relief and fatigue. The rest of the trip was uneventful (thank god).

I went straight to the farm and stayed until I had done as much as I could to save the surviving fishes. We took a terrible beating. Subsequent charters always made profits for us. Jim Briggs came up with what seemed to be a good plan after we had done another charter. The charter price had been raised to over $3,000. Briggs had met a pilot at the airport who worked flying a company plane for one of Florida's big construction companies. He had some ideas and we met to talk it over. That was how I first met Sam Poole. Sam and I were about the same age. We had both been in World War Two and there the similarity ended. He was a bona-fide hero. At 19 he was a full Colonel in the 8th Air Force. At 19 I'd made Private First Class, and then got busted back to Private. His flying exploits in Europe were legend. He was a huge, blond six and one half foot giant "Cracker." If he had been any more Southern he wouldn't have been able to talk at all. He did not enjoy his job (too tame). He told us he knew where he could buy a war surplus Lockheed Ventura for six thousand dollars. This was a Navy aerial torpedo bomber they called the PV-2. The bomb bay could be welded shut and the machine gun turrets removed and then sealed. It had sufficient range to fly from Sarasota to Barranquilla and then to Villavicencio and then on to Leticia. He could take five or six hundred boxes each time. It would cost $6,000 and had hardly been flown. I bought it. Sam had his own deal in Barranquilla where he could profitably resell a full load of baby chicks bought in Florida. That was his deal and he could do it with no pain to us. He would then fly empty to Leticia, and bring back our fish. It sounded great and it seemed fool proof. It would save us money and make us independent. I had no idea what I was doing, but the price was right. We named it the "Flying Guppy". We spent another $5,000 to make it practical to fly. It was cheaper to own and run than to charter, but not by much. We made fifteen or twenty trips. During this time I learned that while Sam Poole was a bargain, I had to hire a copilot. I also had a bad shock when I got my Esso bill. We had filled up every trip in Colombia. Esso has misled us and charged us a terrible price as compared to what we had been told to expect to pay. Almost double what the same Esso aviation gasoline cost us in Miami. We had made five trips before I got the first bill. We did cut that cost a lot by taking fifty five gallon drums of aviation gas with us to Leticia. Saiz could always use more half drums to store our fish.

About that time Avianca put in the first scheduled flight to Leticia. Our need for a private company-owned plane disappeared. I wanted regular shipments every week of smaller quantities. The fish were better. The freight costs were not a lot higher. I think the final straw was when we needed to replace the little wheel under the tail. It cost $700 and that made up my mind. We laid up the plane and tried the Avianca routes. It made sense. Sam Poole flew the plane to a fellow named Hans Hoffman in Miami who was associated with an airplane resale business. Hans also ran a few planes to Colombia selling cheap fares under the name of Condor Airlines. The Flying Guppy sat and sat. I finally reduced the price down to our depreciated cost ($9,000). It still sat for almost a year. I got a call from Hans late on a Thursday afternoon. He had a cash buyer for the plane who would pay just $6,000. I had to have the papers at a certain bank in Miami before noon the next day. I agreed. He would meet the man I sent, and then exchange payment, in cash, for the signed and notarized documents. It was done without a hitch. A very few days later our "Flying Guppy" became the first plane shot down over the Bay of Pigs in Cuba.

This all happened shortly after Jim Briggs permanently left Gulf Fish Farm. Sam Poole had managed to buy his own plane as he wanted to continue his baby chick business, and he could not afford to fly back empty. Briggs and Sam decided to try to get some fish in Colombia for the return trip. They made a deal with one of the big Chicago wholesalers to take the fish to Chicago. What fish they managed to get were bad and after two tries that plan aborted. Sam Poole also had enough of Briggs and they parted company. They actually came close to making some real money as they managed to find a spot to land in Colombia about one hundred miles north of Leticia where a "new" angelfish was located, and even more important, discus could be easily obtained. This was not a secret and was something Saiz had told us about. Saiz eventually got there and added these fish to his inventory, but they were the first. The angelfish turned out to be what is still called the "Altum" angelfish. The Colombian Altum angelfish actually is a totally different fish from the one we got from British Guiana. This is also called the Altum angelfish. I know there are four types of Angelfish and have been waiting for the last thirty years for the taxonomists to straighten them out (Colombian Altum, original Guyana Altum, Scalare and Dumerell's Angelfish). They brought out the first of the New Altum type angelfish, and some discus. All of the first Altum angels were sold to Hans Schmidt of Tropiquarium in Frankfurt. He gave the surviving fish (less than ten) to his brother Dr. Edward Schmidt-Focke. Edward sent me a picture of these first new Altum angelfish, and I still have it. It may have been an ichthyologist's dream, but was a financial disaster for them.

I still hear from Sam Poole, from time to time, although it has been some years now since our last contact. He was still flying cargo and I hope has managed to make some money. He is a neat guy who I remember fondly.

Jim Briggs had the company's note for $10,000 due two years after the buy out in addition to cash. I saw him again in less than a year when he called to ask me to buy back the note at a discount. He was broke again. He suggested a fifty percent discount; a great deal for us. I had to give him the $5,000 within twenty four hours. I found the money somewhere and I paid off the note. I never saw Briggs again. He went downhill from that point. He died very young a few years later.

When I arrived in Florida in 1956 the largest tropical fish producer in the world was the H. Woolf and Son operation in Gibsonton, Florida. Their business was huge. It was then operated almost completely by Jim

Woolf. I never met Herb Woolf, Jim's father, who had suffered serious health problems in 1952, and died in 1960.

From the first time I met Jim Woolf I have admired him. Over the years the more I saw of him the more certain I was that my first impression was correct. He was respected by his employees, customers, and most impressive by all of his competitors. I have never heard one bad or mean word said about Jim Woolf. He is a quiet, gentle, and extremely creative person who got things done.

The Woolf story is important history. It is a good example of an American dream becoming a reality against apparently insurmountable odds. No matter how hard the Woolf family got beaten down they always managed to get back up. If anyone imagines that the Woolf family's creation of the world's largest producing tropical fish farm was something that happened without enormous hardship they could not be more wrong. At the start if it were not for bad luck the Clan Woolf would have had no luck at all.

Herbert Woolf and Al Wilinski were partners in a pretzel manufacturing business in New Jersey. The business had started in 1928 with the purchase of a small plant in Elizabeth, New Jersey. In 1930 the business relocated to Belmont Avenue in Newark, New Jersey, and operated there as the Preferred Bakery Company. It was the most modern plant of its kind in the area. They made and sold pretzels. They also supplied their customers (mostly taverns and bars) with pickles, olives, and similar items. The business did fine. It generated good profits until the effects of the Depression reduced both the volume and the profit.

No one had any money. All of their customers were in trouble. Most customers could not buy what they needed and they could not pay their previous bills. By 1932 Herb Woolf was looking hard for something to augment the fast eroding sales and profits. The depression deepened. Their business, and everyone else's, was rapidly going downhill.

Jim Woolf was twelve in 1930 when he was caught up in the tropical fish hobby. He was the original hobbyist in the family. In the next years he filled the sun parlor in their home in Union, New Jersey, with more and more aquariums, fish, and plants.

Herb Woolf then got interested in Jim's hobby. In short order he was seriously considering the tropical fish hobby as an alternative source of income. The pretzel business was no longer making profits. One of

Jim Woolf's best fish suppliers was a local Polish woman named Mrs. Veszpremy who bred and sold fish from her home. Herb Woolf got to know her. She was operating from her home and wanted to open a real store. Woolf invested the money she needed and became her partner. Mrs. Veszpremy and Herb Woolf opened a small retail tropical fish and aquatic plant store on Elizabeth Avenue in Newark. They had some eighty aquariums. After three months of expensive lessons in what not to do that first business was dissolved. Herb Woolf did not abandon his idea to become a part of the tropical fish industry. In 1932 he made a major step. This time a large and almost immediately profitable retail tropical fish business was created. This business was located on one side of the pretzel factory. An area 125 feet long and 25 feet wide was converted into a large retail store. The shop was called Belmont Aquarium (the pretzel factory was located on Belmont Avenue in Newark). Belmont Aquarium had over two hundred display aquariums. They stocked, besides the living material, a complete variety of aquarium equipment. Aquariums for resale were purchased from a manufacturer named Winner in Philadelphia. He charged Woolf and Wilinski $1.25 each for a ten gallon tank. They retailed them for $1.95. The normal selling price was $5.00. Business started slow. It grew better every week as word spread that Belmont Aquarium had ten gallon aquariums for $1.95. Jim told me that his father, until he passed away, always tried to figure out why, during the depression, people had money to spend on fish, but not on pretzels.

One good supplier was Albert Greenberg who sent them aquatic plants, wild collected native fish, and a variety of fish that he raised in his Everglades Aquatic Nurseries located in Tampa, Florida. Aquarium Hamburg in Germany supplied a wide variety of wild caught fish they had from Asia, and even at times from Africa, plus a large variety of German tank-raised egg layers. These they were raising in their hatchery in Hamburg. Germany was the center of the tropical fish business. Woolf got the best livebearing fish from Bill Schomburg in Slidell, Louisiana, who operated the largest tropical fish farm in the world (then). The most important item that Woolf bought from Schomburg's (Crescent Fish Farm) was his medium-sized black sailfin mollies. These cost $100 for one hundred fish. They came in pairs and Belmont Aquarium sold them for $5.95 per pair. A pair of the breeding-sized black sailfin mollies sold for $25.

In 1934 Herb Woolf, Jim Woolf, and Al Wilinski took a trip to visit Albert Greenberg in Tampa. Greenberg had expanded his Everglades Aquatic Nurseries operation the year before. This expansion was to a new small farm with dirt ponds that was located on The Tamiami Trail (Route 41) south of Tampa near Adamsville (now Gibsonton). Greenberg indicated he wanted to sell this farm. The idea intrigued Woolf and Wilinski. Greenberg had put Al Wechsler, the man he had brought down from Chicago, in charge. This operation was called Suwannee Water Gardens. The branch operation was not working out. Herb Woolf fell in love with Florida. Greenberg wanted to get rid of Wechsler. Woolf and Wilinski agreed that Wilinski could run the Belmont Aquarium and the pretzel business alone. Woolf planned to move to Florida and develop the farm operation. They would make Greenberg an offer, and try to buy the small farm. The plan was to have the Belmont Aquarium use their Florida produced product, and then as soon as they could, they would add a wholesale tropical fish business in Newark. The deal was done. They owned Suwannee Water Gardens (and Al Wechsler). In 1934 Herb and Hilda Woolf with the then sixteen-year-old Jim Woolf were in business in Adamsville, Florida. Three weeks after they arrived (November of 1934) the pretzel factory and the Belmont Aquarium burned to the ground in a terrible fire. The Newark fish business and the pretzel factory were history. Nothing was saved. Everything was gone. There was no insurance. The partnership was over and the very few assets were divided. The Woolf family was in big trouble. No money, no customer, and little knowledge. The farm had dirt ponds, a few cement vats, a packing shed, and a lot of headaches. They had inherited Al Wechsler, and they had problems with him (as had Greenberg) from the start. They parted company and Wechsler (with financial help from Woolf) relocated in New York City at Two State Street. This was a small shop on the second floor. He specialized in Aquatic Plants. He stayed in New York for three or four years and then returned to Chicago, where he remained in business for many years. Woolf hoped Wechsler would be successful in his own business in New York. They had sent him fish and plants with an open line of credit. The regular price for aquatic plants was two dollars for two hundred plants and you could pick the assortment. Wechsler seemed to manage well, but did not pay Woolf for the material they supplied. Eventually he did make a settlement. This loss added to already abundant miseries.

Early in 1936 they were scraping the bottom of the barrel and future prospects were all bleak. Fred Cochu of Paramount Aquarium in New York City who had been a supplier to Belmont Aquarium was now one of their customers and came up with a great offer. He was an agent for Aquarium Hamburg. He offered Herb Woolf, on their behalf, a job in Los Angeles. Aquarium Hamburg wanted to open a branch. They planned to send their fish shipments via the Panama Canal. This was a long trip that they had tested and felt could be made safely. Herb took the job as branch manager for Cochu and Aquarium Hamburg. Jim was almost eighteen years old (1936) and would be left alone to run the fish farm. If Jim could hang on, fine, but if he couldn't he would then come to Los Angeles (after he finished his senior year in high school) and join his mother and father at the new Aquarium Hamburg branch there. Herb and Hilda Woolf were driven out to California by Fred Cochu in Fred's first new car (a Desoto). Together they planned the holding facility. Herb Woolf was left on his own in Los Angeles to get it done. Everything was ready and Aquarium Hamburg sent off a huge shipment. It came right on schedule via the Panama Canal to Los Angeles. The trade in California was waiting. This depot would be a big help. Fish sent by rail from the east coast to Los Angeles were costly and seldom arrived good enough to be profitable. The frustration of being able to sell and the inability to get sufficient product at reasonable prices in a timely manner should be solved. Good, different, and healthy fish were practically on hand. At this point the lights went out. Disaster struck (again). The powerful Longshoreman's Union called a strike. It happened just as the boat arrived at the dock. Nothing moved. Herb Woolf spent every minute of every day trying desperately to get the Union to allow the fish to be unloaded. After several weeks had passed the shipment was in terrible shape. It was too late when Herb Woolf finally got a release for the live cargo. Unfortunately, the live cargo by then was mostly dead cargo and the smell had a lot to do with their getting the cargo released. Most of the few surviving fish were ready to join their brothers. It was a disaster of monumental proportions. It was an enormous loss for everyone and proportionately largest for Herb Woolf. Aquarium Hamburg and Fred Cochu quit. They abandoned the wonderful new fish depository that never really opened. Herb and Hilda returned to Florida with Fred again driving the new Desoto. A very important event on the return trip helped Woolf raise fish more efficiently. This was a stop at the Crescent Fish Farm in Slidell, Louisiana. William Schomburg had been raising lots of fish there since the early 1920s, and had a big operation. He had been a supplier to Belmont Aquarium in Newark, New Jersey. Woolf for the first time saw a really efficient, successful tropical fish farming enterprise. He learned many things from Schomburg that he later applied on his Florida farm.

In his father's absence Jim managed to keep the farm afloat. Herb now was completely discouraged. He was seriously considering a move back to New Jersey. Jim convinced his father to stay, and as prospects in New Jersey were just as bad, Herb agreed to give it a try. The depression continued to devastate the country. Now Herb asked Jim if he was prepared to commit himself to the tropical fish business, and not later decide to do something else. Jim agreed. The Woolfs, father and son, became 50/50 partners in the business. They had operated under the Suwannee Water Gardens name until then. The name of the business was changed to H. Woolf and Son.

Fred Cochu and his Paramount Aquarium in New York remained their major customer. In 1935 there was a hurricane which had set them back again. They lost much of their crop due to terrible flooding rains (called toad stranglers in Florida). They had tightened their belts and kept at it. Things couldn't get worse. Surprisingly they did just that when they had a devastating freeze that winter. They salvaged what they could and tightened their belts once again. If they were being tested they passed. By 1937-1938 they were producing and shipping enough fish to keep afloat. They were slowly getting out of debt and had enough money to make a down payment on a new Pontiac automobile. Neighbors who had watched the crazy Yankees play around with small fish (that you could not even eat) took a second look. Ponds were still being dug by hand. Herb and Jim dug their share of ponds in the early years. Most were dug, day after day, by one employee, a gigantic black man named Jim. He had approached Woolf and proposed to dig a pond for $7.00. He was hired and given a chance. He was an awesome pool digging man. He dug pools for Woolf by hand for years. The pools were about fifty feet long by fifteen feet wide. The average casual laborer received $1.25 dollars a day. This was a lot of money. Most field workers were paid $1.00 per day. It took two men three and often four days to dig a pond. This cost $7.50 to $10.00. Jim, alone, dug a pond in two and one half days. All of the ponds were connected to a deep free flowing well using either a concrete trough or galvanized piping. The amount of water was regulated by a valve at the well head and the artesian pressure was controlled in that way. Every pool received water (a gallon or two per minute). This kept the fish warm in the winter. The water from a deep well comes up at least seventy degrees. If you have a really deep well it goes up to eighty degrees and above. In the summer when the heat is really oppressive the well water keeps the pond water cool. Without the running well water the fish would freeze faster in the winter, and cook faster in the summer. A screened overflow pipe at the opposite end kept the water level constant and prevented the intrusion of wild fish.

Herb and Jim Woolf were able to hire their first real employee in 1937. Woolf had managed with casual labor until then. This was a powerful man named Charles J. Powell (who everyone called C.J.). C.J. was then, among other things, a prize fighter (who no one wanted to fight). He had trouble finding opponents. He took over the outdoor pond production. He stayed with the Woolf operation until the end. He did his job and they produced good fish. He was respected and admired by all of us who knew him. I know for sure that no one ever talked back to him. We were good friends in the early 1960s when he had started his own farm. At least once a week he would bring me fish. Jack Pearlman, Hank Hansen, C.J. and I would play poker in Hansen's trailer for an hour. Part of the deal was for Hansen to cook and serve lunch. We all enjoyed it, and this included Hank Hansen, who was the world's worst poker player. He lost consistently. We all felt bad about that, but still took his money. The Woolf operation always (almost exclusively) raised livebearing fish in the 1930s. The few egg layers they raised reproduced themselves in the ponds (paradise fish, zebra danio, rosy barbs, and cichlids such as Jack Dempsey, Meeki, and Egyptian mouth brooders). It was after World War Two before Woolf started raising egg layers inside in quantity. Woolf next added imported wild fish for resale. Now they could supply almost all of their customers' fish needs. They never made money with imports as keeping them in Florida's hard and alkaline water presented lots of problems. The solutions were more sophisticated then anyone understood in those years.

Herb and Jim Woolf were on a clear track by late 1937. Their plans were finally coming true. The original farm was completely filled with ponds. They could not expand there. It was much too small. They had a pressing need for more fish. Woolf had to expand production. Jim found a twenty acre parcel in Adamsville (named after Oren and Don Adams' grandfather) with a wonderful free flowing well and more land adjacent to it that could and did handle future expansion. In 1938 they bought this acreage. This became their main farm. Later that same year they bought the adjacent twenty acres. There was enough room now for Jim to build a little hanger and a small landing strip. His interest and skill flying small airplanes developed at this time. The first plane that Jim owned cost $395. He flew it for several years. By 1940 he could afford to trade it. He bought himself a second plane for $900. Jim had his father's support. This tiny aeronautical beginning became, in later years, the major reason for the enormous success of the Woolf operation. Over the years they continued adding acreage and ponds at this new location. At the peak of their production they had 165 acres under cultivation. The land they owned contained almost 1500 dirt ponds. The original (Greenberg's) farm was resold in 1939 to Hans and Carl Jensen from Chicago. Jensen was the manufacturer of the Jewel Aquariums. When that business lost its profitability (the Depression again) he decided to move to Florida and try farming tropical fish. After Hans died, his son Carl continued to run the business and simplified the operation. Their major crops were glassfish and angelfish. These he did nothing more than stock them in dirt ponds. The angelfish breeders were kept inside during the winter months and stocked outside in late March. They bred easily in the outside ponds. At the end of the season (October) the ponds were taken down, the fish that had been raised were sorted by size, and then sold in the next months.

I learned something then that we and most other Florida angelfish breeders missed. Angelfish pairs will do well for, at the most, a little more than a year and often less in normal hatchery production aquariums. They slow down and then are replaced and sold. We all did this, and it was years later before I realized that this was not necessarily the right way to go about it. Carl Jensen told me that some of his breeders had to be ten years old. They were all much larger than any we had set up in breeding production. By taking all of the pairs that slowed down and putting them outside to spend the summer you would in the fall get some additional pond raised fish back, but most important the "used up" breeders would not only be rejuvenated, but had increased in size. This translated into not just good breeders, but breeders that were more productive. Egg production from these "worn out" breeders was almost double what we normally expected.

Woolf now hired a second full time employee. This was Oren Adams. Oren had been making his living with commercial fishing. When Woolf offered him steady work he jumped at it. He worked under C.J. Powell and the operation flourished. There were ominous war clouds on the horizon. Jim Woolf by now (1940) had become an accomplished small plane pilot. He told me that it did not take a genius to figure out that the United States was going to be in the war. He was determined to be part of it, and when he did he wanted to fly. In early 1940 in Tampa the government started training pilots for an expanding Army Air Force. This was done by the Civilian Pilots Training Program. This was primary instruction, and was always conducted by civilian instructors. Jim, one day, was visited by a representative of this group and asked to fill in for one of the two regular instructors who then was sick. He was hired for a month. This was his entry into the government's flying program. Jim had been drawing a wage of $15 a week at the farm. The first week as an instructor he earned $110. He was also flying. He probably would have done it all for free. This was so much money that he is still talking about it fifty five years later. This contact led to his being able to take advanced flying training for himself. His natural flying skills developed. He worked toward and earned his Commercial Pilot's License, and then also received his Instructor's License. He spent many months in the Civilian Training Program. When the United States formally entered the war Jim was inducted into the Army Air Force, and immediately placed into an enlisted reserve program. This enabled them to continue using Jim as an instructor where he was badly needed. Later (1943) when the instructor shortage problem was solved Jim was told that he could make a choice to either be activated into the Army Air Force as a cargo pilot, be assigned to tow targets for the Air Force, or fill an opening to fly essential cargo for the Pan American Grace Airline in South America. Jim spent the last two years of the war as a pilot based in Lima, Peru flying for the Pan American Grace Airlines.

When the war was over Pan American Airlines offered Jim a fabulous job as a Command Pilot. Ten years earlier Jim had promised his father he would stay with the fish business. He declined the airline's offer, and soon he was back at H. Woolf and Son.

Both Oren Adams and C.J. Powell had left Woolf during the war to serve in the Army. They returned after the war. Herb Woolf, with no trained help, struggled through the war to keep the operation going. His salvation was due to his oldest and best customer, Fred Cochu, whose Paramount operation in New York could use all the product they could get. The problem was how. Rail traffic for perishable material was impossible. Fred worked out a wonderful deal with a trucking firm that moved furniture from North to South for the government. They had the permits and they had the fuel, and most important they often drove north with partial loads. Cochu contracted for space north, and as often as they could (about every three weeks), they stopped at Herb Woolf's farm. Herb Woolf loaded the truck with whatever fish he had ready. He packed them in galvanized tin fish cans. The cans were insulated with paper and furniture blankets. No one cared how much the cans weighed so lots of water was used. The more water the better chance the fish had and the more water the slower it reacted to cold or heat. Results were great, and both firms operated in spite of difficult times. The infant tropical fish industry in Florida was, with this exception, just about shut down.

In 1946 transportation by rail was at best unsettled, and usually an invitation to calamity. Cochu continued his truck deal as long as it existed (1947). Herb and Jim were frustrated by the difficulties in getting product to market. The airlines were not able to take much freight. The fish often had to arrive at major airports remote from good potential customers. National and Eastern Airlines were the only ones operating from Tampa and for some time Eastern Airlines would not take live cargo. If space could be had on National Airlines it was seldom for more than six or eight boxes.

Jim toyed with the idea of the company owning their own plane (later this expanded to a fleet of three) and trying to make deliveries north. They bought a single engine Howard that could take 75 cans of fish (packed like sardines). This they operated only as far as the Carolinas. It was not practical, but was a start. This first try did, however, prove the merit to the idea. A larger twin engines plane (Lockheed Lodestar) was purchased.

Jim did all of the flying at the start. He would load the plane in the early hours, take off at first light, and head north. He would be back the same day and often manage to put in additional hours working the farm. They went north as far as New England. The packing medium grew more sophisticated with experience. Every fish can received its own air line with an air stone attached. The first containers used were galvanized cans. These were replaced with square treated waterproof (waxed) boxes. Finally by 1954 they were able to dispense with the plastic air lines and used sealed plastic bags in a corrugated container as we do today. Oren Adams' brother Don was hired in 1949. Don had spent six years in the Marine Corp. in the Pacific. He was involved in all of the major campaigns. Don told me he lived through it with only one problem and that was on Iwo Jima. He left most of his hair there. He still is not sure whether it was the Atabrine tablets he took for malaria or fright. Oren Adams in 1946 spent time at the Paramount breeding operation in Ardsley, New York. This at the invitation of Fred Cochu. Hugo Schnelle, an accomplished fish breeder, and Fred's brother-in-law, had set up the fish breeding program for Paramount during the war.

Hugo Schnelle had been an equal partner with Walter Griem in, what had been until the war, the most important tropical fish business (Aquarium Hamburg) in the world. In 1941 Schnelle had been in New York visiting with Fred Cochu. He elected to stay when the war broke out. He spent the next seven years in the United States living and working with Fred. When the war was over and he could return he decided he no longer wanted to live in Germany. He settled as best he could with his partner (Walter Griem) and spent the remaining years of his life at Ardsley, New York, managing that business for Paramount Aquarium. Hugo Schnelle trained Oren Adams in the basics of breeding egg laying tropical fish commercially. Oren, who was now the manager of the newly created Woolf breeding department, passed his knowledge on to his brother Don. The Adams brothers set the standards for breeding egg laying fish in great quantities.

Don Adams concentrated on raising angelfish, gouramis, and all the various danio species. Don Adams created the All Black Angelfish, but until now has never received credit for the development of this exciting fish. He never asked for or tried for any recognition and watched in frustration as others claimed the credit using his fish as their breeding stock. In trying to nail the priority down now, some forty years later, I became aware of many conflicting claims. Other people had black angelfish on the market the same year (1955) Woolf turned their all black angelfish loose. Don Adams had them more than two years earlier (1953). Woolf did not release them at that time as they were trying to first produce them in commercial quantities. Don Adams started developing the fish early in 1950. It started with a single sport that was close to today's black lace or dusky angelfish. Don held the fish back trying to learn how to produce quantities and get the strain to breed true. We now know that he had an impossible task. No one has ever been able to easily produce black angelfish in quantities similar to normal angelfish. By 1954 he had oppressive amounts of culls (mostly black lace angelfish which also were a new variety) that the Woolf operation had to release to make room for other fish. I am confident that any of Woolf's customers or their customers who used these fish (and they did) as breeders had some all black angelfish almost immediately. The all black angelfish is easily produced by breeding black lace to black lace. You get 25% all black. Most of the all black angelfish sold in the United States for the last thirty years have come from the Far East (Hong Kong and Singapore). Production of black angelfish is labor intensive and the Orient has the advantage in production costs. It is a beautiful and spectacular fish. In 1955 there were black angelfish articles in all three major hobbyist magazines (Aquarium Journal, Aquarium Magazine, T.F.H.) in June and July reporting the new all black angelfish. Five people were all claiming credit. Three of these were customers of Woolf (Otto Beldts in St. Louis, Ludwig in Detroit, and Berkowitz in Philadelphia) who had gotten the culls from Don Adam's black angelfish. Don Adams and the H. Woolf and Son's fish was never mentioned by anyone. Early in 1955 Woolf was selling the fish. It never had any commercial impact for Woolf as large production never materialized for them or anyone else in the United States.

Oren Adams developed lyretail swordtails from one chance cull (a green wag swordtail). He tells an intriguing story about the first Opaline gouramis which he raised and introduced. He was given by their import department five tiny, strangely-marked wild blue gourami that had been a contaminant in a bag of wild *Rasbora heteromorpha*. These had just been received from Singapore. Oren raised these, bred them, and then named them. All of the opaline gouramis that have been sold from Florida came from this stock. No one to this day knows where in the Far East they originated.

The Woolf operation grew fast to become the largest operation in the entire fish world. They soon were shipping more fish than all of the other fish farms combined. Their private air delivery system was refined. The shipping container they were now using was half the size and capacity of the normal fish box used today. The Lockheed Lodestar could handle six hundred of these half boxes. Jim, at the controls, was often packed in so tight that he could not get out of his pilots seat until boxes piled about him were removed. Woolf in the 1950s was shipping the equivalent of five hundred large boxes of their own produced fish each week. The key word in that sentence is produced. I do not think that anyone has ever equaled that production figure. A large part was being delivered in Woolf's own fleet of airplanes. As the volume increased, Jim Durst, Jim's copilot and mechanic, took some flights as captain. Then other pilots and copilots were hired. They had only one accident. It was a miracle that anyone survived. This was with a PV-2 Lockheed Ventura that had been an aerial torpedo bomber in World War Two. It had just been put into service to deliver fish. On one of the trial flights, when landing in Tampa, the copilot hit the wrong switches. He turned off the engines (two). This turned the plane into a rock. They set it down hard on its belly. The crew walked away. The PV-2 was a total loss. This was the same type of airplane I had bought to fly to my compound in Leticia, Colombia. Woolf was now flying twice each week, to the Midwest and north to New England. At times they made three flights in one week. A trip to California was made every third week. The airplane always returned to the farm the same day, excepting the far west trip. The air operation was unique, and no one could compete with it. Woolf never lost a customer except the few that they elected to drop. Customers were standing in line hoping Woolf would be able to sell them. The alternative delivery systems were difficult, dangerous, and often more costly. Imagine a customer living in a town like Indianapolis, Trenton, Charlotte, or Muncy. They would receive information from Jim Woolf, who was then in the air and flying to them, confirming that he would touch down at twelve noon and to be waiting there with a truck. Often, Jim would land and not even cut the engine. The customer would drive right up to the plane. They were given the twenty five to fifty boxes of fish they had ordered. The plane was back in the air heading to the next customer in fifteen minutes or less. The wonderful thing was that it was not more expensive than alternate and unworkable methods of transport. Woolf delivered by air for fourteen years.

The commercial airlines in the mid 1950s were slowly learning that the transport of tropical fish was a big and profitable business. In fact, by the early 1960s, tropical fish had become the single largest air freight item out of Florida. Weekly volume approached 15,000 boxes. It is interesting to note that cut flowers are the second largest freight item out of Florida. A very nice added touch is that human remains are right behind the cut flowers in cargo volume. Eventually commercial airlines cargo capacities improved dramatically and some of Woolf's customers found other suppliers.

The H. Woolf business grew at an amazing pace from the last years of the 1940s until the facility became part of the Hartz Mountain Empire in 1963. Herb Woolf's health problems started in 1952. He had bad bouts of hypertension (high blood pressure). He went to John Hopkins Clinic and then to Duke University. He had some good years, but his health problems persisted. In 1956 he was walking a 45-acre piece of property in Ruskin, Florida, that he was negotiating to buy, to again expand. He had a major heart attack that day after he lost his footing and fell atop a rattlesnake (that did not strike). He recovered from this, but had to slow down. He died after a final heart attack in 1960. The quality of Woolf's fish stayed high. All of the old time Florida fish farmers knew their secret. A rapid expansion in volume combined with a never ending supply of new ponds are the perfect formula for fast growing, highly productive crops of large livebearing fish. By the third year pond production in a new pool falls dramatically.

The Woolf dollar and fish production volume had peaked in the fast years of the 1950s. No new ponds were added as business volume had ceased to increase. By 1956 when the last acreage was bought and put into producing ponds, they were farming almost one 150 acres of tropical fish ponds. The total number of dirt pools approached 1500.

A very subtle change in production and quality took place at this time. The older ponds were playing out and the multitude of new farms in business all were digging new and highly productive ponds. The wonderful and seemingly inexhaustible supply of water in this area had dropped and continues to drop. When fish farms were built before World War Two ponds were dug "three shovels deep". This made a pond less than three feet in depth. Abundant supplies of artesian water provided an unending supply of water under natural pressures. No one ever imagined that anyone ever would be using pumps to get water and, even worse, paying enormous electric bills. This was another important factor in slowing down the Woolf operation. Their electric bills were between two and three thousand dollars a month and water levels kept dropping. Water had been within a few feet of the surface when Woolf first started using it and by the 1960s it was often fifty or more feet below ground level and needed special (expensive) turbine pumps to reach and lift it. An enormous number of new fish farms had been established in the 1950s as the demand for tropical fish could not be filled from the existing farms. There were more than fifty and almost one hundred newly dug fish farms in Florida. Many of the best operators provided fierce competition. Many of these new farmers, as employees, had been trained by Herb and Jim Woolf. The demand for fish was great. Soon there were more farms and fish than needed. Prices eroded fast. Jet planes, expanded air line facilities, plastic bags in cardboard cartons had arrived.

This combination of factors made Jim Woolf receptive to an offer from Leonard Stern to let Hartz Mountain acquire the facility. The timing was perfect for Jim Woolf (which when you think about it was not unexpected as this is a very bright man). He was correct as subsequent history has proven. They worked out a mutually satisfactory deal and Jim Woolf retired in 1963. Herb and Jim Woolf, together, led the way for all the rest of us to follow. They were great role models. Among the best fish farmers today are many who had direct and indirect roots in the Woolf operation. Both Oren and Don Adams are in business with their sons and son-in-laws.

C.J. Powell had a successful farm producing good livebearers. The name Graves is prominent in the industry. George and Robert both were ex-Woolf employees. Four of them stand out. The only tiny one is Robert who is barely 6' 2". The others are much larger.

George Graves was a fish farmer's fish farmer. I always used his fish as a yardstick to measure other people's quality. While George produced a variety of livebearers he is best remembered for his wonderful huge black mollies. This stock came from some of the last and best strains Bill Sternke produced. George Graves used very large and very deep pools. It worked for him. He owned and operated his own dragline and was always re-digging (revitalizing) his ponds. He could put great size on all of the platy *variatus* strains and we all envied him. His fish were in great demand. George developed both the Marigold and the Marigold Tuxedo Variatus Platys. Glassfish have always been a hit-and-miss production item. They are only practical to breed in a dirt pond. The production secret George Graves stumbled on was to poly culture them with his black mollies. George almost always had glassfish in quantity. The rest of us struggled to raise enough for our customers and then bought from him. That last was at times a problem. George often had orders for double what he could produce and he produced a lot of them. If George did not think of you as a friend (I was lucky) he would not deal with you. He sold all the fish he produced to a limited number of customers.

Robert Graves ran a more typical balanced farm and shipped north rather than supply local farmers who shipped north. He always did well with some of the tougher egg layers.

Glen (Googie) Graves was, and is, one of my favorite people. Googie is a hoot. He can be loud and he is always happy. He actually lights up a room when he comes in the door. I haven't seen him in years and would like to see him again. He had great imagination and great ideas. He worked on and produced a number of beautiful new swordtail strains (his specialty) and won many of the top prizes at early FTFFA professional fish competitions.

Cousin Donald Graves is a truly gigantic man. He is soft spoken and very talented. He raises unreal numbers of gouramis and does not raise anything else. He raises all of the commercial varieties. The only exception being *Betta splendens*, the Siamese fighting fish. This fish is too labor intensive to make economic sense in Florida. The great majority of these fighting fish are now raised in Bangkok. As they can be sent with little more than enough water to wet them down the freight is low. I've kept Bettas alive for long periods of time, in small sealed bags, with only moisture in the bags. I also remember drowning them by not allowing them to reach the surface for air. They are a strange fish that requires atmospheric air to live.

I am listing (courtesy of Don Adams) a roster of other Woolf employees who, after leaving Woolf, operated their own fish farms. C.J. Powell, Oren Adams, Don Adams, George Graves, Robert Graves, Don Fanner, Jim Sweet, Marcus Chancey, Pete Chancey, Charley Carver, Gomer Makin, Leroy Baker, Robert Ekker, Joe Givens, Bill Givens, Ed Spivey, and Dan Stansell. That is a list of 17 people and an amazing tribute to the Woolf family as they all have been successful.

While the negotiations with Woolf and Hartz Mountain were going on (1962 and in secret) I had a call from Leonard Stern of Hartz Mountain. I had never met him and he wanted to meet me and talk to me. I spent a day with him at my Gulf Fish Hatchery and we worked out a tentative deal that seemed to make sense for both of us. I would expand my operation and dig more ponds. The additional production would be geared to their needs. Prices would be low, but acceptable. I did not have the financial ability to do any of this and Leonard offered to co-sign the loans I would need from our bank. He was to get back to me, and he did several weeks later. He told me then that the Hartz operation was taking over the Woolf operation. His plans for a joint venture with Gulf Fish Hatchery did not materialize. At that time in his career he was not making all the decisions. Soon after this period he was making the decisions. In the following years Leonard Stern led the Hartz Mountain company to awesome growth and profits.

Often, in later years, I have regretted not having had the opportunity to join the Hartz Mountain live stock operation. What I would have wanted would have been to run it. The operation had massive problems that could have been solved. There were a lot of fish bought that enriched the wrong people. There were a lot of the very best and the most honest employees forced to quit. The ones that stayed had a field day removing and reselling fish and material. Local management consistently protected the bad guys and let the good guys suffer. It may only have been bad judgement, but I think not. They very quickly gave up trying to produce the vast amounts of fish they needed to supply their customers. The enormous production ground down to a trickle. Hartz then was supplying all the fish to Woolworth, Kresge, Sears, Grants, and large numbers of smaller but similar chains. The fish that Hartz provided were of good quality. This statement of fact will surprise most people who saw the product at the retail outlets. Apparently Hartz never put together a workable program to help their retail customers solve the keeping problems. Nothing could ever have been worse than the quality of the tropical fish that the consumer was offered from these Hartz Mountain customers. It fascinated and disturbed me when I visited these stores. No one cared. Good fish were dumped on top of sick fish. Tanks were cleaned only in extremis. When they were cleaned the sick fish were put on top of healthy fish. The solution was difficult, but obvious. If tried it never was implemented. There had to be a simple clear set of rules. Illustrating what I mean has me now describing a small disaster that I caused. After telling a new employee to grab a pail and move the fish in that tank into that tank I walked away. A few minutes later I returned and found her netting the fish and dumping into them into a "dry" bucket. I did not tell her to put water in the bucket. The variety offered had to be drastically reduced to include only the hardiest varieties. The employee had to be assumed to be a cretin and the assumption had to be that the cretin was a different person every day. Great numbers of potentially good hobbyists were driven out of the hobby by buying vast quantities of these almost always sick and diseased fish. It really hurt the hobby. In time the chains slowly and finally dropped out of the live fish business. This was one of the best things that ever happened to the tropical fish hobby. It was a blessing when it happened. It gave the industry another chance to get good healthy fish to the consumer.

In 1959, Emilio Saiz, my Colombian partner, proposed that we open a second compound in Villavicencio, Colombia, and I agreed. This compound worked so well that the next year (1960) Saiz and I built ourselves a six room home on the compound so that we could stay there comfortably when in Villavicencio. We used that house and compound for many years. It was a perfect location. Mainly, we could receive new fish from the east (Rio Meta) in the Colombian Llanos and also from the northeast (Puerto Carena)) near the Venezuela border. Emilio had spent considerable time checking out the areas. The Rio Meta had many great fish and we were going to explore the area for another potential collecting area. Emilio had found a few wild Ramirezi there. That was exciting news. The original importation of Ramirezi cichlids came from Venezuela (only). After the original importation few if any came out. The Venezuelan government made legal export impossible. It is a wonderful fish. It was and is still much in demand. Saiz found the fish near Puerto Gaitan on the Rio Meta. The area was rich in catfish varieties. He also found the royal and blue-eyed *Plecostomus* there. The best discovery was a striking new catfish (*Pimelodella pictus*). This we then called "Angelicus" *Pimelodella*. Today the name polka dot *Pimelodella* (which is a better name) is more commonly used. We had difficulty collecting enough of them as these new catfish sold fast. When Saiz learned it was nocturnal, and could be best collected effectively at night the problem was solved. *Corydoras metae* and a very attractive green gold variety of *Corydoras aeneus* were also available in quantity. Five or six types of *Plecostomus*, all of which were saleable, were found. The best was a small (3 inch) golden-striped *Plecostomus* and also the great bushy nosed *Ancistris* (*A. triradiatus*). Loise and I, along with our oldest son Bill, made a trip to Colombia. We met Saiz in Bogotá. Then we traveled five hours over the Andes by car to Villavicencio. We met Isidro and Manuel, our two best collectors, at our new installation in Villavicencio. We all headed for the Rio Meta where we could collect and sample the potential fish. Afterwards, we would make a decision as to whether or not we needed a third compound. It was the dry season and we could go overland by bus. No real road, but a road was not needed. The Colombian Llanos is flat country. The Villavicencio compound was ready to ship fish. If Emilio was right it would make sense. The most practical way to get there was by bus. If you have never travelled through Latin America by local bus you have missed one of life's true adventures. These vehicles are cheap, uncomfortable, and less than dependable. They carry everything imaginable. There were people aboard with chickens, turkeys, and even a goat. Loise and I managed seats together for the trip and Bill was sitting across the aisle from us with two hunters and their three dogs. It took Bill weeks to get his flea bites under control. He perked up later that evening when we went down to a local stream that fed into the Rio Meta for a bath. Down from us were a group of young naked Indian maidens who were bathing. This was an eighteen-year-old's dream of "life in the jungle" and one of his best memories. Mine is escaping the stream after unsuccessfully trying to prevent shoals of *Exodon paradoxus* from biting parts of me that are usually covered by a bathing suit. It was a fast bath as all I could think about was Emilio Saiz's stories about the dreadful Candiru catfish. Actually at that time I did not believe a word of this story, but later I discovered that his wild tale was completely accurate. Candiru are urinotropic catfish. The attraction is urine as the name suggests. The young Candiru (Vandellia species) are small, naked skinned, worm-like parasitic catfish belonging to the family Pygidiidae. They are nasty and dangerous. The glasslike young (much less than an inch) often appear as a contaminant in bags of Amazonian shipments of cardinal and neon tetras. These fish can and do penetrate the urogenital apertures of swimming mammals. You got it. They swim into and wiggle up and into the body where they lodge permanently. The pain is intense. Dr. Gudger of the American Museum of Natural History reported and documented instances where Indians had cut off their penis to relieve what has to be, and has been described, as excruciating discomfort. I can not conceive of that kind of field surgery though the agony must have been unbearable. That was the very last time I ever entered the water above my thighs in South America. We had arrived late in the day. We set up camp near a small block building Emilio had built to store collecting gear. It also held two army cots and some cooking utensils. Saiz had several big plastic bags of food. These were placed on a wooden platform near the storage hut. He opened them to let the air and heat out. We went for the just described bath while the others busied themselves setting up camp. On our return Loise discovered the two bags of food were black inside with thousands (no exaggeration) of cockroaches. As all our provisions were fresh that was the end of our food supply. Total remaining food was a can of pistachio nuts (husked) and a can of Vienna sausage. There was a small local cantina which only sold warm Colombian Gasiosa (soda pop) and warm cervesa (beer). There was little sleep that hungry night. Saiz, who had a magnificent singing voice, went off and soon we could hear him singing in the distance (at the cantina?). We were exhausted and Loise and I tried to sleep outside on one army cot with my big feet in her face. She had roaches in her hair. She brushed them out with no complaint. She is a lot tougher than almost all of the men I have travelled with over the years. Next day we did some serious collecting. The ease with which we could collect Ramirezi led us to make a quick decision to build a permanent holding facility. This, in spite of the fact that it could only operate during the dry season as many times the rains made the bus and truck transport impossible. We could seine now during the dry season in water averaging 18-24 inches in depth. I collected and preserved in formaldehyde many unknown characins. Later Dr. Jacques Géry found four new species in this group. He named one *Bryconamericus loisae* and another *Hyphesobrycon saizi*. This pleased them both. The dominant fish was the Ramirezi. Usually there was one good-sized piranha in each seine load, but no one was bothered. These red-bellied piranhas (*Serrasalmus nattereri*) have terrible teeth. My experience with piranhas would indicate that there is little danger unless you do stupid things. The huge black ones (*Serrasalmus niger*) from Guyana are the worst and this because they grow the largest. All piranhas are dangerous to handle as they can easily (like a cookie cutter) remove the end of a finger.

In 1955 I took a week long trip up the Berbice River in eastern Guyana. We made a stop at a native village several days up river where I found and bought a baby capuchin monkey from a young mother who was breast feeding it. It seemed old enough to wean (it was). It even came with a name which sounded like "Papaduke". I took it home and gave it to our daughters. This adorable looking capuchin monkey was really disgusting. Jumping on their heads, entangling his hands and feet in their hair, he would hoot with pleasure and then urinate. He seemed to prefer Amy. I think it was her red hair. The more she screamed the happier he got. He thought it a great game. For once there was no complaint when we replaced him with a baby raccoon with more sanitary habits.

Most of the male natives in Papaduke's village had one to three toes missing on either or both of their feet. They lost toes when using a foot as a rudder while paddling their dug outs. I think a combination of the churning water and the underside of the foot being a contrasting color (much lighter) confused the piranha (*S. niger*). It could, and did, easily mistake the foot for a fish in trouble. The toes were neatly amputated by the black piranha. One look at the jaw and teeth of a twelve to fifteen inch black piranha will convince anyone.

During our first night in Manacacias I had eaten the small can of Vienna sausage. I rationalized that as I had been told for years how unhealthy a food this was I would be doing everyone a favor, big mistake. I have not to this day been forgiven. On the river I opened the only other can we had (pistachio nuts) and politely passed them around. Loise took some, gave them to Emilio who took some and then handed them to the boatman whose big dugout we had rented. He emptied them all in his pocket and returned the empty can to me. Everyone was delighted to see me get an empty can for breakfast. We did stop along the river to eat some oranges that had mostly gone wild. While edible they were no treat. They did little to cure the hunger pangs, and even now I can feel the burn from the juice on my mosquito-bitten and burned face.

Back at camp all we could think about was food. Loise and I walked amongst the Indian huts in the settlement (Puerto Gaitan) and soon spied a haunch of meat hanging in a tree to keep it from the animals. It was capybara (the world's largest rodent) and excellent eating. We negotiated and prepared to buy some. The owner cut off a large slab which we then could see was crawling with maggots. The quest for food continued. We kept trying and shortly found a big, newly caught three foot shovel-nosed catfish (*Sorubim lima*) and bought it. It was found just in time as Loise had about convinced me to go back and get the capybara meat. We ate it all after managing to wait for it to be cooked—wonderful white meat. Saiz had scrounged up some bread so the meal was complete. Our food problem was solved.

The collecting was very encouraging. Everything came together and despite some bad fish keeping problems both in Colombia and Florida we eventually made out well. I told Saiz to lean on the Ramirezi collecting and get me as many as he could. He outdid himself. Gulf got 30,000 of them on the first shipment. I later found that the water where we collected the Ramirezi was dead soft, and had a surprisingly low pH of 4.8. The fish came to Villavicencio where the water is hard and alkaline (about pH 8.4). The water was changed and the fish were repacked and then sent to Gulf Fish Hatchery. They had their brains scrambled by the water shock long before we got them. I then put them in water that was on the soft and acid side which further shocked them. I did a lot of dumb things and this happened more often than I care to remember. Almost immediately we had big trouble. I lost half of them in a matter of days. In desperation I released the survivors into large empty dirt ponds that were loaded with live food. Dirt pools provide an effective last resort cure for deadly problems. Of course, this was again a fourth shock as the Gulf Fish Hatchery pond water had a pH of 7.8 or more and was again very hard. It was a terrible disaster. I could not imagine anything worse (there were in subsequent years). I learned a lot from that experience. Eventually I recovered less than one thousand of the original 30,000 Ramirezi. I had lost 29 out of every 30 I had received. The survivors were gigantic Ramirezi. These survivors had grown larger than any wild or tank raised Ramirezi I have ever seen. I showed some of these to Emilio when he next visited. He agreed that he had never seen a wild fish anywhere close to the size of these. I sold the monster Ramirezi for one dollar and fifty cents each. Saiz had billed the Ramirezi for six cents each so the 30,000 cost me $1,800. The one thousand giants brought back

$1500 plus freight. We had a loss, but it was a bargain as it forced us to learn what caused the problems and to try not to repeat them.

Many years later the tropical fish hobbyists in Java had the local rice farmers raise very large Rams by releasing breeders in newly set rice paddies. That would not work in hard and alkaline Florida, but in the soft and acidic Indonesian waters it worked like a charm. These Indonesian Rams are the only ones I have ever seen that come close to the Colombian Rams that survived our first gigantic importation from the Rio Meta in Colombia. I learned a lot of positive things from the experience. Severe water shocks to tropical fish cause terrible losses. The problems you see and treat (tail rot, Ich, mouth fungus) are all secondary infections, and not the real problem. The main problem was water shock. The only way to correct that problem is in Colombia. The second truth is that tropical fish in a dirt pond will grow much larger than any wild specimen ever does. This last gave me the inspiration to start a grow-out business which turned out to be very lucrative. I did not let my competitors know what I was doing and we had a good thing going for many years. I sized fish for additional profit, and made happy customers. Utilizing paraldehyde as a tranquilizer we convinced our Asiatic shippers that we actually wanted tiny fish packed densely. *Pangasius* cats were a phenomenon. These so-called "Iridescent Sharks" grew so fast it was astounding. A baby fish would transform itself into a six inch "show" fish in eight weeks. It became an important part of our business, and in later years, an additional source of income for the industry. It got better each year. The biggest part of the total cost from the Far East is the air freight. The less fish in a bag the higher the per fish cost. The smaller the fish was the more could be packed in the bag and the lower the landed cost. The hardest problem was to convince the shipper this was really what we wanted. The biggest negative (normally) encountered buying from the Far East is the small size of the fish. Here was a customer asking for still smaller and cheaper fish. It worked out very well for us. The shipper could put five hundred small-sized Ramirezi in a box and this would add just ten cents per fish for freight costs. If the number in the box dropped to one hundred extra-large sized fish then the freight shot up to 50 cents per fish. The difference of 40 cents per fish was more than enough for us to make a nice profit. The 40 cents per fish freight cost saving gave Gulf Fish Hatchery another item to sell at a profit.

Jim Woolf (1994)

Herb Woolf (1950s)

Crash at Tampa Airport and everyone walked away - 1958.

Load of fish flying north.
H. Woolf - 1956
Note: plastic airlines.

Oren Adams who Jim Woolf describes as the number one man!

Jim Woolf during the Second World War

Don Adams

Ralph Meyer and Hans Kleinheimer

Hank Hansen

The deadly water shocking of the wild exported fish still is a common occurrence in Colombia, and to a lesser degree in other areas. It is the major reason why Colombian fish have never been as profitable for importers as wild fish received from other parts of South America. The available fish variety is probably the best in South America; the keeping and reselling of the fish the worst. Today Colombia is held captive by the drug cartel and there is little interest in tropical fish. Much of the area where we collected is under the control of the "Cocaine Cowboys" and only a real crazy would try to collect or send fish from that area. Most of the collectors have found other, more lucrative work in the drug business. I made my last explorative collecting trip in Colombia in 1976 just before Emilio Saiz died. You never try to collect fish in the rainy season. I did this that one time, and only then because I had no other opportunity. I arranged to meet Emilio at our house in Villavicencio and then made my only solo trip into the interior. I used a private plane that Emilio had chartered. The plan was for the pilot to drop me off at a Catholic mission in a very remote area on the Rio Muco in the State of Vichada. Emilio had gotten some good vibrations from a report brought back by one of his collectors he had sent for a look. He could not go himself. His heart condition prevented him from any exertion. I stole five days that August to make the round trip. I arranged to take Isidro and Manuel with me. These two were our best collectors, and had been trained at our Leticia compound. The mission was in reality a school. It was staffed by three nuns and one priest. The school would be closed for some forgotten reason while I was there and I could use the facilities. We would stay three days. This included half a day getting there and half a day returning to Villavicencio. The day I was to leave Saiz was going back to Bogotá. I was with him at the airport in Villavicencio when he left. I still vividly see a picture of Emilio being patted down for concealed weapons before going up the stairs into the plane. He shouted to Claudia (Mrs. Saiz) when they had finished checking him and motioned her to him. He then opened his brief case which he had held in his hand while they searched him. He opened the case and handed Claudia his pistol which he had forgotten to leave at home. I was airborne myself about thirty minutes later with Manual and Isidro. My pilot had an old Esso map of Colombia. About half way there he was hopelessly lost. He found a remote cattle station and landed in the field near the only building. He left the engine running and ran to the building clutching his map. He found someone there to give him a direction. I know because I saw him pointing to the east. He ran back and we were in the air properly directed within five minutes. It was wet. The country was completely flooded (this was in August and as expected). We flew down the Rio Muco until we could see the Catholic mission. I made him circle low and slow several times before making his landing so I could get an idea of what was there. I knew the river would be impossible to collect as it had flooded over its banks. I saw what I was looking for and knew where to try. There were three ponds within a mile. They were all close to each other and away from the river. We landed and the pilot agreed to return for me before noon on the third day. Early the next day I was ready to explore the area and determine the potential for tropical fish. We had army cots and mosquito netting provided. I had our own food. We were in good shape. I was too excited to sleep much. I was up and ready to go at dawn. Big mistake! We started and then stopped. The mosquitoes just about ate us alive. We retreated to wait until the sun came up higher. Then the bugs would become bearable. Instead, at about 10 am, it started to rain (a blessing as it kept the biting buggers down). It was terrible walking out to the lakes. I carried my push net, bags, rubber bands and, most important, a face mask and snorkel. Isidro and Manual had two sizes of seines, Styrofoam boxes, my push net, and hand nets. Walking in the knee high grass was fatiguing .We were mostly in water two to six inches deep. I even managed to catch a few fish on the way. One turned out to be a new species of *Characidium*. It was the first fish I preserved.

The closest pond was too small and too shallow and we went on to the largest pond. This turned out to be a collector's dream. It was clear as glass with lots of downed trees to provide shelter for an amazing variety and number of fish. I have never, ever, collected in a spot with more variety and promise. I will try to list the fish caught there. The total area of the largest pond was no more than five acres. I can now only, from memory, list the fish that would have commercial interest. The rest are pickled, and in the Smithsonian Institution's collection. A number of these fish were only seen. The identifications are casual and from my personal knowledge. Three types of *Copeina* (one was a new species), hatchet fish, *Leporinus fasciatus*, several *Anostomus* species, *Leporinus* species, *Characidium* (the new species), angelfish, which I could not capture, and would guess were "Altum", *A. ramirezi*, neon tetra and cardinal tetra (together!!), Severum, Festivum, chocolate cichlids, *Aequidens dorsigerus*, a characin that appeared to be a cardinal tetra, but without any green at all, but lots of red. I tried to bring some of these back without luck. I never saw discus, but would bet that they are in the area. I did find lots of *Crenicara filamentosa*. Catfish were represented by two types of *Corydoras* and I also collected more than a dozen other species including *Loricaria, Ancistris, Plecostomus, Farlowella, Hoplosternum. Otocinclus*, and two types of *Platydoras*. I never wrote this trip up. I have kept it to myself until now. I wanted to first collect it again, and this time in the dry season. This all happened some 30 years ago. My original notes are long gone. I have not and will not be back. It is there still waiting for some one to do it right. Take along a good map and plenty of insect repellent. Do not go in August. The area is virgin ground with tremendous potential.

We did mostly ineffective collecting after this. It was now raining constantly. We were for all sensible purposes blind. The third morning was spent packing and waiting for the plane. I wanted to collect, but was afraid to leave the compound area. The pilot never showed. We sat and waited all day. I didn't have Loise with me to continue our lifelong gin rummy and backgammon battles. That night we collected along the river's flooded edge using flash lights. This has been very effective for me in the past. This night we did not last long as the insects ran us back inside under the mosquito netting. Only fish I can now remember collecting was the largest (a good six inches) striped Raphael catfish (*Platydoras costatus*) that I have ever seen. Our pilot showed the next day about noon. We returned to Villavicencio without mishap. The State of Vichada in eastern Colombia, where we had been, will someday provide a bonanza of new and exciting fish for the tropical fish hobby. Today, I think, you would take your life in your hands to spend any time in the area. The llanos cowboys are now cocaine cowboys.

While thinking about it I will fill in the final chapters of the Mike Tsalikes story (remember him from Leticia?) Appropriate now as I am discussing Colombia, drugs, and the fish business in Colombia. In later years Mike and I always had a distant, but cordial relationship. He denied having anything to do with my arrest and the financial punishment inflicted upon me on my first trip to Leticia. If you believe that I have a bridge to sell you....

Mike and Trudy closed down the Tarpon Zoo Leticia fish operation to concentrate on their animal business. They'd never learned the rudiments of proper fish keeping. Mike had an island similar to our Ronda Island that he had sanitized by removing all predatory animals. He had then stocked it with squirrel monkeys. He fast became the king of the squirrel monkey suppliers. Mike got thousands of wild animals and his captive breeding project was very successful. Squirrel monkeys then sold to the wholesalers for $5.00 each. They sold lots of them. Mike became well known after appearing in several episodes of Wild Kingdom apparently catching and wrestling a gigantic anaconda. He prospered and was known as the "Mayor" of Leticia. His arrest, large fine, and deportation from Colombia in the mid 1970s was a shock, but not really a surprise. Mike had finally been caught dealing in drugs, supposedly cocaine. Later events make this believable. I had a call from Mike several years later from Tarpon Springs. I was trying to retire about that time. I was spending a lot of my time trying to help ex-employees build a business of their own. Mike said he was looking for a tropical fish distributor. He was re-opening his Leticia Fish Compound, and I was the perfect choice as we were such old friends (right?). He wanted to come down next day with his partners and talk to me. The timing was great and I wanted to hear more. Colombia then had few fish and those available were sent from Bogotá and of poor quality. Fish captured, kept, and exported to the States from Leticia in Leticia water would be good fish as they did not have to endure water change shocks. Cocaine and marijuana were the big businesses now. The fish collectors mostly worked for drug dealers (they still do). Iquitos, Peru, had become the tropical fish and animal export center in South America. Emilio Saiz had died a few years earlier. Experience had made me very careful dealing with Tsalikes (remember, I just look stupid). It didn't take me ten minutes to know the deal was rotten. Mike introduced his two partners in the proposed new fish business. They were both Colombian nationals and wandered around the Hatchery apparently bored and not interested in our talks. Strange to say the least. Mike wanted to send up a cargo plane of fish every two weeks. It would land in Sarasota. I wore my normal stupid face and let him talk. I told him I would call him back in a few days and let him know. He left. I called back the next day, did not speak with him, and left a message that we were not able to handle the deal. He had me arrested once. This time what he apparently was offering me was really big time jail in the United States and not just house arrest in Leticia. I never spoke with Mike again. He evidently prospered in his "new" business ventures. What he was doing was infinitely cleverer than smuggling drugs on a cargo planeload of fish. He had for some time been sending, from Leticia, boatloads of rough cut logs. Using state of the art mechanical aids, and new glues he could cut a slab off the side of the log and hollow out a section. The cocaine was put in the hollowed out section, and then the removed slab glued back. It was not detectable by sight, and more important by smell. The quantity of cocaine smuggled into Florida by this method was enormous. It went on for some time until someone, who was unhappy with Mike, informed the Drug Enforcement Agency. Mike Tsalikes was caught. If the D.E.A. had not been tipped off Mike probably could have done it forever. He is serving a life sentence. As far as I know his Tarpon Zoo compounds, Wanderraga's place and our Ronda Island have all been reclaimed by the jungle. Colombia has a better future for tropical fish export than any place in South America. The time is not now. Someone someday will build a great tropical fish export industry in Colombia.

We had another wonderful, reclusive friend in Colombia. He was a Swiss botanist living outside of Cali named Fred Kyburz. In 1954 he had sent a letter to Dr. William Innes. Innes was the original editor and publisher of what was then the finest magazine published for the tropical fish hobbyist. This was "The Aquarium" magazine. Kyburz had found a pretty fish while on one of his botanical collecting expeditions in the Cauca valley outside of Cali, and specifically, the San Juan River drainage. He took a black and white photo and sent it to Innes asking for help. The editor of the magazine then was a bright young fellow named Alan Fletcher. Alan sent the picture to me. Kyburz called it the Emperor tetra and the name stuck. It was a characin identified and described by Dr. Carl Eigenmann as *Nematobrycon palmeri* some fifty years earlier. A second and equally attractive species then called *N. amphiloxus* was also found in the same area. Kyburz had two fish to offer. In short order I became his distributor along with a dealer in the Miami area (Herman Bias of Franjo Fisheries). Many years later Dr. Stanley Weitzman at the Smithsonian found that the original type specimen of *N. amphiloxus* was in reality only a race of *N. palmeri*. There was, however, a new species in the marketplace that was still undescribed. Dr. Weitzman honored Mr. Rosario LaCorte when he described the other species of emperor tetra as *N. lacortei*. I have always felt good about this as "Za" Lacorte is certainly one of the world's great fish breeders and also is the person who pioneered the successful reproduction of the emperor tetra for the marketplace. I have always felt bad about fish that honor truly undeserving persons. Ego and position has often enabled them to get new species of fish named for them. The party that actually discovers the fish has no say in the naming. The taxonomist describing the new species names it. Kyburz sent me fish whenever he could accumulate five boxes. They always came in good condition and sold out fast. I was anxious to meet Kyburz and explore the area with him as I expected there would be other exciting fish (there were not) that he could collect. He had sent me a few specimens of a new fish that was not commercial, but did turn out to be still another species of *Nematobrycon* (*N. kyburzi*). He had had a very bad experience in his marriage (his wife ran away with one of his employees), and he had no use for women. Loise was well aware of this, and as she wanted to collect with me she was determined to make Fred like her. I wrote Fred and told him we were coming. I didn't actually ask him if it was agreeable to bring a "woman" with me. I simply told him we were corning and that Loise could handle herself in the bush in any circumstance (she can and did) and she would be an asset. We were on our way before he could reply. Fred lived hermit-like on the top of a mountain called Bitaco about 15 miles from Cali. He met us at the airport, took us to a nice clean hotel, and then we went to see his home on the top of Bitaco mountain. It was a fairyland. The birds and butterflies were tame and spectacular. As a botanist he had planted wonderful exotic plants everywhere. He served us the fruit of a huge climbing cactus that was memorable and something we haven't seen since. His botanical specialty were Anthuriums. He had discovered a number of new species. He was making available rare varieties to collectors world wide. The house was primitive. His dogs were all over us and full of fleas. We had a great time. By the time the day was at an end Loise and Fred Kyburz bonded, and become lifelong friends. That was a relief. We sat on his porch and Fred mixed "Swiss" Martinis for us. Three parts of Vermouth and one part of Gin. He was convinced the rest of the world's Martini drinkers were barbarians, and only he knew how to mix the drink properly. He had been feeding birds and butterflies for years. The display was awesome then and now is still in my memory. I remember also a small pond in his front yard that he had built to keep fish. He had, the year before, asked me what he could put in his pond as the birds took goldfish as quick as he could stock them. As he liked Siamese fighting fish (*B. splendens*) I had suggested them, and told him they would breed in the pond if he left them alone and planted water lilies, etc. The world would have been a lot better off if his letter or my answer had gotten lost. Several years later with the pond full of all sizes of Bettas the pond wall ruptured during an especially fierce downpour that became a "Betta liberator". The Bettas went down the mountain with a lot of other stuff all washing into the nearest stream that fed the flat lands of the Cordilleras watershed. Siamese fighting fish in Colombia, South America? They did not just breed they exploded. Kyburz quickly had a "new" wild fish to sell. I know about hybridization. This was lowbridization. The Bettas reverted to the nastiest, wildest, least attractive fish imaginable. They chewed each other to pieces when they were shipped. The problem was that you could hardly tell males from females. They had reverted to the wild, short fin type in a very few generations. Hundreds of thousands of these fish were collected and exported from Colombia in the ensuing years. I doubt anyone ever made any money on them. I never did. I hated that fish. I had learned a trick some time before that I employed on these wild Bettas which helped a lot. Bettas can not be tranquilized effectively with regular tranquilizers as it does not last a full day. It takes at least 25 times a normal dose to do it. One phenomenon that concerns Bettas was taught me by Fred Cochu. He claimed, and I did not believe him, that a massive killing dose of copper in solution would not kill Bettas. It would tranquilize them. It works. Unfortunately, I learned this much later. I did not know the trick when I really needed it.

Gulf Fish Hatchery set up a live fish display in 1957 at Jay and George Winters N.A.P.I. show in New York City. The traffic stopper that Gulf Fish Hatchery displayed was a 29 gallon high aquarium full of huge show quality male Bettas (tranquilized with paraldehyde). It created a lot of interest and the start of that first day was great for business. About halfway into the day the tranquilizing agent lost potency. The Bettas were just waiting for that. They unleashed all of their hostile frustration on each other. It was a piscatorial fight to the last fish (I think the survivor then committed suicide by jumping out). This all snuck up on me. Neither Loise nor I noticed the carnage until it was all over. It was a terrible sight. Best I could manage was some ratty looking goldfish for the empty tank.

Kyburz, Loise, and I were off collecting before dawn the second day after we arrived. We collected all day long. We never saw another vehicle or person. The collecting did not turn up anything notable. About noon Loise asked us to stop the truck and not get out of the front seat and to let her go to the back of the truck. She was in the ready position when two cowboys rode up the road. The only people we had seen all that day. She still turns red when she thinks about it.

Many years later her courage was tested when she attempted to repair a leaking commode. She again barely survived cardiac arrest. We were in Kulai, Malaysia. We were there for six weeks living on the fish farm that T.F. Tan had constructed to provide additional fish for his Carol Aquarium operation in Singapore. At that time he was the largest shipper from Singapore. I had just retired and had been hired to do some consulting for him and try to solve his production problems. The "John" was not working. Loise bent over the tank and removed the cover. She had not known that a huge and fully adult Tokay gecko (twelve to fourteen inches) lived there. A bite from a Tokay brings getting a finger slammed in a car door to mind. The Tokay leapt at her and hit her at the neckline and shot down the inside of her blouse. Moving at the speed of sound it worked itself downward looking for the floor. It hit the deck at a full reptilian gallop. It was last seen heading north in the direction of Bangkok.

Some ten years earlier Loise and I were in the bush in Colombia on a collecting trip. Feeling the call that night she left camp and supporting herself on the trunk of a tree was visited by the world's rudest iguana. The unfeeling and uninvited monster dropped out of the tree onto her head. She is credited in Guinness's record book as the uncontested holder of the world's record time for the "dash with pants around ankles." None of her friends were ever sure whether or not she is totally unhinged as she kept going back for more.

We left Fred Kyburz the next day for our Villavicencio compound. We saw Fred again the next year when he visited our home in Bradenton, Florida. Fred Kyburz did not live much longer. He had an advanced case of glaucoma. His vision was terrible. One night in a rain storm he left Bitaco and headed down the mountain to Cali. He was killed in an automobile accident. He drove off the road and over a cliff by mistake.

Business at Gulf Fish Farm, with the help of Jack Pearlmen, was booming. We honed our skills and continued to acquire new and rare imports from all over the world. Harry Rambarran in then British Guiana (now Guyana), who I without hesitation rate the number one shipper ever, consistently gave us large amounts of fish in excellent condition that we could always sell profitably.

Brazil in the 1960s had wonderful fish and terrible shippers. Discus were an important item. Losses for everyone were catastrophic. I had learned to handle bad discus while still in New York, but those fish were at least alive. There is little that can be done when half the discus arrive dead. Discus for years came from the firm of Diaz and Lopez in Belem where no discus are to be found. They were sent in from remote areas as Belem was the best (only) place then for export by air.

Later, when Varig Airlines made regular stops at Manaus, the business boomed. The fish were still very bad, but the availability and variety was much improved. Discus were the worst. I interviewed more than one shipper to try to find out what caused the problem. Eventually, I stumbled on the reason. All of the discus were kept in floating wooden cages in the river. The greatest quantity of fish were inventoried during the dry, low water, season. The fish came to the Manaus exporters in good condition, and kept well in the floating cages. The fish did not keep well in their concrete vats. The holding and packing operations were located one hundred feet or more from the river's bank. The problem was at its worst during the dry, collecting season. All the compounds now stood high above the banks of the Amazon. The Amazon moves dramatically, as much as forty feet, up and down during the year. At the highest point the water, the river and the fish are alongside the compound. At low water, the river and the fish are way down a sharp hill. It is quite an experience to look over the side of a canoe during the wet season and see, just under the surface, the top of a living palm tree. The exporters had good discus in the cages. They destroyed them taking them up the hill and releasing them into the shipping boxes. The Indian help carried the discus up the hills as fast as they could run. The discus were piled into dry nets one fish atop the other. They rubbed each others slime from their bodies on the trip up the hill. This, of course, was not apparent to the exporters. Then, almost all of the fish exporters were totally unsophisticated fish handlers. The first shipper to handle the fish properly in Manaus was Willi Schwartz. It took him years before he got the problem solved. The rest followed suite. The problem was cured. Brazil today sends good discus. It has only been in recent years that a fraction of the wonderful variety of fish in Brazil have been offered. People, mostly German writers, hobbyists, and collectors, have found and made available a wonderful variety of new fish. Heiko Bleher, Rainer Stawikowski, and Arthur Werner have introduced most of the new fish. Rosario LaCorte on his four trips did his share of discovering new and wonderful fishes. Harry Rambarran now is in partnership with Adolpho Schwartz who inherited the Aquario Rio Negro compounds in Manaus from his father. Together they do a spectacular fish business, accumulating fish, and shipping from a large holding facility in Miami—a model operation.

For a number of years Iquitos, Peru, had the largest volume of fish available in South America. We first dealt with an English shipper there, named John Rokes, who did a very good job. I also got good fish from Leo Baumer who is now in Miami importing and handling Peruvian fish from his own collecting compounds. Our third shipper was named Arturo Zamorra. Later on Gerry Entel, whose father and mother, Mac and Sue, operated Sumac Fish Hatchery in Miami, became our principal supplier. His fish were by far the best, and he certainly was the most reliable shipper from Iquitos. I enjoyed our weekly contacts when we placed our orders. Gerry has a great sense of humor and a cute wife (Suzie) who was even funnier than he was. Gerry also was the most imaginative shipper in Peru. He sent collectors into new areas (Pucalpa, Peru) to make new fish available.

The Iquitos exporters were an unforgettable crew. I always enjoyed my visits to Iquitos. Iquitos was a very rough spot then. Women were getting kidnapped on the principal streets in town during the day. One day Loise, who I had left writing letters at the hotel, decided to walk to John Rokes's compound. Anna Rokes had a fit when she walked in, unbeknownst to Loise she had just walked through the most dangerous part of town. A large percentage of the population lived (still do) in boats at the rivers edge. Their homes went up and down with the rains. There was only one real hotel in town overlooking the river. It looked like a movie set for a grade B film. A maitre d'hôtel was posted at the entrance to the dining room. He was splendidly dressed (for Iquitos), wearing a tattered formal frock coat that had seen better days with unmatched pants. At every meal he would seat us and ritually present an elaborate printed menu. He then would tell us what they had to offer for dinner. None of the exciting items on the menu were ever available. Invariably we got fish or chicken. The fish was wonderful, and we ate it with relish. It was usually Paiche (*Arapaima gigas*) or Gamitana (Pacu). This last we feel is the best eating fish in South America. The hotel was seldom busy as no one, in those days, came to Iquitos who wasn't a fish or animal dealer. One year in the early 1960s, Loise and I were there on business. The hotel was very busy. Very important looking Peruvians in various uniforms were constantly in meetings at all hours. Naturally we were curious. We learned that they all were very high governmental figures. One man, in a bemedaled white uniform complete with gold braid, had been educated in the United States. His English was perfect. My Spanish never has been, so we talked in English. He was fascinated by what we did with Amazonian tropical fish and we were invited to eat and drink with him every evening when he was not in a meeting. We knew he was a general in the Peruvian air force. Later we learned he was the Commanding General of the Peruvian Air Force. Two weeks later, after our return to Bradenton, our new friend's picture was on the front page of every newspaper in the United States. He was now the President of Peru, as the Junta that had met in Iquitos (to make plans) had successfully toppled the government.

The Iquitos fish and animal people invited Loise and me to be their guests at a private party at the local Chinese restaurant. I had a terrible seat. I could see into the kitchen. It was not clean enough to be called filthy. Dirt floor with the usual pigs and chickens underfoot. With the help of Pisco Sours I shortly couldn't see the dirt in the kitchen. Pisco is a native Peruvian moonshine that someone sometime decided to describe (as a joke??) as a brandy. It tastes as much like brandy as a mixture of warm Dr. Pepper and lighter fluid. It is, however, an effective anesthetic. The Pisco Sours were used to wash down the first "special" drink that had been prepared for us. The presentation liquid was a sickish smelling, green broth that seemed to be etching the glass as steam rose from the potion. We had to drink it before they would tell us the "secret" ingredient. The group watched us with amusement, so we made sure everyone drank it before we did. The secret ingredient was the ground up penis "bone" of a coati mundi. It was reputed to be a powerful aphrodisiac. We were only allowed to drink one glass which did not present any problem. It tasted about how you would expect it to taste and that was disgusting. I never pressed to find out what caused the steam or what the green glop was and I still am not that curious.

Loise is a talented small animal person. She had been keeping and breeding a wide assortment of wild and domestic small mammals for years. She had recently lost a wonderful coati that she had for many years. This animal, "Thurber", would terrify every zoo person who visited us as coatis are not supposed to be easily trained. They are wonderfully bright and affectionate animals. Her Thurber was a much-loved addition to our family. Various zoo people who visited were very wary of him. He had claws like a bear and could have used them. Thurber never so much as scratched anyone. Thurber loved the car and rode everywhere with Loise. He always draped himself across her shoulders in the back of the driver's seat. He could be let out of the house, and would return at her voice command. He had the run of the house during the day. Loise could take fresh food from his mouth. I never was brave enough to try. He returned to his cage at night and while guests were visiting. He was not destructive. Loise only had to say "It's cookie time" and Thurber would get into his cage and wait for his reward. One time when the phone rang delivery of the promised cookie was delayed. Ever afterwards Thurber sat by the cookie jar and waited until Loise had the cookie in hand and was en route to the cage. Then he would run and get into the cage. At night he had a fascinating twenty or thirty minute ritual. Thurber would take his blanket and wrap it around his body. He was meticulous. It had to be draped perfectly. His long tail (his pride and joy) had to be completely concealed. Thurber would totally enclose his body including his tail. Only his black rubber like snout protruded. He spent a lot of his free run time in the caged area around our swimming pool. We knew why. Some time earlier I released a dozen or so exotic lizards in our pool-side rock garden without thinking a lot about it. Thurber, in short order, caught all of my reptilian munchies. He spent years afterwards looking for more. Thurber would get atop the shower by the pool where he'd learned to turn the water on. A coati can work a lock as well as any monkey. They are wonderfully dexterous animals. Thurber sat balanced atop the shower head and stayed dry while he washed his beautiful tail. This was his great delight. He didn't bother learning to turn the water off, but Loise did try to teach him.

The most fun was when Loise would put our menagerie together. None of the animals were ever mean. They played for hours. I have unbelievable movies of some of their antics. The most fun was when Thurber would get on top of Irving (my mixed breed dog who went to the farm with me every day for 17 years) and ride like a rodeo cowboy on a bucking wild steer. He would stay just far enough back so Irving couldn't reach him. He could not be unseated, and usually would manage to remain intact when Irving would roll over. Irving had to make at least three barrel rolls to unseat him. Thurber then would start a wild running game with Whitney, our Persian cat. A stranger would think mayhem was being committed, but it was only an exciting game they both enjoyed. We all missed Thurber when he died of cancer.

This next trip to Iquitos was partly to buy a baby coati. Leo Baumer had a very young litter on hand. Coatis always have four young at a time. Loise decided to take two of them, raise them together, and eventually try to breed them. They were very, very young and not weaned. Chances for survival were slim. Animals are supplied by the local Indians to the dealers in Iquitos. Babies are taken to the animal dealer. The adult goes into the cooking pot. The dealers take these young animals even though they are much too young to have much chance of survival. They buy them for two reasons. If they don't buy them the animal will certainly die or be sold to a competitor. Often the dealer will be able to save their lives. Secondly the dealers did not want to discourage the Indians. The Indians are the source of all the animals they get. All the stories we have been told about "expeditions" into "the great unknown" to "capture animals" are myths. The "great white hunters" set up camp in a promising area, and then use the natives to catch the animals and bring them to them. Very few animals are collected by the commercial collector. The few animals that they may capture are taken by accident rather than by design. It is good business to buy everything offered.

Using a tiny bottle and nipple Loise found in a local shop (it came from a child's toy set), Loise managed to concoct a formula that the four-inch babies thrived on. We named them Gunther and Francis. They travelled all during that trip in her square straw purse. This included the trip through United States Customs in Miami. The two baby coatis arrived back home fat and sassy. I bought, on that same trip, a wonderful collection of pre-Inca pottery that his brother wanted to sell. Leo's brother, Walter, was an engineer who supervised road construction projects on the west coast of Peru. His hobby was collecting ancient burial pots found in the pre-Inca ruins in the Peruvian desert area where he had worked. Walter Baumer was then planning to leave Peru and return to his home in Switzerland. He needed to raise some money. I bought the collection and some time later donated it to Bradenton's South Florida Museum. Loise and I both felt good about gifting the collection. It has become a major exhibit at the museum. This was my initial exposure to pre-Colombian cultures. It stimulated a life long interest. Harry Specht, Al Klee, Russ Norris, Rusty Wessel, and I on the many trips we have made in the last twenty years have always made a visit to pre-Colombian sites part of our fish collecting expeditions.

Mongolian gerbils (*Meriones unguiculatus*) were unknown in the pet industry in 1962. A few had been imported by one of the laboratories breeding and supplying research animals. They were very superior pets when compared to the popular, nocturnal, hamster. Gerbils had a much better disposition. They seldom bit and they would almost certainly sell well. There was one problem. They were very difficult to breed. Loise who has the patience and interest to work and learn was asked to take on the project and learn how to reproduce these animals. She started with two pairs. During the following year our home was filled by an ever increasing supply of captive bred gerbils. Loise wrote the first two books on the subject. She learned the techniques and passed this information and her produced stock amongst a number of commercial breeders. The rest is history.

Alberto Zamorra was another Iquitos supplier. A good shipper with one bad habit that made buying from him difficult. Alberto made imaginative substitutions that created unwanted costs. He was incurable. His great pride was a local catfish he had discovered that he called "Zamorra Cunchi" (Zamorra's catfish). The name had no scientific basis. The fish had no common name until he supplied it. He took great delight when he realized he forced his competitors to supply their customers with Zamorra Cunchi (*Helogenes* sp.). Zamorra went to Miami every chance he could. This was often, as he was a major shipper and he loved Miami. The cargo planes taking the Iquitos fish to Miami always let the major exporters ride free. He told the girls in Miami that he was an Inca prince. It was a great act and it worked for him. He spent more time in Miami than in Iquitos. Zamorra's brother-in law, Carlos Prentis, was the mayor and an amateur taxidermist. The little museum in Iquitos that he managed was interesting and his taxidermy was good, except for the glass eyes. The eyes were all the same size and the same blue color. I'm sure they were all from one box he had ordered from the United States. Every animal he mounted had the same blue eyes. Some were startling and would stop you in your tracks; a small animal's head with eyes that were relatively gigantic or a large animal's head with tiny little eyes. His snakes, birds, monkeys, fish, and even frogs all had identical eyes. He had mounted the most tremendous "*Plecostomus*" anyone had ever seen. I measured it and it was 47 inches long. I have pictures! Wonder what it was?

The Amazon collectors all had wonderful stories about freshwater sharks 20 feet long, and huge catfish that could swallow a man whole. Sharks do enter the river; great huge marine sawfish have also been found way up the river. The largest of the catfish in the Amazon is the Pirahyba (*Brachyplatystoma filamentosum*) which grows to at least six feet with recorded weights of more than three hundred pounds. Add piranha, electric eels, alligators, anacondas, and the dreaded parasitic Candiru to this list and the Amazon certainly becomes an interesting and exciting place to swim.

The freshwater Amazonian pink porpoise is "Boto" (*Inia geoffrensis*) and is commonly found. It is a folk tale accepted by all the Indians that "Boto" is the reincarnated spirit of people that had drowned in the river. Fortunately, for the Inia population, eating this animal is a serious taboo. If native fisherman had hunted them for food they would certainly by now be extinct. These freshwater porpoises are wonderful animals. They make an exciting exhibit in public aquariums. They are small, live in freshwater, and can be displayed easier than the larger marine species. There actually are four species of fresh water porpoises known. All are river dwellers and native to the Ganges, Rio Plata, Yangtze, and Amazon rivers. My old nemesis Mike Tsalikes in Leticia had been sending freshwater porpoises to the United States for several years with little to no success. The demand from public aquariums was in place and the potential profit worthwhile. Mike had tried every way he thought possible. I had two good friends, Dr. Earl Herald at the Steinhart Aquarium and Larry Curtis in Ft. Worth, who had asked me to try to obtain a specimen for them. They had both tried to get one alive from Mike with no success. Emilio Saiz and I talked about it a lot before finally deciding to give it a try. I had no desire to foolishly sacrifice any of these wonderful animals. I had one advantage that we hoped might make the difference. I could instantly place the animal, on arrival, into a large dirt pond and not into a large concrete vat as Mike Tsalikes at Tarpon Zoo was doing. I thought this was a big part of the problem. I knew for the most part that all the animals arrived barely alive and then only survived a few days. Removing the stress quickly might be the answer. We decided not to try to ship an animal unless it was less than five feet in length. Saiz had watched Mike fail repeatedly, and had a pretty good idea of what not to do.

Larry Curtis at Fort Worth had built a special facility for Amazonian porpoises. He had repeatedly failed to get one alive. He also agreed to charter a small plane to take the animal directly from Gulf Fish Hatchery across the Gulf to the Fort Worth Aquarium. I arranged for the charter of a plane in Florida and set the wheels into action. I could actually land the plane on the farm, and then taxi it alongside the pond where the porpoise was being kept. The animal would be placed in a sling to support its internal organs in a huge coffin-like wooden box lined with plastic over soft blankets. Only about forty percent of the animal would be in water. It would be kept wet with towels and personally attended.

Sam Poole agreed to fly from Colombia as low as possible to prevent any cold or pressure problems. When he set down our Flying Guppy in Sarasota, the Inia would be trucked to the farm. There, in less than an hour's time, it would be released into a large pond. Our first attempt appeared to be completely successful. The animal was just a bit over five feet in length. It settled down in its pond breathing and blowing without stress. It was feeding the next day. Almost immediately a Fort Worth employee arrived. Final arrangements were made to fly it to Texas. Everything went as planned. The animal arrived at the Fort Worth Aquarium alive. It could not have been easier. I had told Larry Curtis that if it died within the first thirty days he could tear up the invoice. It did and he did. I never found out why. He reported that the autopsy showed an infestation of flukes in the blow hole. I later found out that this was not uncommon, and I doubt it caused the death. I was sad and discouraged and decided that if I tried it again, I would keep the animal on hand for a good length of time before attempting to ship it. I would not let anyone rush me.

The next attempt was made to the Steinhart Aquarium in San Francisco. There was no live arrival guarantee and the buyer would supervise the packing and routing. The Inia was to go by commercial airline, but would have Dr. Robert Dempster as its attendant for the entire trip. Saiz secured a very young animal just under four feet in length. This small Inia travelled without mishap, and immediately settled down in its pond. My six year old daughter, Jodi, spent most of her free time at the farm and immediately bonded with the other juvenile. Inia have a few stiff hairs on their snout. She named him "Whiskers" and the name stuck. I kept Whiskers for many months in a one-hundred-foot pond immediately adjacent to the hatchery. He would come to the bank and push about a third of his body out of the water. Jodi spent hours with him in and out of his pond. He came immediately to her call and would lift his head so she could rub his "whiskers". Dr. Earl Herald himself came to Gulf to help prepare the animal for shipment to San Francisco. We all hated to see Whiskers go. I decided then that I would not import more of these animals regardless of the result. Bob Dempster and Whiskers took off for Chicago where a transfer was to be made. Dr. William Braker, the director of the Shedd Aquarium, and a loyal friend of Dr. Herald and mine, agreed to support the transfer and do anything that needed to be done if problems arrived. They did as the plane ran into a heavy snow storm and was seriously delayed. Bob Dempster and Whiskers made it to Chicago in a blizzard. Bill Braker and the staff of the Shedd Aquarium were right there to whisk Whiskers to a temporary home at Shedd Aquarium. It took three more anxious days for Bob and Whiskers to get to Steinhart Aquarium. Later Bob Dempster told me that on arrival in San Francisco the porpoise was in better shape than he was. I never imported another porpoise. Many years later Whiskers died of old age at Steinhart. Years later Earl Herald, and others, made a trip to India to try to bring back the freshwater porpoise found in the Ganges River. I had imported some exciting reptiles from a native Indian dealer named Jerry Anderson. I put him in touch with Dr. Herald to help make arrangements. That part worked out, but they didn't manage to get an Indian Inia back alive.

Anderson also dealt in artifacts and antiques. He offered me a quantity of material that he had obtained on a collecting trip he made to Baluchistan in north-western India. I don't know why I bought the collection. I think it must have been the three hundred year old shields he offered that were made of Indian rhinoceros hide. They were neat. I got three of them. They even had silver knobs on them. I also got some hand-carved leather gunpowder flasks, and several wooden carved and inlaid shot containers. That part was fine. I also got about twenty woven rug type blankets that had been used on camel backs for the past three hundred years. They had a stench that was enhanced by Florida's humidity. Dry cleaning over and over again did not work. Loise tried everything. She gave up and loaded them into my car, and told me that she did not want them back in the house again. I took them to the farm and hung three or four on the walls of my office. Pat Casciano, my secretary, walked in holding her nose, and told me it was the rugs or her. I had ten seconds to make a choice. I then put them high up in the rafters in a dry part of the hatchery as far from people as I could. Then I tried to ignore them. No vermin ever attacked them. I am sure one bite of a ripe camel blanket would kill an elephant. If you can imagine someone distilling the juice from fifty pairs of old sweat socks you would be getting close to their stench. I got lucky again.

We had a lady customer from Arcadia, Florida, who ran a combination pet shop and antique store. I always thought this strange, but it seemed to work for her. She admired the rhinoceros hide shields displayed on the office wall and wanted to buy one. I told her she could have it if she would also buy the wonderful three hundred year old antique camel blankets with it. I told her the blankets were in storage and would smell "musty". I did not bring them back to the office. Pat Casciano, my secretary, was watching me. I took my customer (victim) with me into a well-aired area on the loading dock and brought the rugs to her. She bought them all (with one of the rhino shields thrown in) for enough money so that I had the rest of the goodies without cost. I have always wondered if the obviously cursed rugs caused her to go out of business. I never saw her again, and later heard she had gone bust.

Loise and my relationship with Larry Curtis, then the director of the Fort Worth Zoo and Aquarium deserves its own book. He was and is our good friend although he has avoided us for years. I can not blame him. Larry loved catfish and knew a lot about them. He had an extensive collection at the aquarium and was always looking for new varieties. I sent him many of the rare specimens from Brichard and Saiz.

This story starts with an Australian Blue Mountain lorikeet that I obtained in a trade. I had met Rick Naegele, the first curator of the newly opened Busch Gardens Park in Tampa. Rick had called and came to the farm for a visit. He wanted Gulf Fish Hatchery to set up and maintain two large display aquariums that Busch was putting in the area where they handed out free mugs of beer (heavy traffic). One was to be marine and the other freshwater. I could have them serviced by one of our people when they were en route home from a delivery to the Tampa airport. It was only ten minutes out of the way. We did it for years until they gave up on the tanks and the free beer. Importing Psittacine birds were illegal then and no one bred anything much excepting budgies, finches, and cockatiels. Busch Gardens agreed to trade me a surplus baby Blue Mountain Lorikeet. They had raised some and this one was in surplus. It was a spectacular and beautiful bird. Rick gave it to me in trade for three large lion fish and a few anemones. I wanted it to give to Loise as a birthday gift. I could not wait to make the deal. Big mistake. Loise turned out to be the owner of the loudest and most irritating squawking creature in the bird kingdom. Blue Mountain Lorries are fructivorous (fruit eater). I later learned that word when I finally did what anyone, but a total idiot, would have done before getting the bird. I read about the bird after he was in residence. I knew then that no one in their right mind would ever have one for a pet. It was not only terribly dirty, but constantly dirty. This at all times accompanied by a never-ending, spine-chilling screech. I had already learned about the incessant screeching. As it was a gift, Loise was remarkably calm (on the surface) about the animal. I tried not to notice the noise as it was incredibly beautiful and I hoped a family member. Thinking about it now I must say that Loise is a very nice person. It didn't bother me as I was away at work most of the time. We had five kids in residence that summer plus the usual dogs, cats, snakes, and Thurber (Loise's pet coati). One Sunday morning, while everyone was still asleep, Loise was up cleaning around the bird cage. She unexpectedly became the recipient of a tail switch that lathered her face in unexpected and disgusting bird feces. I was still asleep when she pounced on my moribund carcass screaming something into my ear. "She has to go". I was still trying to figure out which child was leaving, when to my relief I learned it was the fructivorous bird.

We sold the bird to a delighted Larry Curtis at the Fort Worth Zoo and this started the curse. Over the next several years he claimed (I think he may have been right) that Loise and I were trying to destroy him. He was happy to get her Blue Mountain Lorikeet, and paid a good price for it. It arrived in Texas in fine shape, was placed in a wrought iron display cage outside his bird building, and was dead before the day was done. It choked on a piece of popcorn given by a visitor who obviously did not think they were serious about the "Do not feed the bird" sign.

Next came the freshwater porpoise death described earlier. Saiz about then sent me "Pickle". This was a baby freshwater Amazonian manatee. It was a tiny baby, barely two feet long, and unweaned. The mother most likely had been harpooned for food. I am sure we got it just in time for Loise to save it. Loise concocted a formula for it. Then she got me a calf bucket (used to feed baby calves when the mother is not available) for her baby food. It worked like magic. Pickle took up residence in Whiskers' old pond. It was happy and shortly able to feed itself. The pond sported newly introduced water hyacinth and these along with a variety of other foods made the baby manatee look like a fat little gray pickle. Larry Curtis had come for a visit and saw the "Pickle" and wanted her. I had not offered it for sale. I was enjoying having it although, after a couple of months, I realized that even a baby manatee was not a thing of beauty. It also was really low on the mammalian intelligence scale. We were offered a good price which we accepted. I was happy as I felt bad about the bad luck the Fort Worth Zoo was having with our animals. Larry agreed to pay in advance. We, in turn, would keep Pickle for two or three more months while the Fort Worth Aquarium built a special exhibit. I guaranteed live arrival (only). They built a big glass fronted exhibit tank. The animal was wonderfully visible from above and also could be viewed through a front glass panel. The exhibit was decorated with large pieces of drift wood. Pickle was dead that night. She swam to the bottom, jammed herself under one of the large drift wood pieces that had been concreted into the floor. She quickly drowned! ..... We were all sad at the news and wished we had kept her in the pond at the farm.

Gulf Fish Hatchery was now handling a good variety of reptiles and amphibians. I had a shipper in Barranquilla named Jaime Zambrano who sent us baby caiman, and handled baby iguana. He also sent all sizes of boa constrictors, and a large variety of other herps. I'd stopped handling baby iguana years before as the animals were so badly abused before being shipped that only a small percentage could acclimate. The Indians accumulate them for the dealers. They were never fed and were weak to the point of death by the time they were shipped to us. They were doomed. We decided that if we could not get good healthy animals we would not handle them again. We never got good ones and we never handled them. That has all changed now and wonderful, healthy animals are available in almost every pet shop.

Our reptile supplier, Jaime Zambrano, had his shipments cleared through customs and then forwarded by a friend (?) in Miami, who did the trans-shipping for him. Zambrano always swore he knew nothing about the bags of marijuana that were concealed in snake bags in the snake boxes. These bags were nailed down in the rear of the snake boxes. Each box would have four or five bags of snakes in it, plus the "special" bags that were tacked to the rear of the side to be opened. Great plan. I have no idea how long it had been working. What customs inspector would be fool enough to stick his hands into a box of snakes especially since the bags he could see and feel were full of snakes. When it was discovered, by one of the newly employed dogs, we got a visit from the drug enforcement people. We finally convinced them that the "pot" was offloaded in Miami before we ever got the shipments. Thank God!

Some short time afterwards Jaime Zambrano came up with what he claimed was the largest Boa constrictor anyone had ever seen. I could have it for the special price of $75. It turned out to be a real monster. I called Larry Curtis and told him that we had a Boa that was just a shade under thirteen feet. It turned out to be the second largest red-tail Boa ever recorded (alive). He couldn't wait to buy it. We found a late night cargo plane to take it to the Fort Worth Zoo. We repacked it into the special large bag, and the wooden crate it had come to us in, and off it went to Fort Worth. The weather was chilly in Florida at that time of the year and the monster snake was easy to handle. That is one thing I learned after the fiasco at General Aquatic in Brooklyn years earlier with Jardine's sixteen-foot gift anaconda. That, of course, is to cool reptiles down before handling. Cold acts as a tranquilizer. Boas are very different from anacondas. Boas are smaller but much thicker. Anacondas grow much longer (up to 30 feet) and always stay relatively thin. An almost-thirteen-foot Boa is a huge, thick, powerful snake, and much more dangerous than a thirty-foot Anaconda. Either one is large enough to kill a grown and careless man.

Larry Curtis picked up the giant snake at the airport. The cargo flight had arrived in the middle of the night. He had the cargo people load the crate into his nice warm station wagon. To make sure it was alive and that he had time before unloading at the zoo he had brought a pry bar along to open the crate and inspect the snake. He checked and it was very much alive and well. The heated vehicle made it very happy. Curtis had his girl friend with him for company, and took her on a tour (?) of the zoo for several hours, while waiting for his help to arrive to handle the monster snake. It was a warm night in Texas. He did not close the car windows. When the crew arrived to take the snake to its display cage, it had escaped. An almost thirteen foot Boa constrictor is no joke. The snake stayed hidden for almost eight hours while a good part of the Fort Worth Police and Fire Department helped the zoo's personnel search for it. He made the news that day.

The two infant coatis (Gunther and Francis) that Loise had brought back from Iquitos, were now almost grown. They were completely tame and never mean, but they never became real pets. Loise realized that having each other, they did not need her. When out of their cage they streaked around the house and were just too exuberant to be left out for long. This was not satisfactory for any of us. Larry Curtis was asked if he wanted them. They were perfectly tame. The zoo was delighted to get them. The big mistake was made when Dr. Curtis decided on one of his fundraising programs to include the zoo's new additions. Gunther and Francis would be part of the live exhibit he used to spice up his program. The meeting was held at the Nieman Marcus lunch pavilion. You guessed it. Gunther and Francis had no trouble escaping from their cage which had not been properly fastened. Coati mundi are very agile animals. Not only can they undo what you would think is a secure lock, but once free in a big department store recapture was several notches above impossible. They caused a lot of damage. It was late that night, after the store had been closed for hours, that they finally surrendered. The ravages inflicted on the candy department finally slowed them down enough to get them caught. A coati will do anything for sweets. They were then so full of food that they were waddling and hardly running. A mostly hysterical Larry Curtis (I got lucky and was not home) got Loise on the phone. She told me it wasn't easy to understand him as he was blubbering a lot. What was clear was that he had asked Loise for her solemn pledge that no matter how much he begged her, she would not ever let him have any of her animals. If Larry didn't have bad luck dealing with us, he would not have had any luck at all.

Importing from the Far East by air was terribly hazardous as heavy fish mortality could almost always be expected. This remained true until the advent of jet airplanes. In the early 1950s we could import into New York from the Philippines. In Florida, after trying direct imports and failing repeatedly from Hong Kong, Singapore, and Bangkok it became apparent that this was a sure path to the poorhouse. There were few flights. No one in the airline industry paid any attention. If everything worked out (it seldom did) and the shipment made the connections (they seldom did) the airlines would often finish you off by putting the fish boxes in unheated cargo areas and avoid paying claims by calling it "an act of God". Pan American was the worst. The only fighting chance we had was with foreign carriers, and Sabena, Japan Air, K.L.M., and S.A.S. were the most reliable. There were responsible shippers in London (Bowler, Whitwell, Smykala) who handled large quantities of Singapore fish (and later some from Bangkok). They reconditioned them there, and sent the fish on to New York. That worked fine when I was in New York. Buying Far Eastern fish via London trans-shipped through New York to Florida consistently caused losses.

I had met and liked a Chinese dealer from Singapore named Harris Teo. He visited me in New York at General Aquatic Supply about 1953. We had tried several direct imports from Singapore to New York. It was not profitable. When I relocated in Florida he was the first man I wrote to as the Singapore to London to New York to Florida shipments were almost always bad. The alternative was to again try fish from Singapore to Florida via California. Together, starting in 1957, we experimented with small shipments. Results were bad to start, and certain important items like *Rasbora heteromorpha* were unprofitable for years. Concentrating on the fish that traveled the best we could and did import from Singapore. The Singapore fish really helped Gulf Fish

Hatchery sell its own produced fish so there were indirect benefits that were not easy to measure. Teo Way Yong and Sons were the best and largest of the Far Eastern dealers. Harris Teo ran the business with his four brothers. The family was tenth generation residents of Singapore. The family had been in the tropical fish business since the early 1930s, then when they supplied most of the fish that went to Europe and the United States by water.

By the time I entered the tropical fish business the transport of tropical fish by ship was drying up. The better the airline service became the less sense it made for anyone to handle fish by ship.

The very first commercial boat shipment of aquarium fish was made by Paul Nitsche. This took place in 1893. Nitsche was then the chairman of "Triton". Triton was an early Aquarium Society located in Berlin, Germany. The strange thing about this first shipment is that it went the wrong way. It went from Germany to South America. The plan was to get South American fish to Germany. The contact was in Buenos Aires, Argentina, and was with a German friend of Nitsche who had settled there. The fish were to be sent from Argentina to Germany in special containers. These were constructed in Berlin and were made of sheet metal. The containers were sent to Argentina and, even though there was no great interest in tropical fish in Argentina, the cans were filled with ornamental fish. The trip to Argentina took an incredible 53 days. The ship was delayed leaving Europe, and when it arrived in Buenos Aires there was a cholera outbreak that caused an additional nine-day quarantine. The six cans sent were approximately twenty inches square and contained 234 fish. The fish were all cold water specimens and consisted of orfe, sunfish, minnows, goldfish, stonefish (?), and paradise fish. A nameless man accompanied the shipment. He could, and did, aerate the cans with a hand device. The cans were stowed on the open deck. The cans were filled on the 14th of September 1893, and unloaded on the 7th of November 1893. It is a testament to the hardiness of fish that of the 234 fish sent, a remarkable 180 survived. Most of the losses were attributed to salt water intrusion caused by a severe storm that swept sea water over the boat into the cans numerous times. There was no additional freshwater to make water changes. The water was filtered and reused. Unfortunately, little detail is known about this first water shipment of fish. We do know that a return shipment was scheduled for May of 1894, but I do not know if it ever happened. I suspect it happened and was a disaster. There was no further report given in the Triton Society bulletin. However, some of the very first South American fish that arrived in Germany included at least three Argentinean species. These included the chanchito (*C. facetum*), Buenos Aires tetra (*H. caudovitattus*), and the Port cichlid (*Aequidens portalegrensis*). My guess would be that they were bred from the few survivors of a second shipment. I ran into Paul Nitsche's name again in a report (1898) about the very first livebearing fish, *Gambusia affinis*, imported to Germany. Evidently, the sex differences were not known. It took Nitsche three frustrating years of trying to breed all males before he discovered his error.

Harris Teo and I were good friends. He was the third close Chinese friend that I had made in the fish industry. Earl Kennedy in the Philippines was the first, Peter Tsang in Australia was the second. I dealt with Harris Teo for many, many years, and we never had a problem. Good experiences were duplicated over and over. The business transactions we had with Chinese dealers all over the Far East have always been good. As a group, the Chinese fish exporters are the world's best and most efficient suppliers. Certainly they are the most honest. Almost every year Harris came to the United States to visit his customers. He always stayed at our house for several days. He carried with him what he called his "coolie outfit". This was his car-washing uniform. His passion was washing cars. He loved to wash cars. He could never wash cars in Singapore as he would lose face. I am sure we greatly impressed our neighbors when they saw this authentic Chinese car washing machine singing away while washing our three cars like they had never been washed before. He spent the best part of a day doing just this on every visit. It took years for us to learn why Harris always brought Loise a big box of hand appliquéd linen tablecloths and napkins. Loise still has some of them in use. Some years earlier Harris had invested considerable monies in a business in Taiwan that produced these linens. The linen business had gone bankrupt. All Harris could salvage was a vast amount of unsold product that he spent years giving away. I remember our first visit to Singapore. I tried to find out from Harris how the collectors captured Kuhlii loaches. As is the case with almost all of the fish exporters around the world, Harris had no clue as to how anything got caught. All he knew and cared about was that the fish got delivered to his holding compound. He did try and never was able to find out for me. I have tried for many years now, and still do not know how Kuhlii loaches are caught in the wild. Early on I discovered that Kuhlii loaches would pool breed in Florida. I had some that had reproduced in quantity in a dirt pond. I never knew just how many as I never could catch more than a few. I discovered I had them just as winter arrived and lost the pool to the cold before I could learn anything. I did see lots of dead ones then. I determined not to try again until I had some idea as to how to remove them from the ponds. I still do not know how to do this. I learned from Rabaut that a half coconut shell open end down in an aquarium would collect every single Kuhlii loach. A quick swipe with a net as you lift the shell takes every single one, if you coordinate the swipe with a quick lift. Another frustration in my Singapore dealings was my inability to obtain female long-fin glassfish (*Gymnochanda filamentosa*). I knew from Dr. Günther Sterba's book "**Freshwater Fishes of the World**" that only the males had the wonderful elongated dorsal and anal fin filaments. The only fish exported from Singapore were males. No one ever saw a female. I was particularly interested as I felt certain (and still do) that these fish would reproduce in dirt ponds, as three other glassfish species that I tried had all pond bred. I still have never seen a live female. The closest I have come is the color photo (page 500, plate 135) in Sterba's book. Things changed rapidly in Singapore during the period from 1960 to 1980. Wild caught fish now became a small percentage of the product shipped. Produced fish made up almost ninety percent of all the fish shipped. Jet planes cut the elapsed time dramatically. Labor intensive items that Florida could not competitively produce became the principal foundation of a greatly expanded Singapore fish industry. Fancy guppies, other hybrid livebearers, and angelfish became the important production items. Singapore rivals the United States in the production of new items and has introduced many very successful hybrids such as lyretail mollies, red chromide cichlids, albino Kribensis, and wonderful new strains of livebearing fish. All sorts of longfin sports have been made into strains such as longfin Oscars and kissing gouramis. Most disappeared fast (thank God) as they are ugly and no improvement to existing strains.

Until recent years all of the clown loaches shipped came from Singapore. They were imported from Sumatra and a few from Borneo. Now Indonesia can and does send them directly to the world markets.

A young Fred Cochu (1937)

A really bad, but unique photo of Fred Cochu (right) and Herb Woolf picking fish in 1943.

Fred Cochu (second in line) with an almost 29-foot python he sold to the Bronx Zoo in 1940.

Cochu shipment (1935) by water.
Hamburg, Germany to New York City.

PARAMOUNT HIGHLIGHTS

1929 - 1939: over 250 shipments from Germany
1934: Paramount Aquarium, Inc. is founded
1936: Fred Cochu flies first shipment of neon tetras to Lake Hurst, N.J. on the Hindenburg. The lone surviving tetra of the trip became famous and was named "Lonely Lindy" by an adoring public.
1937: The first of 204 expeditions up the Amazon by Fred Cochu for Paramount.
1939 - 41: Fred travels the Far East, supplies rare animals for Frank Buck, and brings shipment of fish from Singapore.
1939 - 47: Paramount worked for the government trapping electric eels
Stocked the Pittsburgh Aquarium Society's new aquarium with fresh water dolphins and other rare fish.
1946 - Fred Cochu explores Nigeria and introduced for the first time the elephantnose, the butterfly, the upsidedown cat, the rope fish, and many others.
1955: Fred Cochu and Paramount discovered and introduced the cardinal tetra
1961: Paramount leads expedition to King Salmon, Alaska for Beluga whales for New York Zoological Society.
1966: Expedition for Niagra Falls Aquarium to Rio Negro for fresh-water porpoises.
1969: Paramount delivered 21 porpoises to Sweden.
1970's: Fred Cochu made several trips up the Amazon to improve and modernize Paramount's collecting stations.

SPECIALS

(In Box Lots)

Corydoras	.18 (150 to box)
Neon tetras	.06 (400 to box)
Silver hatchets	.20 (150 to box)
Gold Tetras	.13 (200 to box)
Anostomus	1.00 (40 to box)
Plecostomus	.35 (75 to box)
Angelicus	.65 (75 to box)
Black mollies	.07 (150 to box)
Sunset variatus	.12 (200 to box)
Redtail sharks	.28 (200 to box)
Show bettas	.59 (25 Minimum)
Glass cats	.49 (25 Minimum)
Select multicolor show guppies	.69 pair (25 Minimum)

Packing: Styrofoam Boxes, $2.00 each

SOME IMPORT PRICES COULD VARY SLIGHTLY
PRICE LIST WILL BE UP-DATED EVERY SIX MONTHS

The AQUARIUM
Color Plate by Wm. T. Innes
THE NEON TETRA
Hyphessobrycon innesi MYERS
November, 1936
Vol. V No. 7
Price, 20c
Copyright, 1936, Innes Publishing Co.

* * * THE STAR OF 1936 * * *

in the Aquarium World

NEON TETRAS

(SEE FRONT COVER ILLUSTRATION)

Here At Last! in sufficient numbers to make it possible for enterprising dealers in choice species to supply their discriminating customers with something *absolutely new and unequalled.*

Wherever shown, this brilliant species is conceded to be the most gorgeous of all small Tropical Aquarium Fishes. In addition to its startling beauty and good disposition, this fish is active and durable.

Once before we brought a small shipment of NEON TETRAS to the United States. On that occasion they came here via France and Germany on the airship "Hindenburg," especially for the Shedd Aquarium in Chicago, where they were received with enthusiasm. NOW we are in a position to offer NEON TETRAS to dealers at a price within the reach of everybody.

Besides the NEON TETRA we received a large collection of other rare varieties direct from South America.

PARAMOUNT
AQUARIUM *Incorporated*
21 State Street New York City

"THE HOME OF THE NEON TETRA IN U. S. A."

ADVANCE INFORMATION

SOME MONTHS AGO, we secured a few specimens of a marvelous little Tetra, which we believe to be the most beautiful fish introduced into the aquarium in many years. Everyone seeing it is most enthusiastic. The color plate on the front page, featured from an advance copy of THE AQUARIUM, gives some idea of its beauty, but not fully. Mr. Innes, who made this color plate, states that it is impossible to portray with printing inks the extreme beauty of this fish. The brilliant green line along the side of the fish, contrasting vividly with the splash of red along the sides (which goes all the way under the fish), makes a startling effect, which has been well described by the word "Neon," as it looks very much like Neon lights.

From the front view, the fish presents the appearance of having two bright little lamps in its head. This is a metallic reflection from the eyeballs.

Whenever a new fish is announced and described in THE AQUARIUM, the sale is very much stimulated. For this reason, we are taking this step to advise you in advance so that you can stock up with some of these wonderful fishes in time to receive orders which are sure to come. Your early response will be much to your advantage.

This fish has two great advantages. It is tough, practically none of them having been lost in shipment over a great distance from its native waters. Also, it retains its color at all times and does not turn pale when frightened, as many fishes do, which spoils their value as show specimens.

This was an expensive fish to secure, and we had to pay a high price to get it. By arrangement with the collector, who is the only one knowing where to get the fish, there will be no further importations for a period of a year. This will assure you that there will be no risk of later shipments from outside sources being sold at cut prices.

PRICES:

In quantities less than one dozen	$3.00 each
In dozen lots	2.50 each
In 50 lots	2.25 each
In 100 lots	2.00 each

PARAMOUNT AQUARIUM, INC.
21 STATE STREET NEW YORK CITY

Gulf Fish Hatchery crew (1962)

Jim Briggs, Captain Sam Poole, and Ross Socolof (left to right).
The "Flying Guppy" – 1958

Gulf Fish Hatchery's Ronda Island compound in Leticia, Colombia (1957)

I think more clown loaches have died before being sold than all other wild caught fish added together. Clown loaches are amongst the most beautiful of all freshwater fishes. They are also among the most difficult to handle. Not only are they susceptible to "Ich", but have no scales to protect their body. They get "Ich", and it then spreads like wildfire on their unprotected scaleless bodies. The standard cures that worked well on other fish did not work on clown loaches. It took a while for us to understand that the Mercurochrome malachite green and other aniline dyes that cured "Ich" were poisoning these scaleless fish. It was a case of curing the ailment and killing the patient at the same time. Heat alone will work. This speeds up the "Ich" protozoan's life cycle to the point where the parasite will die before it can find a new host. The temperature is critical, and just below the point where the fish would die, 90–94 °F will work. By siphoning the bottom of the tanks frequently you can remove the eggs while still in the resting stage (tomites), and before they hatch to become free swimming. If the fish density is high it is necessary to increase aeration as hot water holds little dissolved oxygen. This procedure will work although it is an unsatisfactory solution. The problem is adjusting temperatures delicately, and then carefully monitoring the procedure. There is slight margin for error between cured fish and cooked fish. Clown loaches seasonally spawn in the Djambi River on the island of Sumatra. They are easily caught and astronomical numbers are sent to Djakarta to dealers there who sent them on to Singapore. They were horribly overcrowded and great percentages of clown loaches never made it out of Djakarta. Those that did more often than not had "Ich". The trick was to get them to the United States before they made it to fish heaven. The problem still exists, but is almost under control. I never made money with clown loaches, and doubt that any of the other early importers did any better. I never have visited Djambi in Sumatra. The one chance I did have, gave Loise and me a choice between Sumatra and Bali. I have never been sorry that Loise and I went to Bali. It was an exciting experience. We got to see Bali before they had a large hotel on the island ... charming!

Munuf Talib Ardan was a young Indonesian government fisheries officer who visited us under the auspices of the United Nations in 1959. He studied our Gulf Fish Hatchery operation and later we stayed in touch when he returned to Sumatra. He did not remain for long as a government employee, but left to go into the clown loach business.

He eventually became the largest dealer on Sumatra. I always have regretted that we did not get to see each other again. He sent us, via Peter Chia, our shipper in Djakarta, twelve gigantic, full-grown breeder clown loaches, as a gift. I never knew they would grow that large. I have never seen anything even remotely that big again. I knew I could not get them back alive. They were just too big. I had to leave them. I am sure you have noticed that I have not said how large these giant clown loaches were and I won't. I did not measure them and I am sure they have grown six more inches in my memory in the intervening years. I will say that clown loaches are one of the few fish that grow much larger in the wild than in the aquarium. I did bring with me a wonderful handmade miniature Indonesian fishing boat replica under full sail. It had been made in a glass bottle. The boat has three sails and on the sails are these words "Welcome to Indonesia — Ross and Loise Socolof from your friend Manuf Talib Ardan". It is a gift we treasure and still have in our home.

Ferdinand (Fred) Cochu was the dominant figure in the tropical fish business in the United States and probably in the entire world for forty years. This lasted from the middle 1930s until he slowed down in the late 1970s. I just reread that and it is all wrong as Fred, even in 1994, was still not retired. In fact, he had me chasing around trying to find him a book on raising bullfrogs as that was his next planned project. In recent years he had two cancer operations, and was almost totally blind from a severe stroke, has had his heart stop several times, and he reported that he had to have it "jump started". Until the end he was amazingly sharp. His memory recalled in great detail. His accomplishments during his long life were truly amazing. Our industry members all reap the benefits of his pioneering work. He died late in 1994 at age 84.

He was born in Hamburg, Germany in 1910. He was named Ferdinand after his father who had a mixture of Danish and French ancestors. His mother, Minna, was Danish. He emigrated to the United States in June of 1929, and became a citizen in 1937. The year before leaving Hamburg he worked as an apprentice in an import-export firm. He learned the intricacies of freight forwarding under difficult conditions. This training was of great help to him during his entire business career.

The largest tropical fish business in the world at that time was Aquarium Hamburg. His older sister worked there as the office manager. She married Hugo Schnelle who was an equal partner with Dr. Walther Griem in that amazing enterprise. Fred Cochu spent a great deal of time, starting in 1925 when he was 15, working part time at Aquarium Hamburg. The owners of Aquarium Hamburg, Dr. Walther Griem and Hugo Schnelle, both tried to interest Fred in becoming a permanent employee. Fred Cochu only then worked for Aquarium Hamburg. He worked closely with them for all the years until World War Two, but never again was an employee as generally believed. It was a very good and mutually profitable business association. Fred wanted to see the world. Fish, as a business, were the farthest thought in his mind in the late 1920s. At 18 he emigrated to the United States.

At 17, shortly before leaving Germany (1927), he was present when an ex-Berliner named Bill Sternke visited Aquarium Hamburg. Sternke came there to sell new and exciting fish he had brought to Germany from his newly-built fish hatchery in America (Florida). Cochu met and talked to Sternke about the United States and Florida. The interest he had in visiting the United States was solidified after this chance meeting. The gigantic wild Florida green sailfin mollies Sternke had with him were so outstanding that even seventy years later Fred said that he could still see them clearly in his mind's eye. In later years Sternke and Cochu remained close friends, and often spoke about that strange and fortuitous meeting in 1927.

Cochu had no real plans past getting a job when he arrived in New York, so he could eat regularly and learn to speak English. His first job was as a dishwasher in a run down restaurant. In the next few years he got better and better jobs in the restaurant business as his skills and his English improved. He was a dishwasher at the Roadside Rest in Long Beach on Long Island. Next, he became a busboy at the Bear Mountain Inn in Tarrytown, New York. Before he left that job he had been promoted to waiter. Next stop was as an assistant chef in a restaurant in Rockville Center, Long Island. He then got a big break and, as a full time waiter, was hired at the newly opened Hotel New Yorker in Manhattan. He now was able to earn enough to save money and he did. He was sure that in a few years he could open his own restaurant.

The head waiter at the Hotel New Yorker took a liking to Fred. It was now Prohibition and he gave a special extra job to Fred. Fred was instructed to look for, pick up, and bring to the head waiter any bottle of "illegal" whisky he could find. He was to wait until the owners left their table to dance. Then the bottle, which was almost always under the table, was removed. The owner would complain and Fred would send them to the head waiter. The head waiter would then let them buy their whisky bottle back for a good tip. Fred made a great amount of extra money doing this special prohibition job. He was now earning ten to twelve dollars every night and saving most of it.

Prohibition ended in late 1932 and the big money stopped. It was replaced by the Great Depression. Fred realized that the restaurant business he planned to enter now made no sense at all. While trying to decide what he would do next he took advantage of the opportunity, and made a trip back to Germany to visit his mother. While in Germany he decided that on his return to the United States to try the tropical fish business. He had wonderful support from Aquarium Hamburg. He planned to buy all his fish from them and they in turn would turn over their American customers. The three best customers were Otto Beltz in St. Louis, Charles Tricker in New York, and Garden Pet on Long Island. He returned to New York (1933) and started a business. He had met Christopher Coates, the young director of the New York public aquarium, then located in Battery Park in Manhattan. Coates suggested that Fred locate in the area. He rented 800 square feet in a sub-basement at 21 State Street in New York City. The space was next to the boiler room. He never had heat problems. The rental of $12.50 a week included electricity, water, and heat. He bought material and built angle iron racks. He next bought 40 aquariums of 20 gallons each and filled them with water. This done he left the next day by boat for Germany where he bought and brought back 70 cans of fish from Aquarium Hamburg. He sold them quickly and profitably. The new business was called the Paramount Aquarium, and he never looked back. He represented Aquarium Hamburg, and had their fish to sell. This was the start. It worked wonderfully well. In the next five years a great deal of his time was spent travelling back and forth to Germany by boat, where he personally chose his fish at Aquarium Hamburg. He made, during those years, almost one hundred trips between New York and Hamburg. His business prospered. He hired his first employee who stayed with him until he retired. This was Marius Kramer, an expert fish man, who had been working for the Aquarium Stock Company in Manhattan for $15 a week. Fred gave him $16 a week, and Kramer worked seven days a week, but only a half day on Sunday. Cochu also was buying domestically produced fish for his own account from Bill Sternke, Albert Greenberg, and Herb Woolf in Florida. He also got fish from the many small hatcheries around New York City. Customers were encouraged to come and buy and then take the fish back, using the subway. As many good customers could not or would not come to the Paramount warehouse, he delivered many fish himself, using the subway.

Aquarium Hamburg was then the only large global tropical fish operation. Aquarium Hamburg had since the early 1920s developed contacts world wide. A steady stream of wild fish came to them from all over the world. The Far Eastern fish were transported by Aquarium Hamburg employees who they had trained. At one time in the middle 1930s shipments from Singapore to Aquarium Hamburg came in quantities that reached an amazing 500 German fish cans in each shipment. Shipments arrived about once a month. A record of one such shipment exists and I reproduce the list of the content of that shipment in 1935. 500 *Barbus pentazona*, 2500 *Barbus tetrazona*, 30 *Barbus lineatus*, 12,000 *Rasbora heteromorpha*, 800 *Rasbora maculata*, 400 *Rasbora* species, 3,000 bumble bee gobies, 250 *Gobius sadanundio*, 1,500 Leeri gourami, 4 chocolate gourami, 1,000 kissing gourami, 15 *Betta fasciata*, 500 glass catfish, 3 clown loaches, 800 green Scats, 50 puffers, 120 archerfish, and 80 marine coral fish.

No one could compete with them. Water weight was no problem then as it is now using air transport. The fish cans each held three gallons of water. Each can was supplied with an air stone. The fish were not packed heavy. Water was siphoned and replaced each day. Minimal feeding was done daily when each can was inspected. Fish were packed in quantities large enough to arrive alive, and then to be quickly and profitably sold. Larger items such as archerfish were packed 40 in a can. Varieties such as *Rasbora heteromorpha* were packed 250 to the can. These shipments from Singapore were always accompanied by two Aquarium Hamburg employees. The trip took 18 days. In addition, as the years passed, word increasingly spread about this part time business. Crews from ships worldwide provided people that brought fish to Germany. This resulted in a small and steady supply of other exotic fishes from many independent maritime entrepreneurs.

As early as 1931, Griem had been in West Africa. He brought back the first upside down catfish, elephant nosed fish, rope fish, knife fish, lungfish, and wonderful killifish with exotic names such as Cap Lopez, Golden Pheasants, and Blue Gularis. Unfortunately service and suppliers prevented this area from developing until after World War Two.

Fish from South America, which held the most varieties and most sought after fish, were a problem that wasn't easily solved. Fish from British Guiana and Brazil could be sold in large quantities if anyone could get them. In 1932 Walther Griem and his brother Karl (who lived in Rio de Janiero) made a collecting trip up the Amazon. They learned a lot, collected wonderful fish, and decided to try to organize a steady flow of fish to the United States and Germany. They had caught headstanders, *Metynnis*, Oscars, leaf fish, pencil fish, hatchet fish, *Corydoras*, *Plecostomus*, and all other sorts of new and odd catfish, *Chalceus*, *Abramites*, *Anostomus*, *Leporinus fasciatus*, *Hemiodus*, *Prochilodus*, and many others not known to the hobby. They knew that even at the height of a worldwide depression, all of these could be sold fast and profitably. The most exciting fish Griem brought out was the discus fish. They most likely had never before been seen alive in the United States. A few had been imported into Germany as early as 1921 by Eimecke, but these did not survive. There is no record of any spawning in Europe until well into the 1930s. Griem caught these first specimens in Santarem, Brazil, on the Amazon River. Twelve adult specimens made up the importation. The discus were packed singly. Each in a separate large fish can. All twelve survived. The Griems stopped in New York City, and disposed of a large part of the shipment. Eight of the discus were sold to the Empire Tropical Fish Company at the unheard of price of $150 each. This in 1933, when a normal job paid ten dollars a week. Innes put the discus on the cover of his April 1933 issue of "**The Aquarium**" magazine. In late 1933 the first spawning was reported by Gustav Armbruster, a commercial angelfish breeder in Philadelphia. No fish were raised. Dwight Winter reported in a story in the August 1934 issue of **The Aquarium** magazine that after four unsuccessful spawns he had success with the fifth discus spawning.

When in New York, the brothers Griem met and made arrangements with an experienced German fish man. This was Carl Mertens who was then living in Manhattan. He knew the American fish market.

Mertens would handle the new Brazilian fish from New York City. The Griem brothers first called their new venture H. & K. Griem and operated out of Rio De Janiero. Now, a separate and new company was formed called Amazonica, Inc. It was located at 61 Whitehall Street in New York City. Karl Griem handled the South American end and transported the fish. Mertens would warehouse, sell, and distribute the fish. They were in business early in 1934. They had trouble from the start. They had to learn expensive lessons by experience. Weather was a major problem. Learning the months of the year when they could and could not obtain fish was critical. They made a lot of mistakes. They had problems keeping any quantity of fish alive waiting for the next exportation. Nothing worked well. This, again, was the story of the blind dog in the meat house that could smell the meat and could not find it. Karl Griem, who had health problems, was doing more than he was physically able to do. They did introduce some wonderful new fish. Try as they did, and they certainly did try, they never were able to make frequent shipments. They operated for almost three years and then Karl Griem's health broke down completely.

By this time (1937) Fred Cochu had hired Auguste Rabaut, the discoverer of the neon tetra. They were bringing fish into New York from Brazilian areas much further west for his Paramount Aquarium. Amazonica floundered on. Fred Cochu, on one of his trips early in 1937 found his friend Karl Griem (in Belem) almost dead from typhoid fever. He managed to get him back to Germany alive. Karl eventually recovered. He had had enough of the fish business in Brazil. He was delighted to sell the business, Amazonica, to Paramount Aquarium. Mertens, who Fred Cochu described to me as an ardent Nazi, returned to Germany. From that point forward Fred Cochu dominated the market, and for the next twenty years did a wonderful business, continuously stimulating the hobby with new fish.

In British Guiana in the 1930s there was only a part time shipper and full time bartender named Pincus. He dealt in tropical fish and provided fish to Paramount and Aquarium Hamburg. Again transportation was the problem. Enough fish were seen to convince everyone that British Guiana would one day supply many fish. The Demerara River near Georgetown was alive with a wonderful assortment of tropical fish. Nothing much happened there until ten years after World War Two when Leonard Rafferty and Louis Chung both started shipping fish by air. Until then almost all the British Guiana fish came by water. There were no direct flights to anywhere from Georgetown.

The bulk of the fish taken to the United States from Aquarium Hamburg in the 1930s by Fred Cochu, were tank raised fish. Aquarium Hamburg produced a lot of them. They also were the major buyers in Germany of similar fish raised for them by many small hatcheries. The depression was worldwide. Money was scarce. Aquarium Hamburg thrived and so did Fred Cochu and his new Paramount Aquarium. By picking his own fish Cochu had a tremendous advantage over competition in the USA. The German bred fish he offered were the best available.

In 1935 Auguste Rabaut had brought from Brazil to Paris the first small shipment of an amazing new fish that he had discovered. Rabaut had been scratching out a living in the jungles of Brazil when he happened on the fish. He was then primarily engaged collecting the livers of the caiman. I am not sure who or what for (perfume?). In addition he had his Indians collect specimens of the large and breathtaking Blue *Morpho* butterflies. The market for these two commodities enabled him to almost make a living. One of the butterfly collectors told him that nearby he could show him tiny fish with the same reflective blue color as *Morpho* butterflies. Rabaut was then almost at the western border of Brazil. The little town there is named Tabatinga. Located nearby was the small army base at Benjamin Constant. He took some of these jewel-like fish with him when he returned to France.

The fish were sold in Paris to J.S. Neel of the firm Lepant. The name "Neon" was the inspiration of Neel and it stuck as it described the neon reflections of the brilliant green and red coloration. Neel offered these first neon tetras to Walther Griem of Aquarium Hamburg who went to Paris and bought all of the fish that were there. It was only a small number (less than 50). Rabaut realized that he could do better with these little neon fish than with the caiman livers, and decided to return to Tabatinga to try to get enough neon fish to make a worthwhile profit.

Fred Cochu was in Hamburg at that time buying fish. He saw these first neon tetras. He was, for the first time, going to take a shipment back to the United States by dirigible. Griem asked him to take six living neon tetras back to the United States on the gigantic airship "Graf Spey". These fish were to be a gift to Dr. Walter Chute of the Shedd Aquarium in Chicago and Dr. William Innes the editor of

The Aquarium magazine. This trip did not turn into a disaster. That happened, only days later, on the very next and last flight when the sister airship Hindenberg exploded on arrival in Lakehurst, New Jersey. That explosion killed all the passengers. Fred arrived in one piece. Unfortunately, the neon tetras did not do as well as Fred. Only one fish survived. This fish was named "Lonely Lindy" by an imaginative reporter inspired by Charles Lindbergh. It received a lot of publicity. Dr. George Myers described the fish from the dead specimens. He named the neon tetra (*Hyphesobrycon innesi*) to honor Dr. Wiliam Innes. This was published in July of 1936.

Rabaut, who had decided he had discovered something really good, was already back up the Amazon collecting neon tetras for his own account. He brought the next shipment to New York, as it was not only a faster trip but a warmer trip. The boat docked in Staten Island. He had previously contacted Dr. William Innes, who recommended Fred Cochu of Paramount Aquarium to him as a reliable and honest distributor. Both Dr. Innes and Fred Stoye, who was then an editor of Innes's, and later published an excellent magazine "Home Aquarium Bulletin", were on hand when the shipment arrived. This was big news for his magazine The Aquarium. Cochu paid Rabaut the enormous price of one dollar for each fish. There were four thousand fish in the shipment. In 1936 four thousand dollars was an incredible amount of money. Ten dollars a week for sixty hours of work was a better than average job. Fred Cochu asked for only two things. He needed a week to make payment. He told me he did not have the $4,000 then, but would have had a real problem finding $400. He also had to have all of the neon tetras. Rabaut was happy to agree. Cochu had all the fish (or so he thought) in his hatchery at 21 State Street in Manhattan within a very few hours. He fed them and watched them overnight. The first thing the next day he was ready to sell them. The biggest center for the sale of tropical fish in New York City was on Nassau Street in Manhattan. There were three stores there almost side by side. They fought constantly. They berated each other in the newspaper advertisements. Each store was at war with the other two. They fought rudely and insultingly in their weekly newspaper advertisements which every hobbyist read. They all did a big business. The tropical fish buyers in New York loved it. Prices on Nassau street were always lower than any other place. I spent many hours there in the late thirties buying fish and never knowing which store would have the best and cheapest prices. I was amazed and astounded recently when I learned (almost 60 years later) from Fred the Nassau Street "secret". A man named Al Goldman owned all three stores. His managers would meet several times a week, in secret with Goldman, after each store closed. Goldman would plan his strategies. No one ever suspected the truth. Goldman was Paramount's very best customer. Fred's first phone call was to Goldman to sell him the neon tetra that he had exclusively. Al Goldman listened, and then told Fred he had enough. Cochu told me that he was so surprised he could not speak. When he finally recovered his composure he could only sputter that Goldman was crazy. It could not be the neon tetra as he had them all. He left immediately to go to Nassau Street to see the fish. Goldman had laughed and said "Come on down and see for yourself". The mystery unfolded after he saw an aquarium full of neons at the Nassau Pet Shop.

Rabaut had employed one of the sailors on the ship from Brazil as a helper. The helper was to be paid when the ship docked, and Rabaut and the sailor had different ideas as to what his service was worth. He stole a can from Rabaut to pay himself properly. He had then sold his can of neons to Goldman. Al Goldman generously let Cochu have the fish at a more than reasonable price. Rabaut was at Paramount all day, every day, watching the fish and Fred, and worrying about his money. Cochu had no difficulty in paying Rabaut the $4,000 before the week was out. He sold these first neons for an average price of $4.00 a fish. The neons retailed for $10 each. Fred next worked out an employment deal with Rabaut, and Rabaut became an employee of Paramount Aquarium. This association remained in place until a few years after World War Two.

Innes was doing a feature article on the neon tetra and had an excellent color photograph for the front cover of "The Aquarium" magazine issue of November 1936. Innes printed a special mailing piece for Paramount with two pages of additional information to offer neon tetras to the trade. Neons now were sold wholesale for $3.00 each, twelve or more at $2.50 each, and in one hundred lots for $2.00 each. Paramount Aquarium and Aquarium Hamburg maintained a virtual exclusive on neon tetras for the next twenty years. The wholesale price was 75 cents each as late as 1952. I paid it then. Paramount Aquarium made a lot of money in the neon tetra business. At my own compound in Leticia, Colombia, in the late 1950s, we were still getting all the neons we needed from the same area, and paying one third of a cent each. You can see quickly the great amount of profit Paramount had available. In order to protect his supply of neons he had teamed up with Aquarium Hamburg, and together they shared the expense of obtaining from the Brazilian government the only two permits ever granted to anyone for the exclusive right to market Brazil's tropical fish. They were very expensive to obtain, but were effective for over twenty years. In the long run the permit was a great bargain.

Later Al Goldman (Nassau Pet) called Cochu to complain that he was paying Paramount 50 cents each for *Corydoras* catfish. His competition was selling them for 60 cents each. Fred suspected that Goldman's competition had gotten the catfish from one of the many sailors that supplemented their incomes buying fish in exotic ports, and reselling them in New York. It was an opportunity for Fred to return the favor Goldman had done by backing off on the neons he had obtained from Rabaut's sailor helper. Cochu told Goldman to sell the Corydoras at retail for nine cents each. Goldman was pleased when Fred explained he was giving him one thousand fish as a gift. Cochu accomplished two things. He returned the favor Goldman had done for him, and made his competition in New York sick. They learned that Nassau Pet and Paramount Aquarium would not sit by and let their prices be cut.

About a year later, after the first neons were received, Cochu realized that South America was a piscatorial goldmine, and he had to get more involved. He saw the fish that Amazonica was handling for Aquarium Hamburg from other parts of Brazil and determined to open his own "mine" there. He involved himself heavily in South America and, as there was no meaningful competition, he shortly dominated that trade. His major step was in 1937. He contracted with the Brazilian government to rent the newly constructed state of the art fish hatchery in Belem. The Brazilian government had built the hatchery to raise "Tucunaré" (*Cichla ocellaris*). They couldn't and didn't. In 1936 and less than a year from the start, the government's project was a disaster. The funding was discontinued and the project was abandoned. This was part of the Museu Goeldi (zoological park) and located alongside the river. Belem is the city near the mouth of the Amazon River where the big oceanic freighters arrived and departed. The rent paid was enough to keep the zoological gardens going for Brazil. The already fully equipped facility was ideal for Paramount's first real holding compound. Paramount used it until the end of the Second World War. Fish could now be received from 3,000 miles up the river near the Peruvian border, and conditioned before being trans-shipped to the United States by water.

Early in 1937 a really funny (tragic?) happening occurred at the steamship docking facility in Manaus, Brazil, some 2,000 miles upstream from Belem. Aquarium Hamburg had sent their own collectors to Brazil to reap the neon bonanza. Cochu did not know this, and Aquarium Hamburg did not know that Rabaut had been hired, and was now in Brazil collecting for Paramount. Aquarium Hamburg had two trained collectors (Hans Pietch and Wm. Praetorius) on the way to the Benjamin Constant (Tabatinga) area to collect neon tetras. It took two weeks by boat to get to Benjamin Constant (Tabatinga) from Belem, and then only a week to return (with the current) to Belem. Early one evening on the way down river, the Aquarium Hamburg team had another boat, owned by the same company, tie up alongside of them in Manaus. They were amazed to see on the deck of the boat a quantity of German fish cans. They made inquiries, and discovered that someone (Rabaut) was coming from the collecting grounds at Benjamin Constant. They paid a man to dump the entire load of full fish cans overboard. This was timed to happen just before dawn, and just moments after their boat departed for Benjamin Constant. When Rabaut awoke the next morning his entire load had disappeared.

On the next trip for Aquarium Hamburg, Pietch and Praetorius got drunk in Manaus. Pietch was killed in a bar fight, probably by Praetorius who disappeared. All of the money which Pietch was carrying also disappeared. This was a considerable sum as Pietch carried funds to pay themselves, cargo expenses, and the fisherman for the fish. Needless to say Praetorius never returned to Germany.

On Rabaut's next trip he discovered in Leticia, Colombia, two French convicts that had escaped from Devil 's Island in French Guiana. They then had found their way through the jungles to a safe haven in this remote Colombian port (only a few hours up the Amazon from Benjamin Constant in Brazil) where the neons were being collected near the Amazon River. Rabaut hired them, and they helped protect his and Paramount's interests for years. They supervised the Indian collectors who accumulated the neons and other fish between trips.

Cochu first visited this area in 1937. He quickly confirmed

his commitment to an expanded presence in South America for Paramount Aquarium. His next big step was to join forces with an unusual Colombian Indian (honest, hard working, dependable, and very bright), who had been collecting and supplying fish to Rabaut. This was Rafaele (now you know where the Raphael catfish got its name) Wanderagga. He'd never left Colombia or had shoes on in his life. Together they established a compound on a lake (Loretto Yacu, Colombia) some 40 miles west of Leticia that fed into the Amazon River. This collecting compound could be reached using an amphibious airplane. Cochu wanted his operation to be as quiet as possible and he succeeded. Located here he would never have any contact with anyone. He could fly in all his supplies and fly out loads of tropical fish. Later when he needed a larger capacity airplane he flew into Leticia where there was a well maintained dirt landing strip. The packed fish were sent from Loretto Yacu compound on a large flat-bottomed boat the 40 miles to Leticia. The boat was large enough to hold the entire shipment. It was offloaded onto the Paramount airplane and in the air within an hour of reaching the Leticia air strip. Fish were always packed at night and then transported before dawn. This avoided the terrible Amazonian fish-cooking heat during the day. The fish would be in the air before 9 am, and usually earlier, and not have an opportunity to get hot.

The variety of fish in that area was mindboggling. Few people ever saw Wanderagga or Cochu in the 40 years they operated the Wanderagga compound. This operation was tremendously successful from the start. Originally (1937) Paramount Aquarium had used a seaplane (P.B.Y.) with the capability to land and take off from the lake (Loretto Yacu). This arrangement worked well, but when the volume exceeded the capability of the amphibious airplane that method reluctantly was abandoned. The Wanderagga compound produced the bulk of the fish exported from South America to North America for the next 15 years.

In the fall of 1937 Fred Cochu, on a trip to Belem, Brazil, had an unexpected two day layover in Port of Spain, Trinidad. As always, Cochu started talking fish to a dock foreman named Art Reinbrecht. He was a very bright, displaced American married to a Trinidad native. He told Fred he knew where there were lots of tropical fish. He took Fred to a place called "Pitch Lake". Fred, to his great surprise, found large quantities of easily caught *Plecostomus* and Aeneus catfish. That day the Trinidad Tropical Fish Industry was born. Reinbrecht immediately quit his job and started sending catfish to Paramount in New York. It was a big and profitable business for both parties. Many, many Trinidad collectors who learned the techniques working for Art Reinbrecht found backers. By the early 1950s there were almost 50 dealers in Trinidad. In the next ten years so many fish were shipped that the Trinidad catfish population was threatened with extinction. No one was able to breed *Plecostomus* commercially then. These wonderful fish were easily sold by everyone. The old (and false) reports that catfish ate the dirt from the bottom of the aquarium surely helped them become essential (and popular). Every one had to have a "sucker" cat to eat the dirt. Wisely, the Trinidad government, imposed quotas and seasons. This worked well. It became unimportant in the next few years. By that time Florida fish farmers had learned how to pool breed *Plecostomus*. Taiwan and Hong Kong fish breeders started to mass produce *Corydoras aeneus*. The demand has remained consistent. Very small Taiwanese specimens were selling for as little as three cents each by the late 1960s. Today there is no tropical fish industry in Trinidad. Florida yearly produces and supplies almost all (more than two million) of the world's *Plecostomus* needs. The Far East produces large quantities of small Aeneus catfish. Florida produces large quantities of large Aeneus catfish. This phenomenon has become an economic fact of life as this situation now repeats itself with many similar items. Freight costs become the deciding factor when buying or selling fish. Distant production centers (Asia, Africa) can only overcome the freight factor by packing heavy. This can only be done by shipping small fish. The buyer then must decide whether he wants good sized and usually healthier Florida fish, or smaller and less expensive fish imports. In many cases dealers will handle both.

A World War was on the horizon in 1939. This fact affected Paramount Aquarium. Hugo Schnelle, the co-owner of Aquarium Hamburg who was married to Cochu's sister, was in the United States. He was there to personally transport a large collection of marine fishes destined for the Berlin and Frankfurt Aquariums. He had no desire to even try to return to Germany when Germany attacked Poland. He made his presence known to the authorities (the United States was not yet at war). He stayed with Fred Cochu in New York City for the next seven years. Hugo Schnelle managed better in World War Two than he did in 1917. In World War One he was a sailor on a German warship.

That did not last too long as the captain scuttled his ship in Riga, Latvia. Young Schnelle spent most of World War One in Siberia as a prisoner of war.

Joe Lingg, an important supplier of Paramount, had a fish and plant greenhouse north of New York in Ardsley, New York. In 1939 contact and fish from Germany ceased. This effectively cut off the aquarium fish that Germany supplied to the United States. When Joe Lingg told Fred he had to reduce his present greenhouse operations Fred quickly rented the greenhouse from him. He paid Lingg $40 a month in rent.

Hugo Schnelle agreed to raise egg layers for Paramount. The hope was that he could replace the lost German fish supplies. The Ardsley operation under Schnelle, in a very short time, was producing a quantity of much needed product. Their most profitable item was the black tetra that Cochu had found and introduced just before the war. Cochu managed to buy six acres adjacent to the Ardsley plant at a tax sale for the cost of the unpaid back taxes. The buildings Paramount built there were marvels. It was by far the most modern tropical fish hatchery in the United States. During the war Paramount produced millions of fish there.

With Germany at war (1939) no one in Europe was able to supply Far Eastern birds and animals. Fred Cochu jumped into this void. In addition to his tropical fish business he (for almost two years) was heavily and profitably involved in the wild animal trade. It ended when the Japanese attacked Pearl Harbor. His headquarters were in Shanghai, China. He used the same facilities that Aquarium Hamburg had occupied. Shanghai was a good location. Most of the important collecting areas had easy access to Shanghai by water. The first thing Fred did was to try to locate the Bastian brothers. These men were Aquarium Hamburg's trained animal handlers headquartered in Shanghai. They had completely disappeared along with a lot of animals. The mystery remained unsolved for six years until the war ended. The Bastian brothers who were German nationals (everyone thought they were dead) suddenly reappeared. They were in a prisoner of war compound on the island of Ceylon for six long years. They had attempted to get a last load of animals to Germany. It was a good idea that did not work. The boat that they and the animals had been on was torpedoed and sunk. They were rescued and then made prisoners by the British.

Cochu had good customers like Louis Trefflich and Louie Ruhe who were in great need of animals. In quick order he was in Shanghai and learning the animal business. He took the first load back to Los Angeles as quick as possible. He had a day and a half stop in Japan and while there he visited the Imperial Zoo in Tokyo. He introduced himself to the director who asked him if he could obtain baby chimpanzees. He had them on order from Africa and would be getting them soon into Shanghai. He also knew that he could sell them as fast as they were obtained and did not need customers for chimpanzees. He told the Japanese zoo director that he could not sell him any. He could, however, trade them for the ultra rare and almost extinct Japanese imperial cranes. This became a reality within the year. He supplied three chimps in exchange for four imperial cranes.

Henry Trefflich met him in California and bought on the spot all of the birds from his first consignment. The remaining animals (and Fred) went east by rail in a rented box car. The trip was a great success. No one else was able to supply animals. He had a large consignment of Australian kangaroos arriving in Shanghai. All were sold to the St. Louis Zoo and the Bronx Zoo and the profit from this huge sale paid for a lot of other mistakes.

With Germany out of the picture the demand for canaries was great. Germany had always supplied the majority of the world's canary buyers. Canaries were available in China. Cochu managed to buy all the available birds (5,000) for a big price. He then ran into Gustav Stern from Hartz Mountain who had come to Shanghai to buy these same canaries. Stern quickly found that Cochu had bought them all so Stern found Cochu and offered him a large profit on the spot. Fred outsmarted himself by turning down the offer. Immediately after this his canaries came down with dysentery. The entire 5,000 birds died.

About then (1940) Fred almost followed the canaries. He became desperately ill in Shanghai. He had pneumonia and there wasn't such a thing as antibiotics then. A wonderful Chinese doctor named Ming Leong Fe saved his life. After Shanghai was invaded by the Japanese, Leong Fe managed to escape, and made his way to Hong Kong. Dr. Fe and Fred remained in touch and some years after the war the Cochus were happy to sponsor entry of Dr. Fe's son into the United States and helped put the boy through the University of Florida. He earned a degree in engineering. He lives in Ithaca, New York now and the Cochu family

Gulf Fish Hatchery

P. O. BOX 102
PALMETTO, FLORIDA

TELEPHONES
OFFICE: [illegible]
NIGHT: [illegible]

SOLD TO D. C. E (1956)
Prices

DATE
TOTAL AMT. OF INVOICE

No. Fish		Price	Amount
	LIVE BEARERS		
	MOONS (PLATY)		
	Gold	.08	06
	Blue	.08	05
	Salt & Pepper	.08	06
	Red	.10	04
	Blue Tuxedo	.10	06
	Black	.10	05
	Gold Crescent	.10	06
	Red Crescent	.12	09
	Gold Tuxedo	.12	09
	Bleeding Hearts	.15	15
	Red Tuxedo	.15	12
	WAG PLATY		
	Blue	.10	08
	Fiesta	.12	09
	Gold	.15	12
	Red	.18	16
	VARIATUS		
	Black	.12	08
	Sunset	.15	12
	Red Tail	.15	12
	SWORDTAILS (HELLERY)		
	Green	.08	05
	Green Tuxedo	.10	07
	Brick Red	.12	08
	Gold	.15	12
	Gold Tuxedo	13 .18	13
	Gold Wag	12 .18	15
100	Red Tuxedo	.18	14 40
	Velvet Red	16 .20	16
	Red Wag	16 .20	16
	Mixed		10
	MISCELLANEOUS		
	Whiteclouds	.20	40
	Flounders	.15	15
	Red Ramshorn Snails	.02	—
	Mystery Snails	.03	03
135	Ambassis Lala	.22	17 60
	MOLLIES		
	Black Small	.10	05
100	Medium	.16	12 80
	Sphenops	.10	08
	Gold	.10	10
	Blond Marble	.10	10
	Marble	.10	08
	Latipinna	.12	08
	Yucatan		08
	GUPPIES		
	Common	.03	01
	Gold	.06	03
	Gold Veiltail	.10	08
	Blue Veiltail	.10	08
	Red Guppies	.10	08
	Exotic	.50	40

No. Fish		Price	Amount
	ANGELS (SCALARES)		
150	Small	.12	10
	Med. Large	.25	
	Large	1.00	
6	Wild Angel		1.25 ea
	Black Lace		75
	Black		2.00
	BETTAS		
	Male	.50	40
	Female	.25	20
	Unsexed	.15	12
	Show Males	1.00	
	IMPORTS		
	C. Melanistius	.20	
	C. Punctatus	.20	
	Otocinclus	.20	
	Plecostomus	.30	
	Copeina (Arnoldi)	.18	Less
	Rasbora (Het.)	.28	
	H. Rosaceus	.18	
	Pencils	.20	20%
	Silver Hatchets	.18	
	Marble Hatchets	.18	
	Metynnis, Large	.65	
	Kuhlii Loaches	.28	
	Clown Loaches	2.20	
	EGG LAYERS		
	ANABANTID GOURAMI		
	Blue	.10	08
	Red Paradise	.10	
	White Paradise	.15	
	Kissing	.20	18
	Leeri (Pearl)	.20	16
	Dwarf	.22	17
	Giant	.35	
	Thick Lipped	.35	
	Snakeskin	.35	
	Opaline Sm Blue		10
	DANIO		
	Zebra	.07	04
	Gold	.08	06
	Giant		16
	TETRAS		
	Black Sm	.14	11
	Bloodfin	.18	
	Head & Taillight	.18	
	Von Rio	.18	15
	Gold	.20	
	Serpae	.20	16
	Neon	.20	
	Albino Pristella	.20	16
	BARBUS		
	Rosy	.10	07
	Schuberti, Gold	.18	
	Sumatranus	.20	16
	Cherry	.20	
	CICHLIDS		
	Ramirez, Small	.50	

MINIMUM QUANTITY — 50 FISH PER BAG

TERMS

1. We ship Air Freight.
2. Packing charges: 1-Bag Pack, $1.00; 2-Bag Pack, $1.50.
3. We sell not less than 50 fish of any given variety except Breeders and Bettas.
4. We guarantee live delivery and give extras with count.
5. Our terms are cash on accounts and cash for last invoice when reordering on regular accounts.
6. We are not responsible for fish claimed to be dead on arrival, unless claim is signed by Air Transportation Agent.

PRICES SUBJECT TO CHANGE WITHOUT NOTICE

Breeders of

TROPICAL FISH

Gulf Fish Hatchery

R. R. 1 — BOX 360
PALMETTO, FLORIDA

FARM 6-3115
FARM 6-3322 — TELEPHONES — NIGHT 2-5024

December 26th 1958

We are in receipt of 580 boxes of fish from Colombia. The rainy season is on and the water is very high. Certain varieties of fish particularly Neons will be almost impossible to collect during the next three months. The Neons we have are all large. After these are gone we shall be able to obtain only limited quantities of large and then we shall get the new spawned Neons and these are very small. Certain items are very short and as in the past first come first served.

VARIETY	each	bag	1,000
Abramites headstanders	1.50		
Chilodus headstanders	90	75	
Blow fish-puffers	1.00		
A. U-2 dwarf cichlids	25	20	
" " " large	40	30	
Loricaria-whiptail cat	40	35	
Farlowella-twig cat	1.00		
Hatchets	20	18	
Festivum	35		
A.Maroni-keyholes-lge	65		
Saddle Cichlids	40		
lge electric eel 15"	20.00		
Leporinus species	85		
Anostomus Anostomus	1.00	85	
Anostomus species	85		
Catalina-Banjo cats reg.	40		
" " " lge.	65		
Bloodfins	30	25	
Peruvian Longfins	75		
Bumble Bee Clown cats 3"	1.00		
Black Mettynis	65	50	
Trifasciatus Pencils	22		
Marginatus	20	17	
N.Espei-new barred pencil	40	35	
Harrisoni lge pencils	22	18	
Auratus-diptail pencils	22	18	
Blue tetras	22		
Gold tetra	20	18	

VARIETY	each	bag	1000
Black Caymen	1.25		
Glo lights wild nice	23		
Lge Leaf Fish	2.00		
Shovelnosed Sorubim cats-5.00 ea.			
Neon Tetras large	18	15	12
Corydoras Arcuatus	22	20	
" Leopardus	20	18	
" Linneatus	20	18	
" Rabauti	26	23	
" Julii	23		
" Brocias	25	22	
Talking cats	35	30	
lge 3-5"	65	50	
Tetra Metae-redtail	20	18	
Head and Tails	20	18	
Rosacius	20	18	
H.Pulcher	28		
lge cabbagehead Ancistris		1.00	

a few of these also in stock
Redtail sharks, ~~Monodactylus,~~
Rasbora Maculata,Rasb.Dorciocellata
Rasbora Pauciperforata,Kribensis
breeders, large show angels,
Expected soon-- Archersm scats,Kuhlii
black sharks,Heteromorpha,botia's

Gulf Fish Hatchery
P. O. Box 102
PALMETTO, FLORIDA

DATED PRICE LIST
RUSH

NEWS LETTER and SPECIALS

PRICES EFFECTIVE UNTIL DECEMBER 28, 1962
(OR UNTIL SOLD OUT)

	BAG LOTS	EACH
KUHLI LOACHES (200)	.14	.17
GORDON'S PIGMY HELLERI (200)	.09	.12
CHINESE ALGAE EATERS (100)	.41	.45
SCATS (Rubifrons-Red) (50)	.75	.90
T. BARBS (100)	.15	.18
BARBUS CALLIPTERUS (Redtail)	.14	.17
FLAMINGO GUPPIES (Beautiful) (150)	.18	.22
RED WAG SWORDTAILS (125)	.13	.16
SEVERUM (Poor Man's Discus) (75)	.15	.18
BUMBLE BEES (150)	.19	.23
MELAZONA GUPS (Beautiful) (100)	.30	.40
BLACK PARADISE FISH (100)	.35	.40
KISSING GOURAMI (good size, fat) (100)	.14	.17
FIREMOUTH MEEKI (100)	.10	.12
LYRETAIL BLACK MOLLIES (100)	.55	.75
MEDIUM LARGE REDTAIL SHARKS (75)	.90	1.00
SPINY NOSED EELS	—	.90
BOTIA HORAE (Skunk Botia) (100)	.45	.55
JAPANESE FIRE NEWTS (last this year)	.45	.45
BLUE PLATY (Metallic) (150)	.04	.06
CALICO (Red/Black) PLATY (150)	.12	.15
QUEENSLAND RAINBOW FISH (100)	.18	.22
BANANA PLANTS (100)	.04	.05
PANCHAX PLAYFAIRI (75)	.35	.40

A new African Palmatochromis (P. Pulcher) grows much larger than Kribensis — Adult fish are if possible even more beautiful than Kribensis with lovely blue and lavender hues. Each 1.50; Young Adults 3" 2.50.

Extra Fancy Display Goldfish

We have in stock and plan to stock continuouly a number of extra fancy display Goldfish. These come to us from Koriyama Goldfish Company in Kobe, Japan. They are amongst the oldest and finest Goldfish breeders in the world. All fish are perfect show specimens and guaranteed as represented. Average size is 2" plus so realize these are not baby fish.

ALL GOLD LIONHEADS	2.00
CALICO FANTAILS	.60
CALICO TELESCOPE	.80
TELESCOPE JET BLACK MOORS (Fantails)	.50
CHOCOLATE ORANDAS	5.00

IMPORTANT!

If you intend to order fish between now and Christmas it makes good sense to get the biggest part of them as soon as possible. The very worst time of the year for air transport is the weeks before Christmas as with the Christmas mail, and full passenger loads the possibility of off loading and consequent chilling of the shipment is much greater than at any other time of the year.

August, 1962

Gulf Fish Hatchery

P. O. BOX 102 — PALMETTO, FLORIDA

DATE________

FISH________

CTNS. Lge.________

Small________

TOTAL DUE________

BALANCE________

TELEPHONES:
ORDERS, HATCHERY: 722-2128
or 722-1282
NIGHT CALLS AFTER 4 P.M.
ORDERS — JACK: 746-3307
GERALDINE: 722-4147
ROSS: 746-6707
TERMS — 10 Days Net

SOLD TO ________________

No. Fish		Wholesale Price	Jobbers 10-Box Min.	Amount
	LIVE BEARERS			
	MOONS (PLATY)			
	Blue ✓	.09	.07	
	Salt & Pepper ✓	.11	.09	
	Red ✓	.14	.10	
	Blue Tuxedo	.12	.10	
	Black	.12	.10	
	Gold Crescent ✓	.12	.10	
	Red Crescent ✓	.15	.13	—
	Red Tuxedo ✓	.18	.16	
	Picture ✓	.12	.10	
	Picture Wag	.14	.12	—
	Blue Wag	.13	.11	
	Gold Wag	.16	.14	
	Red Wag ✓	.18	.16	
	Red Calico Hybrid ✓	.18	.16	—
	Milk and Ink	.18	.16	
	Gold Tuxedo	.16	.14	
	S & P Wags	.14	.12	—
	Gold Tux Wag	.18	.16	
	Red Tux Wag	.20	.18	—
	Mixed Platy ✓	.08	.06	
	PLATY VARIATUS			
	Black Nubian	.15	.12	
	Sunset ✓	.18	.15	
	Red Tail Rainbow	.18	.15	
	Black w/Red Tail	.30	.25	
	Marigolds	.15	.12	
	Limia Multicolor ✓	.12	.10	
	7-Spot Limia	.12	.10	
	MIXED LIVEBEARERS			
	(Moons, Mollies, Swords, etc.)			
	1,000 Lots	.05 ✓		
	500 Lots	.06		

No. Fish		Wholesale Price	Jobbers 10-Box Min.	Amount
	SWORDTAILS HELLERI			
	Green ✓	.09	.07	
	Green Tuxedo ✓	.12	.10	—
	Green Wag ✓	.12	.10	
	Brick ✓	.12	.10	
	Brick Wags	.14	.12	
	Gold ✓	.12	.10	—
	Gold Wag ✓	.18	.16	—
	Gold Tuxedo	.18	.16	
	Red Tuxedo	.22	.18	
	Velvet Red ✓	.22	.18	
	Red Wag Velvet ✓	.22	.18	
	All Black ✓	.30	.25	—
	Leopard Hybrid ✓	.25	.22	
	Mixed ✓	.09	.07	
	Gordons Pigmy (live bearer)	.20 ✓	.18	
	Anableps 4-eye Livebearer	2.50 ✓	2.00	
	Half Beaks	.55 ✓	.50	
	GUPPIES			
	Common Rainbow	.04	.03	
	Gold	.06	.05	
	Gold Flame Gups	.30	.25	
	Blue Veiltail	.22	.16	
	Red Veiltail	.24	.18	
	Flamingo (Redtail Female) ✓	.40	.35	
	½ Black Veil Gups	.25	.20	
	Melazona Guppies	.50	.40	
	DELUXE SHOW DELTA TAIL Red Male & Red Female	1.00 ✓	.75	
	DELUXE SHOW DELTA TAIL Iridescent Blue	.90 ✓	.65	
	MOLLIES			
	Choc.-Gold Hybrid ✓	.23	.18	
	Black, Regular	.10	.08	
	Black, Medium-Lge.	.18	.15	
	Large Black Sailfins Trios	1.00		
	Sphenops	.12	.10	
	Marble	.11	.09	
	Green Sailfins, Ex-Lge. ✓	.15	.12	
	Black Yucatan, Reg.	.18	.15	
	Black Yucatan, Med-Lge.	.25	.20	
	Liberty, Red Dorsal ✓	.15	.13	
	Albino Molly	.45	.40	
	Lyretail Moll ✓	1.00	.90	
	Lyretail Moll, lge. ✓	2.25	2.00	
	SCAVENGERS — WILD LOCAL FISH, ETC.			
	Flounders ✓	.16	.14	
	Fundulus Chrysotus ✓	.14	.11	
	Flag Fish ✓	.12	.10	
	Crawfish	.08	.06	
	Giant Bullfrog Tadpoles	.05	.04	
	Fiddler Crabs	.12	.10	
	Mystery Snails, Medium ✓	.05	.04	
	Colombian Ramshorn, Lge.	.12	.10	
	Ghost Shrimp ✓	.04	.03	
	Newts, Aquatic ✓	.15	.12	
	Caymen (in season) ✓	1.25	1.25	
	Water Sticks	.25	.25	
	Mosquito Fish ✓	.07	.05	
	Large Show African Frogs	1.00	1.00	
	African Frogs	.60	.55	
	Pigmy Sun Fish	.15	.13	

Gulf Fish Hatchery - 1956

considers him their grandson. Fred was able to make four "animal" trips before the war escalated. The animal trade became another war casualty. An almost 29-foot reticulated python Paramount delivered alive to the Bronx Zoo made headlines. It had been captured in the Celebes islands. A swarm of reporters met the "Singalese Princess" when it docked in Brooklyn. A picture of Cochu and six other men holding the huge snake appeared in all the newspapers. Cochu was paid the enormous sum of $500 for this leviathan. Fred, after his four profitable trips, was out of the animal business.

During the Second World War things slowed down considerably for everyone in the tropical fish business. Paramount Aquarium was one of the few who survived and prospered. They had a constant supply of good Florida livebearers from Herb Woolf throughout the war. Fred Cochu, under pressure, could always solve unsolvable problems. Nobody in the tropical fish business did more than barely exist. Paramount thrived. He was the only customer Woolf had for his fish during the war. Fred Cochu was the only buyer clever enough to work out the apparently impossible wartime transportation problem. Government permits allowed the movement of personal furnishings for certain people. A truck with special permits and supplied with sufficient fuel coupons went from New York to Florida delivering "personal possessions" frequently. On the trip back north the usually partially empty truck was filled with fish sent from Woolf to Paramount in New York.

The government developed great interest in the biology of electric eels during the war. Just what the program had to do with winning the war remains a mystery to me. It was important for the United States Army to have live electric eels. Fred Cochu spent a great deal of his time working with the United States Army to obtain the eels for them. He also was able to obtain permission to bring in other wild fish as "food" for the eels. There always was a surplus of these "food fish". This provided some of the much desired South American fish that had completely disappeared. None were available from any other source.

In 1946 the war was over. Paramount sent Rabaut to Singapore for fish. Rabaut had been employed working in the Ardsley Hatchery for Paramount during the war. He made one successful trip. Cochu immediately sent him back to make another trip. When he arrived in Singapore he cabled Paramount in New York that the area was experiencing unusual and unseasonably heavy rains. He would be delayed. It would be six to eight weeks before he could accumulate enough fish to return to New York. Fred was immediately suspicious as it was then the dry season. He cabled Rabaut for more information. The cable company could not find him to deliver the message. He next telephoned the Singapore Hotel where Rabaut stayed and learned that he had checked out the day before. The mystery deepened. Cochu next contacted the steamship company where he learned that Rabaut had left the day before bound for Los Angeles. He would dock in California. The steamship company reported that Rabaut had almost one hundred cans of fish with him. Cochu now knew that Rabaut was trying to sneak in a shipment for his own benefit. Within 24 hours Cochu had worked out a complicated plan that could throw a monkey wrench into Rabaut's gears if it worked.

Fish were scarce. Far East fish similar to those Rabaut had with him were the key to the plan. Fred was going to try to double cross the double crosser. He only had to get the right kind of fish to California before Rabaut arrived. That was a problem. The market was bare in the United States. A large customer and friend of Paramount in London, England, named Sparks had a shipment from another dealer coming by water from Singapore. They were due in England the next week. When Cochu explained his problem (and his plan) to friend Sparks he agreed to help. Fred left that same day on a fast boat to London. He bought almost all of the shipment from Sparks and took it with him on the Queen Mary to New York. There he rested the fish for two days. Everything was on schedule. He packed the fish and left by train with the Singapore fish that he had bought in London destined now for Los Angeles. He beat Rabaut to California by six days. In those six days the shipment he brought from London to New York to Los Angeles was sold. It was sold at half the current prices. It was also sold to all of the important buyers with the understanding they would not buy Far East fish from Rabaut when they arrived the next week. When Auguste Rabaut arrived in Los Angeles the market was saturated with good and cheap fish. Rabaut found no customers. The prices he had expected to get had just dropped in half. Not only that, but his fish were not wanted even at the new terrible low prices. He learned that Paramount had supplied the fish. The last blow came next. He was no longer a Paramount employee.

In 1939 Paramount purchased one of the most successful retail tropical fish stores in the world. This was the famous Empire Tropical Fish store that had been owned by Richard Buettner. It was located on the corner of Church and Murray Streets in Manhattan. It was not nearly as big as Aquarium Stock (then the world's largest store) which was just one block away. Empire built its reputation on the most wonderful display of the very rarest fish for sale anywhere. Empire sold only quality fish. They never cut prices. It was Paramount Aquarium's showcase. There were at least four salesmen always on the floor selling fish. It was one of my favorite places as a child. This was a fairyland where I could see, even if I could not afford to buy, all the wonderful rare fish that were illustrated in Dr. Innes's book "**Exotic Aquarium Fishes**". This is where I first met Fred Cochu.

Empire also published several excellent hard cover books on tropical fish. These were "**Life and Love in the Aquarium**" by C.H. Peters and "**Tropical Fish and Home Aquariums**" by Alfred Morgan. Both books sold well and are prized collector pieces today.

Shortly after World War Two, Fred Cochu made a trip to Nigeria trying to make arrangements to set up a collecting station. He stayed for several months and brought back a load of fish to Paramount in New York City. The boat trip transporting the fish took 46 days. Results were only marginally acceptable and that only because very high prices were obtained for the survivors. A lot of fish new to the United States came with his one and only African shipment: elephant nosed Mormyrids, upside-down catfish, African glass catfish, Pantodons, rope fish, featherfins, lungfish, *Distichodus*, and other previously unseen cichlids, Anabantoids, and characins.

With the World War over Paramount quickly resurrected their South American operations. British Guiana (now Guyana) had wonderful fish varieties, but no full time fish dealers or workable commercial airline routes. Paramount helped a man named Louis Chung establish a collecting compound on the Demerara River which ran alongside Atkinson Field, the only large airport in the country. The airfield had been built during the war by the United States. A well kept secret that very few knew was that Fred Cochu was a partner in this fish operation. The Chung family remained the dominant figure in the business in British Guiana for many years. Art Reinbrecht, who was the first and largest dealer in Trinidad (*Plecostomus* and *Corydoras* catfish), set up an operation in British Guiana in 1954 or 1955. His idea was to send Guianese fish to his Trinidad operation, and ship them forward to his regular catfish customers in the United States. While there was no established or scheduled air service to Trinidad there were smaller planes that made regular runs. He could ship ten boxes or so three or four times a week to Trinidad. This worked. I remember getting a few shipments from him this way. Reinbrecht did well in Guyana for several years. Then regular commercial flights were established. This eliminated the reason for his business. He continued his Guyana operation competing with an increasing number of other dealers for a few more years. He then sold the business to a man named Oli Mohammed who operated as General Aquarium Sales. Reinbrecht operated for a few more years from Trinidad until he and his wife, Rose, retired.

In the peak years, Paramount took as many as 800 boxes of fish from Guyana to the United States every other week. It was not until commercial airlines could transport fish to Miami and New York City (1954) that Paramount's control of the Guianese fish supply was breached.

Harry Rambarran appeared on the scene in British Guiana in the late 1950s and he rapidly shared the bulk of the business with Louis and Winnie Chung. Harry Rambarran continuously expanded and his operations became a model for future dealers. Years later he merged his operation with that of Adolph Schwartz from Manaus, Brazil. His father, Willi, operated the Aquarium Rio Negro in Manaus, Brazil. This merger made Harry Rambarran not only the biggest, but by far the best fish handler in the world. Today fish from all over South America arrive at their Miami headquarters. Rambarran next opened a branch in California to take care of West Coast customers. Harry Rambarran is a wonderful person. His success was not accidental. He did everything better than his competition. He is unusually clever. His honesty and his ethics in all business dealings made it a pleasure to deal with him. I admire and respect him. I am happy that we remain fast friends. I was his first customer.

Fred Cochu told me how Mike Tsalikes got to Leticia, Colombia, and then became his competitor in the fish business. Some years after the war, Fred was staying overnight in Belem, Brazil. Belem in those days had just one hotel that wasn't much. More often than not he could not get accommodations. They often had to overnight there with a load of fish destined for Vero Beach. He solved the problem when he discovered that he could afford to buy a room from Madame Jerez who ran the fanciest brothel in Belem. For years he rented a clean room for the night, without the girl, who normally came with the arrangement. He paid $20 (which was the cost for a girl, a good meal, a clean room, and a comfortable bed for a night), and while not a bargain, was by far the best act in town. One night when Fred, with his pilot and mechanic, were overnighting in the brothel a badly frightened Mike Tsalikes found him. Fred had only known Mike, who was an animal dealer, casually. Tsalikes, from Tarpon Springs, Florida had a collecting station in Belem. Mike, at that moment, was on the run. He was being pursued by the Brazilian police. They had caught Tsalikes smuggling rare and protected hyacinthine macaws and Mike evidently was not then smart enough to pay the expected "Mordida" (bribes). He begged Cochu to take him along the next morning when Paramount's plane (at first light) would leave. As he had a valid passport Fred agreed. Mike was allowed to sneak aboard the plane before dawn and escaped from Brazil. He never returned. On the trip north Fred told Mike about the area around Leticia where he and Wanderagga had their compound. Paramount at that time had no interest in animals. Mike assured Fred he had no interest in fish. As a result Fred encouraged him to relocate his animal business in Leticia. Mike did. Three months later he showed his appreciation by entering the fish business competing with Fred. He never made much of an impact in his fish business as his product was inferior. He didn't learn the rudiments of fish keeping, and you can be sure neither Fred nor I would help him. My experiences with Mike Tsalikes have already been described. Many years later (1980s) Mike was caught and convicted of smuggling huge quantities of cocaine from Leticia, Colombia, to Florida. Currently, he is serving a life sentence. Mike Tsalikes developed a clever twist in his last smuggling operation. He imported huge boat loads of roughly cut logs of the most desired varieties of Amazonian hard wood. In Leticia, selected logs were cut so that a chamber could be made inside where large quantities of contraband drugs were stowed. The original wood was carefully glued back utilizing the newest state of the art adhesives. It was impossible to find the seam within which the concealed chamber of cocaine was hidden. Trained dogs that examine cargo entering the United States could not detect the drugs by smell. Mike, almost certainly, would still be in the drug business today if he had not been set up by one of his Colombian associates. The customs people who now knew what, where, and how the contraband was concealed, easily found it. Mike Tsalikes and his drug business are history.

By the early 1950s the commercial airline service from South America to the United States expanded greatly. The need for Paramount's air cargo operations slowly diminished as alternatives materialized. Fred Cochu had moved his import operation (Schnelle remained in Ardsley, New York, running that branch) in slow degrees to Florida. He first bought twenty acres in Ojus, Florida (now North Miami). He stocked his first fish ponds and prepared to build extensive holding facilities. His acreage was next to a creosote plant. The noxious fumes, from that operation, quickly poisoned his pond fish. He had to relocate and sold out at a loss. He then moved to Vero Beach where he remained. The small airport in Vero provided perfect facilities for his airplanes. The farm he built south of Vero Beach produced lots of product both for the Ardsley operation and direct sale to his customers.

The supply of wild caught South American tropical fish grew tremendously. By the 1970s an amazing five to six thousand boxes of wild caught fish were sent weekly to the United States. The great majority of these fish came from Colombia, Brazil, Peru, and Guyana.

Auguste Rabaut went into business for himself in the late 1940s. He was the very last of the collectors that transported large amounts of wild fish by water. His fish all came to New York City. I was fortunate to be on the scene in New York then and for two or three years bought fish from him. He operated from a base in Singapore. His terminal was in Brooklyn, New York. He set up an inexpensive (low rental) hatchery with a quantity of twenty and thirty gallon aquariums. They remained without fish for all, but at the most, ten days a year. Rabaut made an average of two, sometimes three, trips a year between Singapore and Brooklyn. His son-in-law was contacted on the ship's radio by Rabaut when he was a day or so from New York. The tanks were then filled. When Rabaut arrived the fish were released into the waiting aquariums. That same day all of his wholesale customers were called. This included those who would drive a long distance to see and buy the fish. Buyers came from places such as Baltimore, Philadelphia, Buffalo, Boston, and, of course, the majority came from the metropolitan New York area.

All aquariums were empty within 24 hours. If any fish were left they were those few that were too sick to be moved. The fish were counted, packed, paid for, and departed with the buyers at a very rapid pace. Most fish went by the tankful. As soon as the customer had a paid bill he was allowed to help pack his own fish. Prices were never questioned and were not negotiable. A good number of the items were only available from Rabaut. The fish were in amazingly good condition when one considers the length of time they had been abused in transit. Rabaut was an expert in his field. From memory now I can remember wonderful clown loaches, bumble bees, Kuhlii loaches, oddball *Rasbora* species, Scats, *Monodactylus*, archerfish, spiny eels, snakeheads, halfbeaks, T barbs, clown barbs, Hexazona barb, climbing perch, *Gobius sadanundio*, walking catfish, glass catfish, *Clarias* catfish, chocolate gouramis, and many *Rasbora heteromorpha*.

In 1955 or 1956 Rabaut retired. His method of operating had become extinct. Improved air transport did him in. I was able to get Rabaut alone more than once to talk with him. My General Aquatic Supply was only ten minutes away from his holding facility. He was a fascinating man. I wish he had written a book, or that I had a better memory of the stories he told me.

He once told me how he had caught freshwater seahorses and lost them all. Rabaut had been working with a fine meshed net swishing through some fine leaved aquatic plants trying to get live food for his hungry fish. He was then waiting for a small plane to pick him up. He did not catch much live food, but did catch small (baby??) freshwater seahorses. I was not the first to hear the story. It was a well known tale that had been dismissed by almost everyone. He said that the baby freshwater seahorses did not survive the trip. Most people thought he had probably caught freshwater pipefish, which are similar, or that he had invented the story to keep his customers close to him in case freshwater seahorses materialized on one of his shipments. I have collected many marine seahorses. I knew, from his description of the collecting area, that it was just where juvenile seahorses would be found.

I thought about his story many times, especially when in future years, some new fish appeared that no one had anticipated (remember I am the guy who dismissed "red devils" as a myth). I always (almost) believed his story. I never could convince myself that he could have invented this phantom fish. This was the man who had discovered the neon tetra, and if his story was made up I would have to know why. He was in business for another three or four years, and why he never went back to try again remains another unanswered question. Perhaps he did and could not again locate the fish. I also was sure he knew the difference between a seahorse and a pipefish.

Dr. George Myers, at Stanford University, knew Rabaut as he was the discoverer of the neon tetra, and Myers had written the formal description. When Rabaut, who was then in San Francisco, phoned him and asked to visit, Myers set up a meeting. This was probably a couple of years before I (early 1950s) had heard the story. Rabaut told Dr. Myers the same seahorse story with no details as to where this had happened other than in "Asia". Auguste Rabaut wanted Dr. Myers (in the name of science) to arrange financing for a collecting expedition. He wanted $10,000. George Myers felt the amount not unreasonable, but explained to Rabaut that universities just could not do that type of thing. He could not help. That was the last contact they ever had. Dr. Myers published an interesting two page report about this in 1979 in a publication of the California Academy of Science. This was more than twenty-five years after his "seahorse" meeting with Rabaut. I'd never seen or heard of this paper. I stumbled on a copy of it in a lot of reprint material that had been sold to an employee of the Shedd Aquarium. This fellow sold his library to me. I am going to let Dr. George Myers's words tell you what happened next.

"In November, 1977, I stumbled on a confirmation of Rabaut's story of a seahorse in fresh water. I was looking up some references concerning other literature in the Zoological Record when my eye alighted on the citation of a paper published in 1916 by the Paris Museum of Natural History. It described a hitherto unknown species of freshwater seahorse, *Hippocampus aimei* (Roule), from the Mekong River. Two specimens were collected by a Dr. Aimé in 1910. They had been caught close to the rapids of Kenmarat, in that part of the river that forms the boundary between Thailand and Laos. One was a male and the other a female."

This strange saga is almost unbelievable. The most unbelievable part is that no one to my knowledge has yet gone to try to collect them (44 years after Rabaut first told his story). There is a good chance that this fish may now be extinct, but someone must try.

I had accepted an invitation to visit Singapore to be the keynote speaker at the 1993 Aquarama meeting. My friend Heiko Bleher, probably today's most successful tropical fish collector/explorer, would be there. We planned to attempt to collect freshwater seahorses after the Aquarama meeting. Several months before the meeting I suffered a second heart attack and then a repeat of a 1983 open heart surgery. This last time they did seven bypasses. This was almost ten years after my first operation. Perhaps this time it will last twice as long as they doubled the number of bypasses. I didn't make it to Singapore that year. I feel fine now, but a trip like that can no longer be done easily. I will not be able to go. Heiko has been told (by me) to go. He says he will. When he finds out I am telling everyone what I know he will move a little faster. Heiko Bleher in action moves faster than anyone I've ever known. These last years have been hectic for him as he has been almost totally occupied trying to get his wonderful new magazine Aqua-Geo off the ground. I hope this is not the end of the story as it will be interesting to know what will happen next.

The first fish farmer in the Vero Beach area was a gaunt and sober man named George Florshitz. George had moved to Florida in the late 1930s from Long Island, New York. He was an excellent fish breeder. He was one of the first successful breeders of neon tetras in the United States. He settled in Vero Beach, Florida, and went into partnership with a man named Schlesinger. The partnership was haunted for years with a hated nickname. Florshitz and Schlesinger were very strange names for rural Florida. They quickly became "Horse S .. t and S .. t Slinger". George was normally taciturn. This did not improve his disposition.

His name was a lifelong problem for him. One evening he called us (person to person) and got Loise on the phone. About then the telephone operator became hysterical. She could not get herself to even try to say Florshitz which would identify the collect caller. Her supervisor finally had to get on the line. I wonder if the girl got fired. I hope not.

In later years Florshitz raised a very limited variety of excellent fish. He made the trip from Vero Beach to the Tampa area once a month and brought fish to me, Joe Leone, and Jim Woolf. George Florshitz could consistently raise large quantities of Siamese fighting fish in his outdoor dirt ponds. He sold them unsorted as "unsexed" Bettas. They were almost an inch in length, and arrived tearing each other to pieces.

We would jar up the males, and grow them out. The balance, mostly females, was sold as unsexed Bettas. Florshitz also raised angelfish and only sold them in medium and large sizes which were always wanted. His Rams, white clouds, Leeri, and moonlight gourami were always of good size.

There was only one real tropical fish dealer in Bangkok in the 1950s. This was Somphongs Lekarre. His quality was not bad, but was erratic enough to make importing risky. We bought a lot of fish from Somphongs when he was the only act in town. Fortunately, for both of us, the most wanted fish were also the hardiest. When we stuck with the various *Labeo* species (redtail, redfin, and black), gouramis, Bettas, spiny eels, fire eels, tire track eels, and algae aaters we did fine. Bangkok had a *Rasbora heteromorpha* look alike (*Rasbora hengeli*). This was much wanted as *Heteromorpha* was always in short supply. *Rasbora hengeli* invariably came in bad. The Kuhlii loaches were larger than the Singapore species, but travelled badly. All these problems cured themselves in time with the advent of more sophisticated methodology, shippers, and faster jet transportation.

Hong Kong had been a tropical fish exporting center for many years. People like George Bing (Hong Kong Aquarium) and Ceylon Aquarium were experienced shippers who were in business since the early 1930s. Hong Kong and Singapore shared the business almost equally in the 1950s. Hong Kong's fish volume forged dramatically ahead in the early 1960s when they started producing and selling huge volumes of small egg layers at very low prices. Small egg layers had been supplied by Germany for years, but even with Germany's lower air freight costs to the United States they could not compete. German fish were small. The Hong Kong fish were still smaller. This German trade dried up and was gone by the mid 1960s. Hong Kong volume forged ahead until a new source arrived on the scene. The new exporting center was Taipei, Taiwan. Rapidly, Taiwan removed a lot of the Hong Kong volume while Singapore expanded into high volume shipments of beautiful fancy guppies and angelfish. Taiwan could and did supply fish that were not easily available from other sources. I always started an order to Taiwan by buying silver dollars as these tank raised fish (*Metynnis hypsauchen*) were then only available from Taiwan. Taiwan offered cheap lyretail mollies. I couldn't raise enough at Gulf Fish Hatchery. By buying the very smallest size of lyretail molly I could get them packed heavy enough to make grow out in dirt ponds a profitable venture. A baby lyretail molly can be sexed when born as their tails are square when compared to the round tail of normal black mollies. Regular and albino *Corydoras* were the other special items that Taiwan offered at three pennies each. This made ordering easy and when we needed weight we would fill in items normally taken from Hong Kong at similar prices and quality. This hurt the Hong Kong volume the most.

Florida also suffered as Taiwan had large livebearers available when Florida farmers (in late winter) had sold down all of the stocks of better sized fish. In past years, customers had to make do with fish that were not nearly as large as they wanted. Taiwan had large livebearers to sell and sell they did. They sold to Florida's customers on the West Coast where it made the best economic sense. The part that hurt the most was that the Florida customers were happy to pay higher prices than Florida was getting, when they had large fish. By the mid 1960s Hong Kong and Singapore volume was about equal again and Taiwan, Bangkok, and Djakarta were all shipping considerable amounts of fish.

Here is where the fish farmers in Florida found themselves at that time. A new scourge arrived that further depressed an already stressed industry. This was the rapid development in California of a tropical fish trans-shipping industry. Freight rates had continued to escalate. If enough freight was ordered at one time the freight rate from the Far East to the United States dropped considerably. This "window of opportunity" opened for several enterprising California businessmen. They consolidated orders and had those all arrive in California on one waybill. The large weight of these consolidated shipments provided them with a considerably lower freight rate. The trans-shipper broke down the orders, opened and examined the bags, and even could help fish in trouble. At the least they could and did re-oxygenate and remove the losers. The shipments were then sent on to individual destinations on the first available flights. Orders could be as low as four boxes which seemed to make sense to even medium sized retail stores. The stores buying the bargain fish took quantities far in excess of what they needed. The average retail store did not have the experience, knowledge, or room to properly care for these overstressed fish. Invariably their bargains cost them more than buying from Florida. Most retail stores tried once and then gave up this semi-direct method, as the promised bargains were ethereal.

More than five hundred large retail pet outlets appeared in the new and (then) very large "discount stores" throughout the country. Most are gone now. Names like Arlans, Korvette, Spartan, Ames, Kings, and Robert Hall were among the largest. The discount stores often rented space to people with some experience to operate the pet departments of these huge stores. Livestock, when it managed to get there alive, was sold as fast as possible (before it died). Sick, small, and diseased fish were the rule not the exception. The magic word was "cheap". Fish were sold like underwear, soap powder, and Jello. The lower the price the more product you could sell. New hobbyists were attracted at a phenomenal rate as things were discounted heavily.

The new all-glass aquariums were selling in the most popular sizes (ten gallons) for as low as $2.98. I remember Martin Weintraub (Martin's Aquarium in Cherry Hill, New Jersey) then (and still) one of the best and largest retail stores had a huge sign on his front window that read "If you paid more than $2.98 for a ten gallon aquarium you paid too much".

The poor quality of cheap dry goods kept pace with the poor quality live stock. Japan was making vibrator air pumps that could be bought for less than $2.00 each. They usually were retailed for $2.98 each and often at $1.98. They were terrible pumps, and did not do the job needed (but they were cheap). Huge amounts of product were sold at low prices. Quality deteriorated from an already low point. Prices at every level kept dropping. More people entered the hobby than ever before. More people left the hobby than ever before. This was the direct result of the buyers' inability to maintain an aquarium setup that was based on low price and lower quality. The setup either broke or died. Basements and attics across the United States were stocked with empty aquariums and equipment.

Florida fish producers quickly went from "trouble" to "real trouble". A large number of factors, none of which were good, came together in the 1960s to slow down the Florida fish farming industry. Florida's fish farmers found themselves in the worst shape in their short history. They'd had it all to themselves for years with business only getting better every year. Incredible as it seemed to us then, all of this eventually made the Florida industry (those of us who survived) the strongest and the best in the world.

I got caught up in the frenzy to see who could sell fish the cheapest. One of my largest and certainly my toughest customer was the Chicago Bird and Cage Company owned by Sid and Bill Meyers. The brothers had leaseholds in some of the finest department stores in the country. They were the first to perfect the use of fish as a weapon to attract volume. Their prices on dry goods were more than adequate to give them large profits. Live tropical fish were used as bait and it worked. They advertised what they called "Super Sales". The amount of fish they consumed was enormous. They wanted cheap fish. The size and quality was not as important as it should have been. The most critical consideration was price. The next most important thing was for the fish to be reasonably hardy. They rotated shipments to their stores over a two or three month period, and did it twice a year. Meyers would "hold court" at trade shows, and there he would beat up on a number of fish farmers (including me). We all came to him in hopes of making a profitable sale. Meyers played one of us against the other. The producers quickly learned that quality fish were way down on Chicago Bird and Cages priority list. They talked quality, but wanted price above everything else, and then they had to be assured of dependability. The end results were ever lower prices for the suppliers. The suppliers had a customer who did pay his bills to the lucky (or unlucky?) producers. To get an order you had to be prepared to sell Chicago Bird and Cage at production costs or below. It certainly was not the fault of Meyers if the sellers were stupid or desperate enough to sell too low, and I do not fault him. They, and soon imitators of their "super sales", contributed to the problem the Florida industry was experiencing. Chicago Bird and Cage sold enormous amounts of fish that were, for the most part, small, weak, and unattractive. New customers entered the hobby at a record pace as the low prices sold product fast. The poor quality quickly made more ex-hobbyists with unhappy memories.

Florida had more fish farmers than needed and they were producing more fish than the market could absorb. The Far East producers were doing lots of volume by selling cheap, small, and unattractive egg layers that ended up being sold through the discount stores. Prices kept going down and the quality went down with it. Florida sold zebra danio for two cents each and mixed color swordtails, black mollies, small Platys and sunset Variatus for three cents each. Florida farmers developed a reputation for cheap, sick, and small fish. We earned it. Millions of this type of inferior fish were sent out to customers. Very few Florida farmers could economically resist the pressure. I was caught up at the start of the craziness. Fortunately for me I sold my Gulf Fish Hatchery at that time, and for three years became a spectator. Meyers (Chicago Bird and Cage Company) then bought his own farm in Ruskin, Florida and produced his own fish. He had found that the suppliers he had were going broke, and his most dependable supplier (me) had just sold out. Meyers had found that many suppliers did not or could not perform as they had agreed. Fish that had been ordered six months before were not there when needed. The sellers, if they had a chance to sell the fish for more in another direction, did just that. This gave Chicago Bird and Cage major problems. We always stayed friendly. They never were able to get their own farm to do what they wanted it to do. They sold it a few years later.

A really talented and bright woman named Mary Terrill bought that farm from Chicago Bird & Cage. It then became Ruskin Tropical Fish. Mary was an excellent fish farmer, and became a good friend. She was one of my favorite people. Mary studied fish all her life, and had an excellent library. She did a really good job with the farm and raised some outstanding quality fish. Mary was an animal person and always had a strange assortment of "pets" around that she was trying to breed. I can remember Galagos (bush babies), gigantic African bullfrogs, lemurs, and Mata Mata turtles. I also remember her four huge, noisy, fierce-looking dogs that I am sure ran off many visitors. Her recent death from cancer surprised us all. It hit her fast. She did not take care of herself, always had a cold beer handy, and if you were her friend she was always there to help. Her sons run the business now and I wish them well. They had a good teacher.

From 1960 to 1975 Florida struggled. The fish farms that survived included the few that tried to concentrate on quality and maintained better prices. In 1966 I reentered the fish business. I wanted nothing more than to raise and ship fish. I wanted a business where I could spend my time not doing "business". I wanted to spend the bulk of my time raising new and better fish. The less I had to do with collecting money, checking invoices, worrying about payrolls, borrowing money because customers wouldn't or couldn't pay their bills, and similar business regimens, the happier I would be. I thought about this a lot and got an inspiration that developed into an idea that turned into my ten best and happiest years.

Before I had sold Gulf Fish Hatchery some three years earlier (1963) I had a very good customer in Toledo, Ohio, then called Toledo Broadway Distributors. They had seven stores when we first started supplying them. They seemed to be doing everything right. They were early leaseholders in large discount stores. They operated full line pet shops in these huge stores. The seven stores they operated were all doing well. In the next three years, while I had been on the sidelines, they had expanded to 27 stores. They needed reasonably priced, healthy fish in large quantities. They were running into the same problems that Chicago Bird and Cage had experienced. They could not depend on their suppliers. The business was run by Phil, Walter, and Stanley Treuhaft. Phil Treuhaft was the youngest, and he was the president of the company. His father-in-law was Louis R. Romanoff. Mr. Romanoff was a prominent Toledo attorney. He retired from his law practice to become the chairman of the board of Toledo-Broadway Distributors. They changed their name to PETCOA Industries. All of my dealings were with Lou Romanoff and Phil Treuhaft. I set up a meeting (1966) to let them know my ideas. We met and I laid out my plan. This was for a joint venture into a tropical fish farming business. They enthusiastically agreed with my ideas. Our association would solve their livestock problems. These problems were daily becoming more serious. I told Lou Romanoff that I had to be given a completely free hand. I have always been able to organize and run things. I stipulated (and they agreed) that while I was winning (making a profit) I was to be left alone. If ever I did not make a profit, then I would be subject to their directives to correct it. In all the years we were associated they left me alone. We always operated profitably. PETCOA would program me as to what they needed. I was then left to work it out. This was exactly what I wanted and what I did best. I kept our prices lower than could be found from any other source. I asked PETCOA for $50,000 and agreed to match it as start up capital for Ross Socolof Farms (the name of our new venture). I had no problem getting a line of credit locally which we all guaranteed personally. We were in business as equal partners. We all knew what we wanted and we were now aimed in that direction. I embarked on a new adventure. Great excitement! I bought 80 acres of land on a dirt road that was about to be paved. I bought the land for $400 an acre. The acreage was on Moccasin Wallow Road north of Buffalo Drain in Cabbage Slough. The address was really exotic and seemed the right place to build a fish farm. I only intended to use 25 acres for the farm. The rest was there if PETCOA continued to expand. It was a wise move. They did and we did. I had the first ponds dug, fertilized, and stocked within two weeks. We had a crop ready to ship that included almost all of the important items in four months time. The very best employee that I had at Gulf Fish Hatchery was a man named Jerry Adams. He was hired first. He could and did everything. He was tireless and enjoyed what he did. He was always there before any other employee and did not leave until everything was done. Fred Small was the second key employee at the start. Fred was something special when it came to living things. I have never known anyone who was so completely tuned into nature. Clarence Adams, who was Jerry's brother, was the third person hired and he ran the field operations with Fred Small. All of these people had worked for me before at the Gulf Fish Hatchery.

Ralph Meyer was the first person I knew in Florida. He had been a combat military policeman in Germany during World War Two. While there he had met and married a wonderful lady. Analiese and Ralph Meyer came to Florida from Detroit. He had been born there. Before he went into the army he had made a living playing in a jazz band, Ralph was an accomplished musician who played a variety of instruments. He had been invited to Florida by some Detroit friends whom he described as former bootleggers. They had operated the speakeasy where Ralph played in the band. In Naples, Florida, they built and operated a roadside tourist attraction called Everglades Wonder Gardens. It was an unusual attraction as the animals all were kept well. Ralph spent his first year there working for the Piper brothers who operated the "zoo". He fell in love with Florida. All of his spare time was spent catching and selling exotic Florida snakes. He walked the highways every night with a head lamp and caught a variety of snakes that he easily sold. Snakes stay on road surfaces as the days cool off. The road retains the wanted warmth. Ralph was another one of those very rare humans who was tuned into nature. The Meyer family took a big step and relocated in Cortez, Florida (near Bradenton). That is when we first made contact (1954). He saw one of my General Aquatic advertisements in a trade magazine. He wrote to me and enclosed a price list of marine fish and invertebrates.

The Meyer family ran a small retail petshop, caught and sold marine fish, and even managed to sell a few fish that they bred. Guppies were always Ralph's favorite fish and he worked on one strain for years. This became his well known and much wanted "Colorama" guppy. He raised this strain all the years he produced fish. He was catching local marine tropicals and by 1954 had started shipping them to wholesale customers in the North. He shipped marine fish to me at General Aquatic Supply in New York. His best marine item was wonderful huge seahorses. In addition we received baby trunkfish, dwarf seahorses. triggerfish, spiny boxfish, cowfish, sea robins, spade angelfish, filefish, pipefish, baby starfish, hermit crabs, anemones, horseshoe crabs, and even an occasional butterfly fish.

Ralph, years later, owned and operated a small livebearer farm. He had sold it in 1963, and gone to work for the same people who bought my original business. He was never happy there and he was delighted to join my new operation. He was a talented wood worker. He designed and constructed the entire office area at Ross Socolof Farms. When it came time to lay out the ponds we did it together. He stayed with me for almost three years. When the business grew and expanded, he asked me to listen to an idea he had been toying with for some months. We (PETCOA and I) would sell him a piece of our property. He would spend the next year developing it and continue to work for me every day until noon. At the end of the year he would be in business for himself. He planned to give me first choice of any of the fish he had for sale and raise any items we wanted. Ralph Meyer working a half day was better than most full time employees, so I agreed. It worked out wonderfully for both of us. Ralph and I, in the almost 50 years we knew each other, never had a cross word or disagreement. He died in 1993 at 83. We had a wonderful last visit some weeks before he died. He was a very nice, talented, gentle man who it was a pleasure to call "friend".

While we were clearing land and preparing for pond construction, we were already constructing a building for the office and hatchery. This structure would be 6,500 square feet and planned so that it could easily be expanded when needed. We did everything ourselves. That included all of the construction. I employed the same two people Jack Pearlman had used to build the new building at Gulf Fish Hatchery. They could build anything and they did. All of the labor was done by our own employees. Rose Kerchoff and her son Butch came aboard next. They both had worked at Gulf, and Butch had been doing construction work for years. I think he, Fred Small and Jerry Adams built more than half of the building. Rose ran the inside hatchery starting just as soon as a roof was put up. None of us ever worked as hard before and I honestly believe none of us ever enjoyed work as much. It was a wonderful time. A beautiful small fish farm was completed and operating in an amazingly short period of time. I had made contact with most of my overseas suppliers. Emilio Saiz was in business for himself in Columbia, as he'd purchased the fifty percent I had previously owned in his business. He was a major supplier. In less than four months the hatchery was full, and best of all, a lot of the fish were from our own production. We did our own welding and constructed heavy angle iron racks. I set in about 1200 of Joe Cooley's low forty gallon aquariums. The most important reason I had located the farm on Moccasin Wallow Road was that Manatee County had a major pipe line (three foot diameter) carrying raw untreated water from the county's reservoir to a treatment plant eight miles away. The line ran in front of our land. Manatee County was delighted to contract with us and sold us great amounts of this soft, acid, magic raw, untreated water at a very low price. It had sixty pounds of pressure behind it. We did not even need a pump. Hank Hansen had located some years earlier on the line. He discovered the value of the water and told me about it. Priceless and rare (in Florida) is the best description I can come up with to describe the water quality. It even had a desirable brownish cast from natural tannic acids. Almost all of the natural water in Florida is hard and alkaline. This is great for cichlids and livebearers, but tough on almost everything else. The hardest commodity to find in Florida is good breeding water (soft and acidic). This type of water is critically needed to breed the majority of egg laying fishes. The better the water, the better the results. At Gulf Fish Hatchery I had a special truck with huge wooden barrels atop the flatbed that we would send to a remote stream of good breeding water. We pumped it in and then out at the farm daily. This was expensive, but water of a quality suitable for breeding was critical. This was done by most farmers that bred a variety of egg laying fish. Our raw county water would test medium to soft in hardness and had a pH of 6.6 - 6.8. It was particularly important and helped us tremendously in keeping large quantities of imports. All the Amazonian, Malaysian, and Thai wild fishes come from soft and acid waters. Few Florida suppliers offered a variety of these imports as they had water problems that gave them great losses and bad quality. We always had all of the supposed "difficult" fish and constantly expanded our variety as we had to have everything available for our own PETCOA stores. The quality of our fish was excellent. If a store wanted a freshwater stingray, an African lungfish, or an Indian climbing perch we had it available.

PETCOA put me on their Board of Directors, and made me a vice president of the parent company. I ran the farm operation and was included in most corporate decisions. I attended all the board meetings in Toledo which gave me an opportunity to sit down and plan future supply strategies. That's when I got to know Jack Canfield well. He was the PETCOA livestock buyer and the man who had to solve their livestock problems. Jack was in his early twenties. He had grown up working and managing a PETCOA pet shop. He became PETCOA's best store manager. He was well suited for the big management job he eventually received. Jack and I became close friends then and still are. It took me a few years to convince PETCOA management that Jack was the best possible person to promote to top management status. The fact that he was so young made them hesitant. In the meantime they had an overabundance of incompetents doing important jobs badly. When PETCOA finally did give Canfield more responsibility he performed better than anyone else in the Toledo operation. Jack and I travelled a lot, visiting various stores whenever we could find the time. Together we were able to reinforce our observations, and tried to pinpoint serious retail problems. Unfortunately, no one was listening, and the problems escalated.

The next years were exciting. PETCOA expanded rapidly. While they did not make the profits expected, the banks had great confidence in the operation and encouraged them to expand and they did. The Ross Socolof Farms operation solved their livestock supply problems. Less than five years after I joined the company, PETCOA was romanced by Wall Street. The business had an exotic appeal. PETCOA needed large cash infusions to continue to expand. They needed money to pay for the new stores that they had already opened, and others they could open. The original seven stores I had first sold to in 1962 had now expanded to sixty units. Large discount chains like Korvette were anxious for PETCOA to open more units in their stores. Unfortunately, they never were given the good stores, but always got the slow volume Korvette outlets.

In 1970 a decision was made to float a stock issue and sell shares to the public. I was called to Toledo after the decision was made and presented with an unusual problem. The underwriters had informed PETCOA that they could not proceed while only owning half of a fish farm. PETCOA had to buy me out or sell out to me. It was really no decision. I had little choice. I agreed to stay with the company and turned in my stock. This solved the problem and PETCOA owned all of Ross Socolof Farms. In exchange I would receive three hundred thousand dollars in unregistered stock at the offered price. This meant I could not sell my shares at that time, but eventually I could. If the stock rose in value I could benefit greatly. The original investments that PETCOA and I had made had been repaid. I had no cash investment in the business and had a very good wage with an excellent bonus incentive.

Our fish farming horizons expanded when it became apparent that PETCOA was having problems getting livestock other than fish. They asked for our help. Jack Canfield and I designed the program. We both realized how much time, effort, and money would be saved by having additional needed items come on one shipment to the stores from one place. We were already handling baby caiman, baby green turtles, Carolina newts, aquatic African toads (*Xenopus levis*), and aquatic Congo frogs.

I started expanding the variety of herptile items. Emilio Saiz in Colombia could get me baby Anacondas, Caecelians, Mata Mata turtles, Surinam toads (*Pipa pipa*), and a constant supply of one of a kind less common lizards and snakes. The stores took them all. I next added Boa constrictors and other snakes that I could get from our baby caiman suppliers in Barranquilla, Colombia. The baby caiman, baby river turtles, and all sizes of Boa constrictors were most important. Tegu lizards, cheap and nasty snakes like Cook's tree Boas, Cribos, and Spilotes were tried and discarded. Red and yellow legged tortoises sold well. Emilio Saiz next expanded his shipments to include various monkeys and other baby mammals. I made contact with several animal dealers in the Far East and soon we had a variety of these animals available to the stores. Ross Socolof Farms continued to sell to other buyers. The expanded line helped make this business more profitable. Our own stores always represented more than 85% of our sales.

Loise and I made a trip at this time to Villavicencio. We stopped for a few days in Barranquilla on the way back to Florida. My fertile imagination soared when I saw three unbelievable huge tadpoles. I had a vision of a new and probably unknown gigantic frog. These monster tadpoles were more than eight inches long. I measured them as I did not believe my own eyes. The tadpoles were larger than any tadpole I had ever imagined existed. The biggest one was easily four or five times the mass of the huge Florida bullfrog tadpole. I couldn't wait to own them and take them with me to Florida where I would build an empire based on this new monster animal. I estimated that an adult would be about ten pounds. The amazing thing about them was they appeared to be still growing. They did not show vestiges of rear or front legs which all tadpoles show prior to an accelerated metamorphosis into the adult form. This apparently was an unknown "King Kong" frog. I had no idea what they were and neither did the Sanchez Brothers (Jose and Edison), our suppliers. These were the only ones that had ever been brought to them by their collectors. I told them I could use lots of them and to try to get more. I got two of the three back alive. I soon discovered, as I examined them each day, that as they grew older they shrunk in size. They still did not have any of their legs erupting. I then started asking questions and reading and soon I discovered that I had tadpoles of the seldom seen paradox frog (*Pseudis paradoxa*). This is a really unique animal and one I had no knowledge of before this encounter. Imagine using two hands to lift one tadpole. I tried for years to get more. They were hard to collect and harder to handle and ship. I never saw another. After they were first discovered, herpetologists looked in vain for these never to be seen giant frogs. The paradox is that paradox frog tadpoles, unlike every other tadpole, grow to an incredible bulk and then they shrink down and down becoming smaller and smaller. When they metamorphose they become a two and a half inch adult of a rather nondescript green and brown frog. Another of my expected fortunes went up in smoke.

While expanding the range of reptiles and amphibians we could offer, I found a German collector in South Africa named Mueller. He was a wonderful and expert shipper. The animals he supplied us were very different. I think John Woods, our South African supplier of *Xenopus* frogs, introduced us. I had done well selling horned toads which we had gotten from Mr. Baty in Texas. He had for some years supplied our General Aquatic Supply in New York. They disappeared as an item when they became scarce and, were fortunately, then protected. The demand for horned toads remained. It was useful to be able to get an affordable look-alike horned "toad" from South Africa. The genus is *Cordylus* and the species was *jonesii*. There were more than a dozen species of *Cordylus*. This one was a four to five inch placid pincushion and apparently was easy to collect. As a result it was the most economical to buy. It was a spiny lizard. Not as bizarre as the American horned toad, but a satisfactory substitute. We sold many of these, and even raised a few young. The young would appear in the holding cages with some regularity as *Cordylus* lizards bear their young alive. The seldom seen and quite rare *Cordylus giganteus* is called the "stargazer". This lizard is a massive twelve inch animal. When resting it would position its head tilted upward (stargazing). A very elegant-looking animal. It was easy to understand how it had earned the name. The few specimens we were able to get were quickly purchased by our zoological park customers. I regularly imported three tortoises from Mueller. The pancake tortoise is flat in shape and looks as though it had been run over by a steam roller. It is collected under rocks and brush in the daytime where it can, because of its unique body shape and pliable carapace, crawl in, and under rocks and brush to avoid the fierce hot and dry daytime sun. The second variety was the hingeback tortoise (*Kinixys erosa*), and the beauty was the leopard tortoise (*Testudo pardalis*) which sold the best. They grow huge. None of the snakes Mueller sent us sold well. The most interesting was an egg eating snake that could unhinge its jaws allowing it to swallow (whole) the eggs that it preferred as food. When the egg was completely engulfed and on its way into the stomach cavity, the snake would break the egg by constriction. South Africa has a gigantic ten inch plus millipede. It is harmless, spooky looking, and really impressive. Think of a big armor plated Cuban cigar with great quantities of legs running its full length, and you will have an accurate picture of this bizarre insect. It was a good display item that sold well.

I read somewhere that the island of Taiwan has more species of poisonous snakes than any other place of comparable size. I believe it. Most are unattractive and rear-fanged poisonous. The best item from Taiwan was the baby soft shell turtles (*Trionyx* species) which could be had, 500 or 1000 at a time, during the season. They also offered the small Reeves turtle and we sold many of these.

Thailand has snail-eating turtles that do not bother fish. The only problem was the size. Most would be in the four to seven inch range. 'These were too large to sell well. I tried for many years to get animals that were three inches or smaller. I always was assured they would be small. They never were. Thailand has wonderful turtles. The most interesting are the star turtles. This turtle has a corona of spike-like projections around its entire body. This creates a star. Albino soft shell turtles (*Trionyx*) turned up from time to time and we had, over the years, a total of five of these beautiful rare animals. They all went to public aquariums. Pythons are the most attractive of the large constrictor snakes, although they do not have the best dispositions (red tail Boas do). We bought and easily sold many small-sized specimens. We learned a lot about handling reptiles and PETCOA never had to go elsewhere for a supplier. Shipping the wide variety of animals saved tremendous amounts of money on freight costs as, they all went as "tropical fish" on the waybill.

Our daughter Jodi spent more time at the farm than any of the other children. She has always been tuned into animals. She is as "simpatico" with all creatures as is her mother. Jodi earned all her spending money at the farm. She worked every Saturday and most of her summer vacations. She even learned rudimentary business procedures. Loise set her up in business, when she was about ten, as the "J0-SEW" Snake Bag Company. She made all of our snake shipping bags for years. Loise made her prepare invoices and we paid her by check. She had her own bank account. She paid cash for her first car when she was sixteen. We sold Boa constrictors by the foot. An eight foot measure was nailed down on our packing table to measure snakes. Jodi handled snakes without fear, and knew just what she was doing. I don't think she ever got bit or, at the least, never told me if she did. She delighted in bringing her macho boy friends out to the farm where she would haul out a nine foot Boa for them to play with. This almost always turned a pseudo-macho boyfriend to Jello.

We had a very early and totally unexpected freeze in 1969. The Boa holding cages had not yet been protected from the cold. The snakes were all frozen to death (or so I thought). Before we could dispose of them we saw some slight flicker of life in a few. We sorted the dead from the potentially live and then draped the dead over a pipe where they hung looking like ropes of limp spaghetti. I put the ones with a suspected spark of life (or a reflex?) back in a cage to observe. The only reason I didn't dump the dead ones was that our son Mark was then into taxidermy. I had promised to keep any large dead snakes for him. Incredibly, as the day heated up, they all came back to life. We did not lose a single Boa. Everyone was delighted (except Mark) after recovering from an unbelieving awareness of what we had all seen.

Yugoslavia had a state owned export business that among other things had a reptile section. The farmers collected and then sold the native tortoises (*Testudo hermanni*), and other reptiles and amphibians to this central collecting agency. I had had a few small shipments in previous years. We had no problem selling the tortoises which were the best items offered. They were of a small enough size (three to six inches), easily fed, hardy, attractive, and made good pets. When baby green turtles were banned in the United States the demand for any alternate item was great. I had no difficulty keeping tortoises and decided, as the price was very attractive, to try to buy all the tortoises that they could supply. We could easily hold them until sold and this even if it took several years. I anticipated a problem obtaining them in the future (that was the only thing I was right about). I could have all available and the number was huge. I knew tortoises live almost forever, so I plunged ahead. Ten thousand tortoises are a lot of tortoises. That is what they had and that is what I bought. I had a vague idea that I might try breeding them, and this despite the previous year's tragedy, when I tried to breed Louisiana sliders.

Never being able to obtain enough baby green turtles Elwyn and I decided to establish a breeding colony of our own. Elwyn went to Louisianna where he bought 500 breeders from our Louisiana suppliers. He then had them trucked in. The main farm had a huge pond that had never been fully utilized. The large size, depth, and shape made it impractical to ever pump and reset. It had been created when the farm was originally dug and the reason for the size was the necessity to obtain a lot of fill to raise and level the terrain in that immediate area. By doing this we were able to construct normal ponds in the area. The only use for the oversized pond was to breed Jack Dempsey cichlids (*Cichlasoma octofasciatum*) in it, and at the same time create large black mollies. Enough Jack Dempsey cichlids, that are kept hungry, will eat every baby black molly. The black molly population, as a result, would never become large enough to stunt themselves. That is what normally happens and keeps the industry's available supply of premium sized black mollies always in short supply. As large mollies were created, removed, and sold they were then replaced with equal numbers of regular sized fish to grow out. This colony would continue undisturbed in our new turtle breeding pond. The addition of water lettuce (*Pistia stratiotes*) provided a favorite food for the turtles. Just as we were content that we had done everything right, and were looking forward to our first crop of baby green turtles, the Department of Interior totally banned the sale of baby turtles in the United States and we were out of the baby green turtle business.

This bad omen should have made me more cautious before proceeding with my plan to own all of the Yugoslavian tortoises. I wasn't listening, and I bought the 10,000 tortoises. We had to pay for them in advance. There was no turning back. I arranged for the tortoises to come into New York by water. That was easy, but getting them to Florida in an affordable manner was not. I discussed it with John Zara who was running our reptile department. John had been the director of the Mesker Park Zoo in Evansville, Indiana before coming to work for us. We had met years earlier on an expedition to Guatemala. John's suggestion was to fly someone to New York, rent a large truck, and be waiting for them on the pier in Manhattan. As soon as the tortoises had cleared customs and were available this person would load and head to Florida and the farm. I agreed before Zara realized that he had just volunteered to do it. We then convinced Ed Hartley, who was breeding fish for us, to make the trip with him. We then constructed a large facility adjacent to the main building for the tortoises. The pen was made on a concrete pad with a chain link fence set into the concrete to prevent anything digging in or out. About 15 inches of soil was added, and then sod was planted. Before the tortoises left Yugoslavia their future home had a luxuriant growth of grass established. The animals would be packed tightly in light weight wooden crates. This would have bothered any creature except a tortoise. My previous experience indicated that any mortality would be insignificant.

By driving straight through John Zara and Ed Hartley would be at the farm in twenty four hours. Everything was ready. The heroic pair were at the pier in New York, waiting and watching, in the rented truck when the animals were offloaded from the cargo compartment. The entire shipment came off the boat intact in one huge load carried dockside inside of a gigantic steel meshed cargo net by a massive crane.

Tragedy struck when the equipment malfunctioned. The huge load dropped the crates of tortoises, like coconuts, onto the pier.... Bedlam. Tortoises were escaping in every direction. Later John and Ed described a truly nightmare scene. Intact crates were placed in the rear of the empty truck body as a wall to contain the escapees. Everyone on the pier was chasing and catching tortoises, and then dumping tortoises behind the makeshift barricade inside the truck. An exception was notated on the waybill. It was a full and sloppy load. John called me then and explained what happened. I advised him to get off the phone, and head home, and we would worry about claims later. From time to time John called to tell me where they were. Usually they were some place they did not want to be. The trip was a horror as John discovered he had rented a truck that was not large enough. The load weighed more than was allowed on the highway for the trucks rated capacity. They had to stay off of interstate highways and move as fast as they could using secondary roads where they hoped they were either legal or lucky. If an additional impetus for speed was needed, the stench that was fast increasing from the cargo was an effective spur. They arrived about midnight half a day later than expected. Jerry Adams and I were at the farm to meet them. We put the tortoises in the pen. Jerry claimed he could smell them before he saw them. The extent of the disaster became apparent when the back door of the truck was opened. Great waves of nauseating stench engulfed us. John Zara and Ed Hartley had done their part and I sent them home. Jerry and I unloaded the tortoises. I had neglected to provide any light which was critically needed. I fixed that by positioning my car with the headlights providing almost adequate light. We carried individual crates and then filled sacks with loose animals into the pen and released them. The impact of the fall had banged many animals together. This caused cracked shells without breaking the crates open. The bulk of the injuries and subsequent deaths were from internal injuries. Often no apparent damage was done to the shells.

Several hours later we had done all we could. I sent Jerry Adams home as there was nothing more that could be done until morning. I remained to spread some fresh food around the pen and hose the tortoises down one more time. The sun would be up in a few more hours, and then we could examine the animals carefully one by one. I checked the tortoises one more time and after locking the pen door bent down, butt end up, to shut off the water supply. I was deep in thought about the terrible loss we faced, when things went crazy. With no warning a massive unknown thing moved in and caught me right between my spread legs and up-ended me. My head bounced off the chain link fence and I hit the ground hard. The miracle was that I did not die of fright. I screamed in terror. Whatever it was left. The only other time I can remember being that frightened was on a trip down the Berbice River in (then) British Guiana. That time I was making my way afoot, on the bank, alongside the river, looking into the water. I almost stepped on a huge sleeping caiman. I spooked the animal before I saw it. It reared up, not three feet from me, opening up a set of jaws big enough to engulf a row boat and hissed violently. I looked at a huge set of gleaming white teeth and blindly turned and ran into a tree which felled me. I recovered and prepared to be eaten when I realized that the gator had gone the other way. That was the feeling I had when this great nightmare beast plowed into my rear. It was a huge pig. We found the tracks in the morning. This enormous boar had been seen several times near the farm. It always managed to escape before anyone could get a gun. It was one of five piglets that Jerry Adams had tried to raise years earlier in a corner of the property. His pen had not been baby pig proof and his animals had escaped. Now, years later, this great beast had his revenge. I am sure he had been watching Jerry and figured this was his chance to get even. He just didn't know that he had missed Jerry by fifteen minutes. Never saw the beast again. We looked for it for years. He probably had heard that I don't get mad, but I do get even.

Our expanded reptile department was doing well and operating smoothly. PETCOA next asked me to think about importing birds. The sale of birds was increasing. Laws had changed. We could now import Psittacine birds that had been quarantined abroad. This would include the small Quaker and bee bee parakeets from South America. These rather nondescript green birds were inexpensive which is what made them so popular. They were an important promotional item. PETCOA sold these, on sale, in the thousands. In addition they also wanted a variety of large parrots, lovebirds, conures, and macaws. Other wild birds were needed. The most important was the Greater Hill (talking) Mynah birds from India. I had handled Mynah birds in the early 1950s before I got to Florida. I had learned where to get them and how to care for them. In short order we were in the bird business in a big way.

In 1953 when I was operating at retail in the General Aquatic Supply business in New York a lady had come in wanting to know if she could trade her Mynah bird for other merchandise. She had bought it there as a baby some years earlier. She suggested a $25.00 cash credit which was about right. She used it to buy something else. I had asked her if the bird talked. She said yes. I had no idea of what "yes" or "talk" covered. This turned out to be a genius Mynah. I did not know this that Saturday afternoon when I took it home. I planned to observe it over the weekend to see if it could talk. I switched on the Dodger game, on the car's radio, just as the national anthem started. I almost drove off the road when I realized that the bird was singing along. I mean all of it. It showed us a wide repertoire that night which included "My name is John L. Lewis, and I am a Mynah Bird". The next day I sold it to a wealthy neighbor who chanced to visit. He had to have it so I let him have it for $500 which in those days was an enormous price. He had two poodles. When his front door bell rang, the Mynah would bark exactly like a poodle. He had confused visitors when after entering his home, they realized that his two dogs had stopped barking, and that the third barking dog was a bird.

I needed additional managerial help at Ross Socolof Farms and needed it bad. I had been looking for some time for the right man. A young school teacher named Elwyn Segrest, then living in Belle Glade, Florida, was one of our suppliers. Belle Glade is a small farming community on Lake Okeechobee. Elwyn had been raising angelfish in his garage to make extra money. He had one customer that took his production. This customer was Fred Cochu from Paramount Aquarium now in Vero Beach. When Fred realized he could not sell all the angelfish that Elwyn produced he suggested Ross Socolof Farms as a customer. I agreed to take the surplus. Elwyn was doing a good job. He was able to bring us fish every other week. He also had good local contacts through his students who he had organized to get us Florida king snakes, red rat snakes, and corn snakes; all of which we needed. I realized that Elwyn Segrest was ready to give up teaching, and we talked seriously. We made a good deal. A good deal is a deal in which everyone gains, and no one loses. Elwyn became the executive vice-president of Ross Socolof Farms. Elwyn and I learned a lot together, and had a lot of fun. We worked many long and hard hours. I bought Elwyn's equipment. He moved his aquariums, himself, and his family to Bradenton. We also received from this transaction a wonderful bonus in the shape of a man named Joe LaFlam. Joe had worked with Elwyn in Belle Glade. He was a very experienced fish hobbyist. He had bred a lot of other types of fish. LaFlam joined the company as a fish breeder. He was a quick study. In less than a year LaFlam became our best fish breeder. He was always experimenting. In one six-month period when he was working with danios, he made eight new varieties. I think all are still being produced. We then got from Czechoslovakia a new longfin zebra danio. When the new danios arrived I gave them to Joe LaFlam. After just one week of conditioning he produced enough young so that he had almost ten thousand young breeders grown out and ready to reproduce in less that four months time. Joe LaFlam put long finage on both the spotted and the gold danio. He also made during that period a pink danio, a new type of gold danio, a blushing danio, and then all sorts of wonderful combinations such as the longfin pink blushing danios. He was the first one in Florida to breed commercial quantities of silver dollars (*Metynnis hypsauchen*). This was a major contribution to our program. Our silver dollar production eventually exceeded some five thousand fish each week. Big, well-conditioned silver dollar breeders could produce vast quantities of eggs. From our most successful spawning we raised over four thousand young.

LaFlam also discovered two interesting mutations. Joe worked both of these for almost a year without ever producing another (this experience is more a rule than an exception). Maybe someday someone will have better success than he did with a fantail spotted danio, and then again with a fantail tiger barb.

Loise had an old friend who moved to Bradenton from Clearwater. He was a Scotsman by the name of James Savage-Jones. He was a sculptor, and an actor, and he needed a job. I always needed help, and Jim was hired. Jim was a favorite employee, and at the same time, one of the worst. He was tried in various jobs. He ended up as a truck driver for deliveries and pick-ups to the Tampa airport. He also was the end man on the packing table. He had terrible eye sight, and often went without his glasses. He was unconvinced that he couldn't see normally. I learned not to let him count fish. He couldn't come even close to being accurate. When things slowed down on the pack-out table Jim would walk up and down it, on his hands. If he lost his audience he would next try a bit of Shakespeare, and if that didn't work he would charm us all singing wonderful Scottish and Irish ballads. Everyone loved him. One day he pulled the gasoline pump out by the roots. He had forgotten to unhitch the nozzle. I was increasingly nervous about his driving skills. I became even more nervous after he took off about three feet from the corner of our bird building. He had turned a little too tightly. Not wanting to hurt his feelings I delayed the inevitable decision to move him to another job. This decision was made easy. He stopped driving when he took down most of the Eastern Airline cargo building in Tampa. Jim stayed in Bradenton and was always our friend. He was in great demand acting and singing in all of our local theater productions. He was very good on stage. He did at times drink a bit too much, and he never knew his lines. No one could tell as he could fake it to perfection. He always looked, and was good. He often would unglue other actors who were waiting for cues that never came. A chance to be the assistant manager of our local theater sent him from us. I think we were both relieved.

My fascination with new fish has more than once been my undoing. My brain has a habit of freezing solid when I hear words such as different, only, new, unique, etc. I received some (new, only, different, unique) "Marble" kissing gouramis from Harris Teo in Singapore. No one had them. We were the first. Kissing gouramis are prolific fish and easy to breed. Good spawns from large breeding pairs could produce 25,000 eggs. I determined to capture the marble kissing gourami market. Just as soon as we had them large enough to breed we leaned hard on the production of our new, unique, only, different marble kissing gouramis. The breeding department did a great job. I anxiously watched lots of them grow, and just as soon as they were big enough to market I planned to set the gears in motion and make everyone rich. Just about then I took samples from the pond stocked the earliest and containing the largest of our marble kissing gouramis. I got sick. I had blindsided myself again. I saw something so obvious that my senses could hardly handle my stupidity. My stomach clenched as I faced reality. Marble kissing gouramis were not going to sell. They were not going to sell no matter what I did. They would not sell because they were incredibly ugly. It was so obvious it gave me an immediate sick stomach. They looked like a soiled diaper that had come to life. I was a late learner, but now was absolutely correct. They did not sell. In fact it got worse as I realized that in my blind cupidity I had not produced nearly enough normal, easily sold, and much wanted pink kissing gouramis. I had about 25% of what I needed. It was the end of August and we had also run out of time to produce more. Kissers are among the tropical fish most sensitive to cold. First thing I did was give all of our marble kissing gourami breeders to Donald Graves, so I would never be tempted again. I then traded all I could for normal kissers. I still had many, many marble kissers left. We sold them out as fast as we could; selling them for less than normal pink kissers.

An interesting observation that I made, over many years, has been the recognition that tropical fishes slowly have adapted themselves to be able to withstand more cold. Charles Darwin's "Survival of the Fittest" is certainly true as far as tropical fish are concerned. I monitored water temperatures every winter for almost thirty years. A maximum/minimum recording thermometer is a good investment. Kissing gouramis can take at least ten degrees more cold now than they could in 1956 when I saw them die from cold water as early as mid October. Breeding purposefully from the survivors or by accident (as the other potential breeders had died from the cold), over a period of years made the fish hardier. In 1977 a bad freeze killed every guppy of every kind with the exception of a very few baby gold guppies. Thousands of their siblings and all the adults were dead. Using these few survivors we produced a strain of golden guppies that could, and did, take this much cold. Hybrid livebearers are much more sensitive to cold than the wild forms. Over the years the hybrids have adapted so that today they can survive previously killing temperatures. In a period of thirty years evolution has made life easier for the Florida fish farmers. An ever increasing variety of cold sensitive fish have adapted to now survive previously killing cold spells.

I have tremendous admiration for the ability of tropical fish to survive. If you contemplate what these tiny creatures are physically subjected to, you can not help wondering how any of them survives. One amazing story comes to mind which illustrates what I have said. I drove to the Tampa airport to pick up fifty or sixty boxes of fish coming from Iquitos. That was a very tight squeeze for my station wagon, and I removed the back seat and the spare tire from the well to use the space for three boxes. About a week later I noticed a strange odor. I rode home with the windows down which cleared it up. Getting into the car the next morning the stench was really serious. I rolled down the windows again, and when I got to the farm I searched for the cause. When I opened the well I remembered what I had done. I had put three boxes of half dollar sized wild angelfish in the well and forgot to unload them. Two of the bags provided the odor. The third bag was perfect. They were packed one hundred to the bag and had been packed for nine days. There were just three dead fish in the surviving bag. The rest were hale and hearty.

I almost did it again when LaFlam came up with an albino gold barb. Fortunately, by then, I had learned that you must ask yourself a question that goes something like "Why would anyone pay a premium of two or three times the normal price, to buy an albino gold barb that is very similar in appearance to a normal gold barb which itself sells poorly. When you get the answer which is ''They would not", you pay attention to yourself.

As captive breeding of tropical fish expands we find ever increasing mutations. These mutations come and go and mostly go. The reason was obvious and one I discovered the hard way. They are usually ugly and not really "that" different. They can not justify a premium price. Some hang around selling just enough to make them worthwhile. The golden Ramirezi is a good example. It breeds as easily as the normal Ramirezi, and now sells for about the same price. A similar item like the albino Kribensis is now about extinct. Almost everything about albino Kribensis is similar to the golden Ramirezi. The difference is in the retail price. It is harder to reproduce, and had to be sold at a premium price. An albino "Krib" cannot justify any premium in price. Most "longfin" strains (good examples are Oscars, kissers, black mollies) are ugly. Valuable creative time spent fixing these monstrous strains would have been better employed if the discoverer had stepped on the sport when first found.

It is a great thrill to find a color sport in the wild. The longfin and albino sports must disappear quickly in the wild. I have never found one. The impediment of excess finny baggage slows them down to the point where they soon become hors d'oeuvres for a bigger fish. I have sent Dr. Joanne Norton of Ames, Iowa most of the livebearer color sports we have caught in the wild. She has used them to create a number of new fish. As of this writing she still maintains the race of blind cave mollies I brought back from southern Mexico many years ago. In that group were two golden morphs. The wild golden sports survived only because life in a cave protects the brighter colored fish from normal predation. She has made these into a pure gold strain. Joanne Norton is an amazing lady with infinite patience and great skills. Her work over the years in creating new strains has made her one of our most outstanding aquarists. Her published "recipes" for breeding angelfish varieties has made an exact science out of what had been great mysteries to most fish breeders.

One year collecting in Colombia I caught a beautiful all blue *Cichlasoma severum*. That was forty years ago and I still dream about it. It died several hours after I caught it.

In Chiapas, Mexico I caught a strange, beautiful ghost-like firemouth cichlid (*C. meeki*) that had bizarre blushing gill plates and little body colors. It retained vivid, blood red on the gill plates. This one I got back alive and it lived. It never would reproduce.

Dr. Harry Specht from Sarasota, Florida, is one of my closest friends, and certainly my favorite travelling companion. We have gone on many collecting expeditions together since our first trip together to Spanish Honduras in 1973. His tropical fish interests center around livebearers and killifishes. He has been very active in the American Killifish Association and recently was chairman of their Board of Directors. Together we collected most of the fish sent to Dr. Norton. This included races of mollies that had red finnage, orange finnage, yellow finnage, and even flag patterns in their tails. Harry and I collected a race of wonderful, huge spotted green swordtails from Princess Margaret Creek in Belize. The first went to Dr. Norton. I then set them up for production. These were the first new race of green swordtails pond bred in Florida in fifty years. The result was amazing. Years of inbreeding had severely stunted all of the Florida green swordtails. I gave stock to Howard Groff, The Hennesseys, Mary Terrill, Googie Graves, and others. This same Princess Margaret Creek in Belize contained one "blue" swordtail. Harry Specht saw it first, and the chase was on. Three hours later an almost dead and mostly drowned Specht had to give up. The fish won that time. It didn't happen often. I've been on collecting trips with an assortment of wonderful and tireless people such as Dr. Albert Klee, Russell Norris, Dr. George Barlow, Jaap de Greef, "Red" Nichols, Jim Langhammer, Jeff Gee, Jurgen Kasprick, Harry Specht, and Rusty Wessel. Rusty is an incredible collector. When he gets on a project he turns into an aquatic pit bull. With skilled collectors like these the fish never had a fighting chance. We have never used poison to collect fish. Harry and I went back to that same location several years later and, not surprisingly, could not find his "blue" swordtail. Perhaps you will have better luck.

My interest in pre-Colombian civilization is shared by Harry Specht. Every trip to Central America we have made has always included visits to interesting ruins. We have been to all the major sites, and a great number of the lesser known ruins. We even found some minor ruins in the jungle, an exciting event.

The all-gold angelfish is an interesting story. I was involved in it from the start. Henry Wingate, who operated the Lakeland Tropical Fish Hatchery in Florida, first discovered all-gold sports. These showed up occasionally in his regular angelfish grow out vats. He never was able to identify the pair that produced the occasional golden fish. The first ones appeared during the 1958-1960 period. Wingate set them aside to try to breed them. From first to last he worked with these few fish trying to get a pair to produce gold angelfish. He never did. Actually he probably did, but he never knew it. He just didn't kept them around long enough. I do not think he found ten gold specimens in a period of ten to fifteen years. It always was a low priority project with him. He never discovered that almost all gold angelfish turned gold after seven to ten months. He was selling the fish before they turned gold. The few he got were, in reality, the best as they turned gold the earliest. There was talk for years about occasional gold angelfish. I am sure these were fish from Wingate that later turned gold in some hobbyist's aquarium.

A very talented fish breeder from Milwaukee named Carl Naja was a customer of Henry Wingate. Carl knew what to do when he had one of the normal Wingate angelfish turn gold. He kept them all, and eventually more turned gold. He raised these and bred the first pair of gold to gold angelfish about a year later. He was the person who learned that these first gold angelfish looked like normals until they were almost grown and then some changed to gold. Some never changed. He did not sell a fish for almost three years. When he sold them he did it all at one time which was very smart. He sold for cash in advance and everyone had their orders sent out the same week. He got good prices. Carl Naja was a regular customer and friend for years. I was one of the first to place an order. He charged fifty dollars each for the larger sizes. I bought fifty of the young fish that had not as yet turned gold and some never did. I also bought twenty of the much more expensive young adults that had or were in the process of changing to gold. My bill was well over one thousand dollars. I felt good for Carl. He was one of the few who managed to recapture his investment in time and then make a good profit while introducing a new, beautiful, and immediately popular gold colored angelfish to the hobby.

It probably is time now for me to forgive him for waking me up in the middle of the night a few years earlier. He had bought some of the largest wild discus (we used to call these "dinner plate") I ever handled. These were robust monsters… easily nine to ten inches high. He wanted to try to breed them. I told him that he was completely wrong to try with adult animals. He should raise some wild babies if he wanted to try to breed wild fish. That was what the 3 AM phone call was about. They had just finished spawning. He knew I really wanted to know that he was right and I was wrong.

It was a strange coincidence that Peter Wong, another friend and a supplier from Hong Kong, came up with a similar looking golden angelfish at about the same time that Carl Naja introduced his fish. The Peter Wong angelfish was not nearly as bright a gold color. This Hong Kong development did show gold as soon as it matured which was a big advantage. I eventually grew some of the less attractive Wong Gold angelfish to breeder size and crossed them into the Wingate/Naja strain and ended up with one hundred percent all-gold angelfish that had their adult coloration from birth. In fact I can still see, in my head, that first spawn when it hatched, and then two days later rose from the bottom of the tank in a large mass of all gold babies. The Wong angelfish never did catch on. It became extinct some years later. The cross is today's gold angelfish.

A very talented fish breeder named Francis (Bud) Goddard lived in Lakeland. He bred many seldom bred species and delivered once each week. We worked together on different projects for years. He came up with the first albino angelfish, in the very early 1960s. I arranged to have it photographed. The fish was male and blind. If it had been a female I think it would have reproduced with success. It died of old age and never was able to fertilize an egg although many different females laid eggs by themselves in his presence.

Ross Socolof Farms had just doubled the size of the buildings. Now I was going to add another large building and a grow-out area with additional concrete vats. This would be another 7,000 square feet. The space would be used to raise angelfish. I had an expert angelfish breeder to design and supervise production (Elwyn Segrest). He did a wonderful job. While we did have major water problems that took many months to solve Elwyn eventually raised an enormous amount of angelfish. We were at our peak when we produced 12,000 a week.

The new bird business boomed. John Zara designed the cages and the layout. We had hired a young man with some experience to help him. He was a very hard worker. We were well pleased with him. Expensive supplies were disappearing. The thief was really good at it. I hate to think of how much he stole. I still would not know if he hadn't been seen in the act by Clarence Adams who gave me the information. The method developed was clever. He had some animals at his home. He asked me if he could take home the banana peels, the outer coverings of the cabbage and lettuce. This plus the other trimmings we had no use for to feed his animals. Why not? He placed the items he was stealing on the bottom of the can and then covered it with the fresh vegetable material he had permission to take. Brine shrimp eggs in gallon cans, peanut butter (for the birds) in gallon size cans, electric motors, and new air pumps all went home with his gift vegetable trimmings.

Over the years I had other serious employee theft problems. The girl who first ran the office was embezzling. A new employee, named Pat Casciano, her assistant at the time, discovered it and came to me. It evidently started as a minor bit of pilferage. The embezzlement accelerated as she got away with more and more. First a few stamps: and then lots of stamps, and then a company check to the post office to buy stamps (and the balance in a blank cash money order). She had been raising a few angelfish at home. She made out invoices for two and three times the correct amounts and wrote herself checks which I signed. Next she forged invoices made to look like the "Micky Mouse" type we daily got from local suppliers. She kept the checks and endorsed them and cashed them.

I hired a friend named Aaron Feldman who was living in Bradenton. Aaron had been in the retail tropical fish business in Chicago (Bit O' Tropics) and had a partner named Bob Troy. Aaron and Bob were customers of mine when I was in Brooklyn and he was in Chicago. They did a big business and any profits they made Bob Troy lost by being the world's worst fish buyer. He always wanted quantity prices on rare and expensive fishes. If elephant nosed Mormyrids were $5.00 each he wanted to buy fifty of them for $4.00 each. Often he did and almost always he lost his shirt. He had the price, but could not keep the fish long enough to sell them profitably. Instead of buying the six or so elephant noses he needed, he had to have fifty and never was able to sell half of them before losing them. Repeat this scenario week after week and your business is heading for the garbage dump which is what eventually happened. Aaron realized this, and left before things really got bad. He was now living in Bradenton and working for a boat manufacturer as a book keeper. We were very lucky to have his help. He worked nights. After several weeks of examining all of our books and records he had a picture of the extent of the theft. We were insured. I had both the sheriff and a representative of the bonding company that carried our insurance concealed in the bathroom in my office when I confronted the thief with the evidence. Just like in the movies. I had complete restitution within 24 hours, a signed confession, and a signed document the insurance company prepared. She agreed not to ever work for anyone where she handled cash or wrote checks. The most frightening revelation was when she told us she had been experimenting making and trying forgeries of my signature on large checks. The sheriff had from her the voluntary admission that she had made, and the bank had cleared, many checks that were in multiple thousands of dollars that I had never seen. These were all legitimate invoices that we had owed. We were lucky to get out of that with a whole skin.

This story does not end here although I never saw her again. She surfaced about five years later. She had returned to town and taken a job with a local insurance agency. Again she embezzled. This time for an admitted twenty thousand dollars, and again she got caught. The insurance company that employed her did not have her bonded. That was a hoot. They did not even bother to check the master computer list that insurance companies all share identifying known thieves. Her name was there. Our insurance agency had the name and information put there years earlier. She got away with it that time as her employers did not dare prosecute. Can you imagine what their clients would think? They would look so stupid if their customers ever learned what they had let happen to themselves.

Pat Casciano developed into a very competent employee. She had a natural grasp of mathematics, and picked up the intricacies of bookkeeping fast. She was guided by Aaron Feldman, and soon could do complete profit and loss statements. As our business grew she became more and more important. Eventually she ran the entire office and became the company's treasurer and personnel director.

One memorable thievery incident was inexplicable. The thief did not need the money. He came from a wealthy family. This time, after the smoke cleared, we ended up better off than before and I will tell you how this strange thing happened. When we constructed the second major pond area (another 40 acres) at the main farm I left one acre undeveloped. This was hammock land that was just too high and rough to try to clear. It also was very heavily wooded. It was easier to leave it undeveloped. The more I looked at it the more I liked the idea of making a small, virgin parkland out of this small densely wooded hammock. I needed some dirt so encircled the land with a moat making an island. I ended up with what we first called Monkey Island. I had learned somewhere that monkeys could not swim and I stocked it with squirrel monkeys. There were always occasional imperfect and unsalable monkeys. This was an ideal place to stock them. We had accumulated about two dozen and this was what we put on the island. A great idea. Saiz was sending them to us regularly from our Leticia compound. I am not sure how, but by dawn the next day they were gone. If monkeys cannot swim they most certainly can fly. Monkey Island then became Goat Island, as I put a pair of African pygmy goats on it that were in a family way. We soon had four and more came later. I had traded an albino lungfish that Pierre Brichard had sent to me for the goats.

I used my daughter Jodi's old pram (a small sail boat) as a means of getting from the mainland to, and back from, the island. It was a wreck.

Main building complex Ross Socolof Farms (1973)

Ross Socolof Farms (1973)

Dr. Jack Gratzek

Ross Socolof Farms
P. O. BOX 1321 - BRADENTON, FLORIDA
33506

Telephone Area 813
776-1211
Night 746-8122

BULK RATE
U S POSTAGE
PAID
PERMIT NO. 116
BRADENTON FLORIDA

Return Postage Guaranteed

SOCOLOF'S FIN 'N FARM CHAT

Vol. 1 No. 7 November 1975

1 Tortoise & Turtle Pen
2 Amphibian & Reptile area
3 Aquatic Plants
4 Parakeets, Cockatiels etc
5 Breeding: Danios, Koi, livebearer genetics
6 Angelfish breeding
7 Livebearer inventory
8 Egglayer breeding
9 Imports and egglayer inventory
10 Guinea pigs, mammals etc
11 Water treatment plant
12 Truck loading and storage area
13 Offices & Laboratory

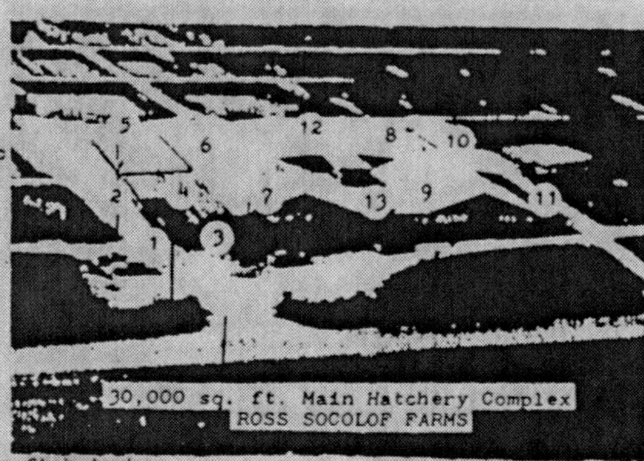

30,000 sq. ft. Main Hatchery Complex
ROSS SOCOLOF FARMS

Use cutouts below on your fish tanks

DEALER PRICE & INFORMATION

	SPECIAL PRICE	BRED AND RAISED HERE	EFFECTIVE ship dates
Gold Barb (Barbus schuberti) Handsome and hardy. Easy to keep, breed and feed. Peaceful egglayers that will go well in any community tank.		.09 ea.	
African Malawi Cichlids Four varieties available - P. zebra, I. sprengerae(Rusty), P. microstoma, P. tropheops(Gold). - Mouthbreeders.		Bred & Raised here .64 ea.	11/3 to 11/14
Brick Swordtail (X. helleri) Beauty accompanied by a good disposition makes this livebearer a most popular fish		Bred & Raised here .07 ea.	
HAMSTERS Whether you choose the Golden shorthair, the Fancy shorthair, or the Longhair Sandy-Bear, you'll have a great pet.		Bred Here Golden 60¢ Fancy 65¢ Longhair 1.65	11/3 to 11/28
Moonlight Gourami microlepis Rare, majestic. Seldom available. Bubblenest builder. Non aggressive. Native of Thailand.		Bred & Raised here .22 ea.	
Gold Wag Platy (X. maculatus) Gives birth to living young - 30 to 100 babies at a time. No bad habits. Gold with a black tail.		Bred & Raised here .10 ea.	11/17 to 11/28
Scissortail Rasbora trilineata Active and interesting. Moves in small schools. Hardy and peaceful. Rightfully named as the tail resembles a scissor.		Bred & Raised here .09 ea.	

Stanley Druce (left) and Aaron Feldman

Pat Casciano and Judy Edwards

Part of 10,000 Yugoslavian tortoises (1974)

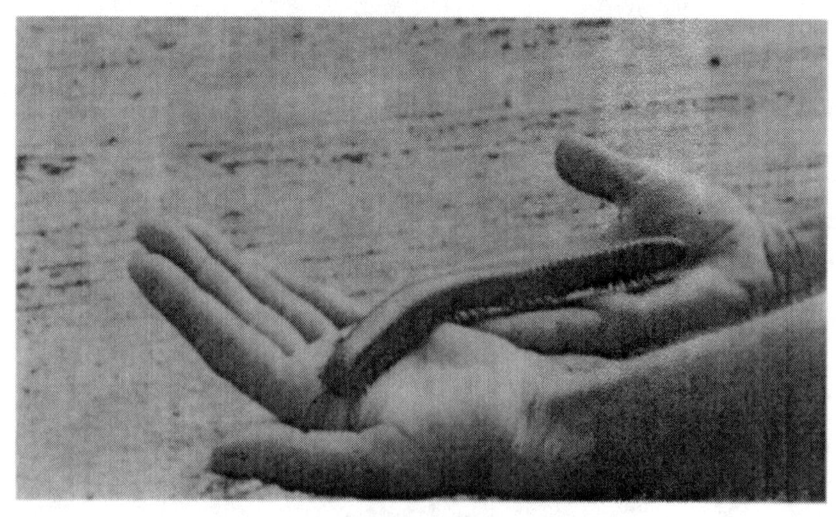

South African millipede

Jim Savage

Elwyn Segrest

"Bud" Goddard

Colonel John Hanan

Johnny Williams and Dick Acheson

Fran Hanan, Dick and Jean Burke, and Ross Socolof (left to right)

"Thurber" the coati with "Irving" the dog

Loise Socolof resting after collecting all day on the Rio Meta in 1962.

Russell Norris – Belize 1973

T. F. Tan - Loise Socolof
Kulai, Malaysia - 1982

Loise with rhinoceros iguana

Dick Stratton on right of Jim Langhammer

Jaap de Greef, Harry Grier, Ross Socolof, Heiko Bleher, and "Red" Nichols

"Rusty" Wessel and Dr. Harry Specht

F.T.F.F.A. Awards Banquet — Ice sculpture is of a *Pseudotropheus socolofi* with Ross Socolof (1994).

If it was left in the water for long it would fill up and sink. We pulled it to the bank and when we used it would jump in and push off the twenty plus feet to the Island. It worked fine until it disappeared. I doubted that it had flown away unaided to join the monkeys. I wondered who would want it enough to steal it. That was the biggest mystery as it really was in terrible shape. It was upsetting as we would have to replace it with something that cost money. Before we arranged to do this it was suggested that we look at the home of one of our employees where we might find our boat and a lot of other interesting things. Elwyn knew where he lived, and we drove out together at lunchtime. We parked the car in the driveway and walked around the back where we found our boat. It had been completely overhauled. It looked better than when it was new. The thief had fiber glassed and then painted the boat. We also found a large number of aquariums, plastic boxes, expensive nets, two seines and other goodies. I called the sheriff. He came right out and arrested the thief. He got off without serving time in jail although found guilty (grand larceny?).

I had been having a terrible time getting enough baby boas. I couldn't get them for ages, and when I finally got a shipment they had somehow all escaped. We found baby boas for months inside the hatchery. I found one between two aquariums where I could not reach it. I had my face right up to the two inch space trying to figure out how I would ever get at it without draining the tank. The boa solved the problem by striking me in the face, getting its mouth tangled in my beard, and neatly capturing itself.

Several months later I hired a boy for the night pack-out crew who had previously worked in Gibsonton for Hartz Mountain. He had experience working pack-out on a fish farm. I thought myself lucky. No one bothered to check his references. I did not know that he was out on parole after being arrested and convicted of stealing fish from another fish farmer. He had been working for us only a few days when I finally got a much needed shipment of one hundred and fifty baby boa constrictors. Almost all were pre-sold, as we had been taking back orders. The new employee waited until the pack-out crew was finished and everyone had left (about 4 am). He then made his way back into the empty building. He stole all one hundred and fifty of the baby boas. The theft was discovered two or three hours later when the regular work day was starting. Someone mentioned that the new employee had an interest in reptiles, and had showed a particular interest in the baby boa shipment. We got fast action after a call to the Hillsboro County sheriff's office. They went to the address we had and learned that our suspect had taken off just an hour before they got there. The best information we had was that he might be headed north to New York City. We made the evening news again. One hundred and fifty stolen boa constrictors is a little different from the more mundane murders reported daily that dull our senses. In time the theft was chalked up in our loser's column. A year passed. We had forgotten the loss. The wheels of justice, during all that time, had been slowly grinding forward. It took more than a year for the routine request from the State of Florida to the New York City police to check out the address they had supplied. Guess who answered the door and who was returned to Florida in chains, and who was eventually convicted of grand larceny? Right! The good guys, much to our collective amazement, won that time.

As the number of PETCOA retail outlets increased the easier it became to sell exotic live stock. We tried to fill orders for anything wanted provided it was to be delivered into responsible hands and was not dangerous. I had a request for a tame otter and, coincidentally, had one available to us from our Singapore animal shipper. It was a small animal and I had been assured it was tame. It arrived and was mean as hell. No one could get close to it. I called the store to tell the manager what I had, and to tell him I was going to sell it to one of the zoological parks. He called back after he had spoken to his customer and he still wanted it. I spoke to the customer myself to be sure. He wanted the animal and seemed to be a responsible adult. He got the animal. A week later he called me back to let me know he had three bonuses in the form of new baby otters. No wonder she was mean—probably labor pains.

What seemed funny at the time, but reflecting now, was really a potential disaster. PETCOA was getting ready to open its biggest store (in Toledo). Phil Treuhaft, the president of PETCOA, called me and needed something really unusual for the opening. I had recently been offered an Asiatic spectacled bear and I mentioned it. Phil liked the idea and told me to order it. The plan was to send it up for the opening. Phil agreed with my suggestion that we donate it to the Toledo Zoo after the first week or so. It arrived and was an almost full grown animal that didn't like any of us. It also was a male, so cubs were not imminent.

We were delighted to send it to Phil. That same night Phil Treuhaft had a call from the Toledo police to let him know that they thought something was loose in the store. They could hear a noisy something moving "things" about inside. Phil thanked the policeman, and told him that he would take care of it. At this point he did not know what was loose and suspected a puppy. Phil is a very sophisticated cosmopolite and the last person I would expect to be a hero. He was a hero that night. He had no choice. In fact he was almost a dead hero. He related his adventure to me on the phone the next morning. He had let himself into the store with his master key and flipped on the lights. Phil had completely forgotten about the spectacled bear. As a result he had no idea what the huge creature was that he had awakened when he let himself into the store. About then he figured out what it was. Instead of leaving the way he came, and calling for reinforcements he tried to force the bear back into the cage from which it had escaped. This was not smart and anyone except Phil would have known this but he knew nothing about animals. He had found a broom and with this he gently guided the bear back to the opened cage. He was doing very well, and later reported he was even enjoying his bravado. That lasted only until the bear wanted to go in another direction. He whacked it with the broom to get its attention. It worked. He got the bear's full attention. Then the bear charged him. Now it was the bear that was trying to cage Treuhaft. Phil kept trying to get back to the front door to escape. The bear was now intent on stopping him first and, apparently, having him for dinner. He was not bitten, but was clawed several times before he got out of the store. The store opened without the bear that left just as soon as the zoo people had caged it and taken it away.

PETCOA could not get enough guinea pigs, and we could not buy enough to supply our demand. Charley Padgett, one of our employees, raised them as a side line. We took the production. When he decided to go out of the guinea pig business I bought his inventory of live animals and the cages he had been using. I built a long narrow building separate from the main complex, but still close enough to get water and electricity. Guinea pigs do well in colonies. The cages were five feet long and three feet wide. We used all of his animals for the nucleus of our breeding herd. We were in the guinea pig business. After watching the numbers for a year it became apparent that the small litters and long gestation periods dictated a resale price a lot higher than the trade had established. They are delightful pets and while hard to profitably raise, we were performing a needed service and had fun doing it.

I have always enjoyed keeping amphibians and most of them sold. We imported fire-belly newts from Japan. They were reasonably priced, beautiful, and easy to keep. They sold well as did the Carolina newts we got from various dealers along the Eastern Seaboard. The farther north they are collected, the larger the animals. The only other salamanders we could regularly obtain were large tiger salamanders. We obtained these from a dealer in Stillwater, Minnesota.

The largest living amphibian is the giant salamander (*Andrias japonicus*) from Japan. These extremely rare and long lived animals reach almost four feet in length. In China there is a huge, but comparatively tiny, relative called the Chinese giant salamander (*Andrias davidianus*). This one does not quite make it to two and a half feet. I saw some displayed in an aquarium in a restaurant in Hong Kong. This seemed very strange and interesting. I asked about them and learned to my surprise that they were not on exhibit, but were an exotic and expensive delicacy which was available for dinner on special order. I got busy the next day and, with Peter Wong, we tracked down the source. Peter is best remembered as the man who developed the "Wong" strain of golden angelfish. Peter also was the manager of the Chinese Country Club in Hong Kong. His head chef pointed us in the right direction to get giant Chinese salamanders. We found that they were periodically imported from Red China and came by train. They would cost five dollars each from the importer. They were all sold as they were unloaded from the train. I asked Peter to try to get me fifty of them, and add on a profit depending on the time and effort he had to expend. I never got fifty (which is just as well). I did get 28 of them. They were very impressive large animals. Quickly, we learned that they hated the sight of each other. Two giant salamanders kept together would fight to the death. This meant tying up 24 large concrete vats. We lost four before finding this out. We had others that needed to heal from wounds inflicted on their bodies by their brethren. The second and more painful lesson was learned when I handled one. I received a terrible, unexpected, and painful bite (from an animal without teeth). They clamp down vice like, and hang on. I think they learned how to do this from a Tokay gecko. I learned that screaming stimulated them to turn the pressure up another notch or two. Obviously, they would make terrible pets. I reconciled myself to not making a fortune trading in giant Chinese salamanders. Ross Socolof Farms managed to dispose of them outside of the pet industry to zoological parks, and not to restaurants, that were delighted to have them. That made me feel good. That was the only thing that made me feel good about Chinese giant salamanders.

We kept on building buildings. By the time we finished, Ross Socolof Farms had 30,000 feet of covered space at the main farm. The original 80 acres were full of ponds. We tried, but could not buy additional land contiguous to the main farm.

Ken Blaising, who had owned and operated Midwest Aquarium in Chicago, was my second customer when I entered the tropical fish business. He was a long time friend, and had then just retired. He had several years earlier bought a farm about two miles from us, and had there a small livebearer operation supplying himself. Ken no longer needed a fish farm. We bought the property. The farm had almost thirty acres with a fair sized holding and shipping building. Joe LaFlam ran this satellite operation for us. We were able to convert the building into a breeding hatchery. Joe kept an eye on the field operation, and bred a variety of gouramis. The fry were grown out there in the dirt ponds. We utilized all of the land by digging several hundred additional ponds. The great majority of the ponds constructed there, and everywhere else on our farms, were 100 feet long and 20 feet wide. The deepest end averaged six and a half feet in depth. By the time we finished digging there were close to 1,200 fish ponds on the five farms.

When I had time to think about it I realized that while I was enjoying the challenge of what had grown into the largest fish farm operation anywhere, I was fast loosing touch with the things that gave me the most pleasure. In the early years, I had come to work, kicked off my loafers, and then spent hours and hours with the fish both inside and outside. The last thing I did before leaving the farm was to clean the dirt from my feet, and put my shoes on. Now my feet were not dirty at the end of the day. As the business expanded I found myself spending more and more time in the office. Always, while driving to the farm, I dictated work memoranda to the staff. These tapes were dropped off on Pat Casciano's desk first thing in the morning. By 9 AM they would be distributed. One day, in a rare quiet moment, I came to the realization that what I had originally planned was no longer happening. I started thinking that I would try within the next five years to somehow extricate myself from being a businessman, and again become a fish hobbyist, and little did I know that wheels were already turning for such an eventual happening.

Now there were over 40,000 square feet of inside space in secure buildings. About half of the space was devoted to holding wild fish, our produced fish ready to ship, amphibians, reptiles, birds, and small mammals. An area almost as large was devoted to breeding fish that were either raised inside until sold, or were transferred outside to be raised in dirt ponds. In all we were utilizing more than 6,000 aquariums most of which were the "low forties" that Joe Cooley had designed. Three feet by six feet concrete vats were the size I decided were most practical. We build a total of three hundred of these and used them for holding fish, reptiles, and amphibians. As we now had four farms in addition to the main farm complex we installed a radio system with the base at headquarters. Every vehicle was linked to it. We even had contact with the trucks that delivered product to Tampa. It was a big help as it saved a great deal of time.

An expanded bird department had been constructed. The United States Department of Agriculture was allowing Psittacine birds to enter the country. They had been prohibited entry for years. The wild caught birds had to come from approved quarantine stations in foreign countries. The birds were to be fed antibiotics (Tetracycline) in their food for several months and strictly quarantined. This would eliminate the various viral and bacterial diseases (like Newcastle disease) that could and did periodically decimate huge chunks of the United State's commercial poultry operations. It worked well enough to prevent most outbreaks, but there were two serious problems. One problem was the smuggling of birds. Lots of illegal birds came in mostly across the Mexican borders. A smuggled bird looked like a quarantined bird. A hundred red headed parrots could provide the thief with an easy five thousand dollars. The risk was minimal, and if caught, the punishment was trivial. These birds were all potential disease carriers. The smuggling has slowed down over the years with better enforcement and larger fines, but it still continues.

The second and much greater problem was that it was easy to cheat the quarantine inspections in foreign countries by bribing the inspectors. A lot of sick birds entered the United States that, in actual fact, had never been quarantined. The law needed to change. It was done after a few bad years, and several bad Newcastle outbreaks amongst commercial poultry producers. The quarantine stations were all relocated to the United States. Birds were tested on arrival, and sick birds were promptly destroyed. Tight inspection at relatively few and controllable stations effectively cleaned up the influx of diseased birds. We built extensive holding cages that were properly designed to be easily sanitized. This we did before the quarantine stations had been relocated into the United States. We were off and flying (pun intended). We brought in birds from all over the world in big numbers. We did really well with the birds from Asia; from Calcutta, Singapore, and Bangkok where most of our birds originated. Our fish suppliers all helped me to locate responsible shippers. The Indian Mynah birds were a big item. African gray parrots and several types of lovebirds were always healthy. The problems were only with birds from Latin America. The Psittacine birds that came from Paraguay were disease time bombs. One awful shipment stands out in my mind. It consisted of several thousand birds including a large number of parrots and one thousand of the Quaker parakeets. The shipment was a nightmare with about ten percent of the birds dead on arrival, and most of the others were weak and droopy. It looked like Newcastle disease. This turned out to be a correct guess, but it was some time before we knew this for a fact. This would have been impossible if the birds had been honestly quarantined in Paraguay. They were sold to us by a Miami bird dealer, who (I later found out) had good prices and a terrible reputation. This was by far our worst experience. I called him immediately. I told him I was going to return the birds to him as they were not as represented. They were weak, sick, dead, and dying. I also told him my bird manager thought they had Newcastle disease. He said it could not be. He pleaded with me to keep them as he then had no available facility to keep them. Fortunately, the shipment had been put in a remote area on arrival. We immediately set up a mini-quarantine area for them. We kept everything, and everybody away from them. This prevented other problems. I was assured by the dealer that our expenses would be deducted from his invoice. I next called the State of Florida's research laboratory and arranged for them to do a rush analysis on sample sick birds so we would know what the problem was, how to treat it, and if it was Newcastle disease what to do.

I immediately started the tetracycline therapy which helped. It turned out to be Newcastle. The next weeks were heart breaking as these poor birds died in large numbers. We did the best we could. I kept the dealer in Miami informed. About six weeks later the plague ran its course. We added up the cost of the disaster. I gave the information to the dealer in a letter along with payment. His loss was considerable as two thirds of the birds had died. I would never do business with him again and told him so. I was stunned and upset several weeks later to be served with a summons. I then discovered he was now suing Ross Socolof Farms for mega-thousands of dollars. He had created a very imaginative scenario that painted a fantasy picture that gave me the shudders. I had very little experience with lawsuits. I had complete confidence in my friend and attorney, Frank Arpaia, to protect me from this Miami goblin. The case did not seem to be complicated. We seemed to have enough solid witnesses and correspondence to defend ourselves. As time progressed I realized from the questions the judge was asking, that he had absolutely no idea of what it was all about. I then started to get nervous. The Miami lawyer sounded totally convincing to me. If I had not been the defendant I would have been convinced that the defendant (me) was a dead beat who was obviously trying to defraud this poor innocent bird dealer. When the lawyers had both finished the Miami lawyer asked the judge about how long it would take to make the decision. He surprised all of us by saying that he had already decided that I was innocent. The Miami lawyer was or acted stunned. This blow was immediately followed by the statement that they would have to pay all of our expenses, and also the court's expenses. I actually felt sorry for the poor sap. He had to pay some $5,000 in costs plus whatever his lawyer had charged him to come to Bradenton. Frank did say to me, as we walked back to his office, that he thought the judge had no idea of what it was all about, but was convinced I would not do anything wrong. I left with a good feeling.

Shortly after this problem foreign Psittacine bird quarantine stations became history. The dealer in Miami eventually went out of business. I would suspect he was unable to compete in a legitimate market.

The best thing that happened to the pet industry as a result of the availability of healthy wild birds was that birds were now more expensive to buy. This higher cost gave impetus to domestic breeding programs. The availability of healthy captive bred birds increased dramatically in the next few years. It made tame baby birds available in ever increasing quantities. This program, more than anything else, stimulated a renaissance in bird keeping. Everyone was a winner. The quarantine procedures were lengthy, expensive, and best of all effective. More captive bred birds are produced every year resulting in less and less dependence on wild caught birds. This is a wonderful way to go.

The same thing is now happening with reptiles. Bird breeding knowledge had been available as an exact science for many years. The breeding of reptiles had been mostly a mystery. The last ten years have seen a phenomenal breakthrough in the reproduction of snakes. An amazing and wonderful selective breeding program has created dozens of color morphs that breed true and are breathtakingly beautiful. The incredible feats, of the hobbyists who have become commercial snake breeders, must embarrass the PhD fraternity of herpetologists. Best news is that greater variety and more reasonable prices on the rarest items are a reality. It is only a matter if time before wonderful animals like Galapagos, Aldabra, radiated, and star tortoises (all available now) will be affordable. They are all being bred. It gives me a great feeling of satisfaction. I am sure you all share my pleasure when you think of what the pet industry now is accomplishing in creating, by captive breeding, much healthier fish, reptiles, and birds. Replacing the need for wild caught animals by captive breeding has arrived and it keeps getting better.

PETCOA by 1975 had over 140 retail outlets. Our business was booming. We had to supply more and more fish, birds, reptiles, amphibians, and small mammals. We were shipping an average of over 500 large boxes of tropical fish each week, and the biggest part of this we were producing. The retail operation was floundering and losses were a lot greater than I was ever informed of. I was spending more and more time trying to help. I could pinpoint problems that concerned the retail store operations. My years of supervising retail supermarkets for my father were put to use. Volume was down, profits were down. I passed on my observations to PETCOA management in Toledo. It was no secret that with few exceptions, all of the newer stores fell far short of glowing estimates of potential volume and profit. There were, of course, several outstanding stores and a number of talented store managers, but the overall profit and volume picture was grim. I had no idea of how bad things had become. I had volunteered to make several trips through the chain with Jack Canfield. Canfield and I always arrived without anyone expecting us. We found a retail operation that was totally out of control: high turnover in personnel, almost no training, great inventory shortages, and dirty stores with livestock that was abused. Obviously, somewhere along the way, management had taken their eyes off the ball. The tight, well-run retail operation that I had joined in 1966 as a partner was now, ten years later in 1976, floundering badly. A chilling and upsetting reaction to some very hard and clear reports Canfield and I made was ignored almost completely. A great number of the operating echelon were frighteningly incompetent. No one paid a bit of attention to our reports.

Things at the farm continued to run smoothly. Elwyn and I had just received the results of the current Ross Socolof Farms Annual Statement of Operations. We had made almost three hundred thousand dollars profit which was a lot in 1975 dollars. Our only operational problem was in paying our bills promptly. Money was tight at Ross Socolof Farms. Our billings to PETCOA were not getting paid in the usual timely manner. I dismissed this as a temporary situation and had been assured that they were getting the retail disaster under control.

I had a phone call from Phil Treuhaft early one morning in 1976. I got a real shock. He had called to tell me that PETCOA had filed for bankruptcy (chapter eleven) late the previous day. I had no idea PETCOA was in such deep trouble. No one had bothered to tell me. The only bright spot for Ross Socolof Farms, Inc. was that it was not included in the bankruptcy. All of the stock in Ross Socolof Farms (PETCOA owned it all) had been pledged as security to the Toledo Bank and Trust to guarantee loans they had made to PETCOA. I was now a wholly owned subsidiary of a bank. The company stock I had received for my half ownership turned to dust. Less than an hour later I had a call from the president of Toledo Trust. That same evening I was on a plane to Toledo to meet with my new employers. It was a really strange day.

All Toledo Trust wanted was for me to buy the farm operation. Any deal that would eventually come close to bailing them out would be considered. I would not have to put any money down. I was not interested. I had originally put the PETCOA partnership together to avoid the type of business I would be stepping right into again. I wanted to stop doing "business". We talked for hours before they finally realized that I would not be a buyer. Toledo Trust advised me that they would honor my employment contract. It had another three years to run, and provided a very good income. As part of the deal I asked for and they agreed to sell me one of the two smaller farms for my own use when I completed my contract. They hired two outside appraisers and then averaged their estimates. I could buy either farm I wanted. I ended up buying the farm PETCOA had originally bought from Ken Blaising.

I agreed to help Toledo Trust find a buyer. This was their primary priority. The second priority was that I cut expenses as the volume diminished and at the same time convert the operation to sell to any wholesale and retail customers I could find. During the transition PETCOA had agreed to continue to buy all product from the farm while they were selling and closing stores. This all came to pass. We were able to keep operating without losing a stroke and the bank did not then take additional losses. The bank eventually found a buyer. I stayed with the new owner for a year or so and then, in 1981, I left. I was getting close to sixty.

The last years I spent at Ross Socolof Farms gave me some welcome time to devote to the FTFFA (Florida Tropical Fish Farm Association), which I had been forced to neglect during all the PETCOA years. I was elected to the Board of Directors, and served under the then President Johnny Williams. I realized that Florida as a tropical fish producing center had a terrible image. The perception was universal that Florida produced a lot of bad fish. It was no longer true, but this kept prices depressed. The fish were getting better, but they were not yet good enough to recapture all of the business lost during the previous years when nothing seemed important but trying to undersell everyone else. I had been working on an idea as to how to remedy this for some time and presented my plan to the board. My idea was to create a showcase for Florida produced fish. The 130 members of FTFFA would all compete against each other in a multitude of categories in a gigantic fish show. I asked the board to let me run the show at the next annual meeting. This might turn out to be an annual event. It would be a true professional fish competition. FTFFA members would compete against each other for awards, recognition, and cash. An early and enthusiastic participant for the plan was Allen Levey who gave the concept his full support. He funded a valuable cash award each year. This was the Edward Levey Breeder's Award honoring his father who was an industry pioneer. It is given each year to the person who has made the most significant contribution to the breeding of a new species of tropical fish in Florida. This was followed, through his efforts, by other cash donations from other progressive pet industry manufacturers. The professional fish show was an enormous success, and did what I had hoped. Florida regained its reputation for producing the best tropical fish in the world. It was also true.

People now believed in Allen Levey's often repeated message to anyone in the industry who would listen. The message was simple. Everything starts with live tropical fish. It is to the benefit of the pet industry to support the Florida fish farming community. Some forgotten genius (David Boozer?) in an inspired moment suggested that we invite Allen to become a permanent member of the FTFFA Board of Directors. He agreed, and he has served for the past fifteen years. His advice and council have been great assets for all of us in the pet industry.

The experiment became a reality because Johnny Williams, Richard Atchison, Fran Hanan, Joe Diaz, Gary Cooley, Howard Groff, Arlen Wetherington, and David Boozer, our executive director, made it happen. The key ingredient was exposure for the show. We utilized the talents of Dr. Harry Grier, perhaps the world's best fish photographer. Harry has, for many years now, taken pictures of all the prize winning entries. From the start, the results of the show along with his wonderful pictures of the winners were supplied to all of the trade magazines, and all of them ran them. The cumulative result of the Professional Fish Show, after sixteen consecutive years, has firmly established the standing of Florida tropical fish. It inspired a real competition amongst the members to see who could produce the best new strains and raise the most beautiful fish. It raised the quality of the Florida produced fish to new heights. FTFFA membership can now truthfully boast that they produce the best fish in the world. Recent shows have had between five and six hundred entries in as many aquariums in more than forty categories. Judging is done by eighteen or more experts who have no commercial interest in the individual entrants. Although I retired in 1983 I still help with the show, and enjoy the once a year contacts with my friends in the industry.

These last years have rolled by, and I am enjoying my retirement. I look back at a career filled with great rewards, friends all over the world, a bit of personal recognition, exciting travel adventures, while I was doing the job I loved doing.

My dreams all came true. I was able to make a living while WORKING AT MY HOBBY! I could ask for nothing more. The years since have been good to Loise and I, and we have enjoyed quieter times together.

CPSIA information can be obtained at www.ICGtesting.com
Printed in the USA
LVOW11s0203120214

373250LV00001B/1/P